The Invisible Power

True Stories of a Police Officer

English Translation of
Mithya Ami Satya Ami
(False Self, True Self)
A book in Bengali

by
Debdas Chakraborty
Commandant of Assam Police (Retd)

Yuvaan
books

Yuvaan
books

An Imprint of Unbound Script

The Invisible Power

ISBN : 978-81-19745-16-6

Published by **Unbound Script**
Plot No. G-20, Basement,
At Seven Wonders Business Centre,
B-10, G Block, Preet Vihar, Delhi, 110092

E-mail : books@unboundscript.com
Website : www.unboundscript.com

The Invisible Power
by Debdas Chakraborty

Printed in India

Price: 399/-

Kalpayogi Mahavatar Babaji
Yogiraj Shyamacharan Lahiri Baba
Ma, who is the inspiration behind this book

DEDICATION

To those unsung policemen who remain steadfastly committed to their duty and serve the Nation, expecting nothing in return.....

CONTENTS

Foreword by

Shri Sanjay Baniwal

IPS, DG TIHAR

My Maa has been the most profound and guiding force of my life or rather my lifetimes. Her love and guidance has made me overcome my fears of losing her, the one I love most. She has guided me and changed the course of my destiny a number of times during my 37 years of service as a Police Officer.

I have never found or experienced anyone like her. She is unfathomable, someone whose dimensions and powers always leave me astounded. She has always insisted not to trust the spoken words but to trust the experience one has. Based on the facts of my experience, I have no hesitation in saying that there is no one like her and can never be another one like her. She is unique.

As a Police Officer, I feel extremely privileged to write this 'Foreword' about the work of Mr Debdas Chakraborty. This book is about his experiences and how he got divine help when he needed it most from

Maa, without even asking. This is my experience also with Maa. She knows and knows everything which has happened and is likely to happen. She forewarned me many times about ensuing tough times and guided me to fight and survive tough times.

I have no doubt that my friend Mr Debdas Chakraborty would have also experienced the same things. The only thing I am sure about is in any of the chapter, there is not an iota of exaggeration or misrepresentation of any kind. It is as it was.

And I congratulate him for undertaking this arduous journey. It is very difficult for a Police Officer to pen down his experiences and I am sure that readers will read it with open mind that whatever is written is was the way it happened. The interpretations of all the anecdotes mentioned in the book, are expressed in true words.

Faith is a matter which is intrinsic and I appeal all the readers to have faith in Almighty and the benevolent nature of Mother like Maa and experience this book through the eyes of an ardent believer, Mr Debdas Chakraborty. I have been a witness to many events which normal person would call "miracles," but Maa made them seem very ordinary. She operates always at a very different plane. I welcome to the readers to experience the subtle interactions of a devotee with Maa in his personal and professional work. May you enjoy it.

(SANJAY BANIWAL) IPS
DIRECTOR GENERAL (PRISONS)

Foreword by

Dr. M. N. Nagendra Prakash

Ph.D. (Med. Sociology)
Dip. (Applied Psychology)
Dip. (Med. Informatics); Corporate Trainer

The book "The Invisible Power" is the reminiscence of an Assam Police Officer, who chose to pen down the experiences of his service career nearly after 23 years of his retirement, that too due to the inspiration of a spiritual luminary.

Though some of the events recounted by the author, Shri Debdas Chakraborty, are more than 50 years old, yet it would appear as though the incidents have occurred just now. In spite of the lapse of time, the clarity, accuracy and sharpness of recollecting the stories and events in a systematic manner is amazing.

For instance, the operation to rescue the two abducted managers of a Tea Estate from the clutches of the dreaded militants, from the dense forests of Karbi Anglong (Chapter 1), single-handedly keeping at bay a group of a few hundred marauders (Chapter 5), a magic lantern guiding the police to a remote village of Kakodonga forest that had been attacked by militants (Chapter 9), sudden change of mind as a result of which a dreaded dacoity and kidnapping of a newly married woman and a probable communal riot as a consequence, was averted (Chapter 13); last moment drama, which was entirely out of script, in cracking the gruesome and sensational murder of a child (Chapter 14), etc. The author attributed the success in all these cases to an 'Invisible Power,' which guided the police at the crucial moment. The reason given by the author for such attribution is not easy to push aside or ignore as the stories unfold.

The incidents at Borjhar airport due to the student agitation (Chapter 7), mob furry in Lumding after elections (Chapter 16), widespread arson and violence in Aamteka/Amguri (Chapter 18), unknown facts about the Chinese aggression of 1962 (Chapter 20) and the author's divinely ordained relief (Chapter 18) are not only absorbing but also thought provoking.

Perhaps this is a rare autobiography of a police officer, who has been through a panoramic spectrum of policing work, as it opens a dimension hitherto not exposed to the public. The book underscores the complexities, struggle and the superhuman effort involved in surmounting the various obstacles that invariably arise in the course of police work.

The document reveals the depth of feeling, concern and dedication to duty and a sense of humanitarian values. As public, we never get to realise the circumstances in which the sincere police personnel perform their duties. We only have a general dislike and negative attitude towards them, which is largely promoted by the media and the movies.

The method of empirical presentation is well followed without any scope for prejudice, subjectivity or bias. All the events are factual and the stories have been presented without any exaggeration. Nor does the author wilfully undermine any functionary of the Government, the Police or any group or community.

This book highlights how a police officer can bring about positive changes by being dedicated to one's profession, upholding the function with honesty of purpose and remaining focused in spite of all adversities.

The narrative style is absorbing and the writing simply takes the reader along, as if they are on the spot. I am sure that the reader will experience every moment and feel as though the reader is present with the author, as the stories unfold.

Perspectives on

'The Invisible Power - True Stories of a Police Officer'

- Lalita Iyer Bhattacharjee

It is an honour and pleasure to give my perspectives on the book by Mr. Debdas Chakraborty, Commandant of Assam Police (Retd.), fondly known as 'Debu Kaku' to our family. Debu Kaku is the first cousin of my father-in-law, Promode Ranjan Bhattacharjee and as is typical of most Bengali families, cousins are often considered as siblings where Debu Kaku was like a brother to my father-in-law, Kaku[1] to my husband and me, and Dadu[2] to my children.

Debu Kaku has taken a decidedly different track when talking about his career memoirs - he writes about his practical experiences and "paradigms" that have been unique to his journey. The motivation and inspiration for this book is unique and noteworthy. Following Debu Kaku's meeting with Ma[3], he embarked on this project. His initiation influenced him through various stages in the recent years, as

1 Paternal uncle
2 Grandfather
3 A spiritual luminary of highest order

in this case, through his spiritual education and psychic liberation to explore and elaborate his ideas and experiences as a Police Officer. Ma who instilled the thought in Debu Kaku's mind to let the world know about his true experiences as a police officer, enabled Kaku to narrate what he learned, and how he handled his experiences, and his daily exposure to human misery and conflict. As an officer of the Assam Police, the location of Kaku's stories centre around Assam, a state in the northeast of India.

A key feature of the life of a police officer is that he remains patrolling throughout his career. This was also true of Debu Kaku who considered himself a law enforcement officer with a larger, fundamental duty to serve mankind, to safeguard lives and property, to protect the innocent against deception, the weak against oppression or intimidation, and the peaceful against violence or disorder. Respect for the constitutional rights of the nation was central to his work ethos.

Police work is rife with stress and tension. Debu Kaku also faced energy shortage with sleep deprivation, long shift hours, societal isolation, and continued exposure to negative human elements. Given that he was in constant danger, he was also overly suspicious of everything and everyone. Despite the challenges of law enforcement, the love for his job was abundant and evident.

The book points out that corruption was unfortunately a reality in the police department and many acts that he witnessed reflected the misuse of authority for personal gain for himself or others. The author discusses the complexities of defining corruption, its impact on police organizations and the quality of police service, its magnitude, comparative differences against other sectors. The weakness of the judicial system also influences the corruption and to that end, the book highlights that there is punishment for corrupt police officers and likewise, rewards for honest ones.

At this point, it must be reiterated that police work also affects and sways one's behavior to a greater degree of positivity, too. Indeed, those attributes are inculcated from experience and tend to become permanent character traits. By and large, the police department is proud to have numerous such honest police officers and police workers. The police career of Debu Kaku is an example of honesty and integrity. The author reflects with satisfaction and says "I feel joining the police force was perhaps the best decision of my life". Rightly, the residual payoffs of a police career outweigh the bad.

Coupled with being stern, cops can also be friendly and humorous. But cop humor is often misunderstood as brash, or downright disgusting. It becomes a part of a policeman's daily life where the book points to humor being infused and internalized in the job and daily undertakings. This is understandable, as humor buffers the shroud of reality that police officers face in societal problems. The common citizens are shielded from the horrors that the police world encounters. The incidents, events and experiences remain in the mind, and it harbours images, voices, screams, visions, smells, and dreams which have been influenced by the police officer's career. These are held in a "tiny little space" inside the head often referred to as "Pandora's box" [4]which complicates one's moods and influences. There are occasions when friends or family want them to share their darkest moments, but the police officer usually leaves them contained. This is evident from the book where it is revealed vividly and is a testament to his ability to compartmentalize his work so as to not interfere with doing his duty.

Being posted in the difficult region of Assam and Meghalaya, he witnessed problems and day-to-day issues in the areas of border disputes and settlements in the Northeast of India. As is well known, the states of the Northeast were largely carved out of Assam, which had border disputes with several states. The bifurcation of the two states, Assam and Meghalaya is also witnessed in the book. Assam's border disputes with Arunachal Pradesh and Nagaland are still pending, and to that end, the book illustrates the troubled and challenging context of the region in the

4 Loving K (2016). Uniform stories. The pros and cons of being a police officer. Despite the negative impacts of law enforcement, the love for the job is abundant.

1990s. Debu Kaku had evoked the resentment and resistance of some fellow colleagues, but remained bold, brave, and buoyant in his approach. The real-life experiences described in the book are addressed with an authoritative, yet balancing role that he displayed. This was by no means an easy task, given the top-down attitude of his seniors. Youthful innocence, obedience, and simplicity were also hallmarks of boyhood qualities at that time. It is interesting, how a police officer can use these qualities to advantage in life-threatening situations and valorize his leadership in a supportive way. These are noted in the book.

The book which is set in Assam brings to the fore the ground realities of one of India's vulnerable regions. The unique geo-climatic conditions of the northeastern region had made Assam and the surrounding areas very prone to natural disasters like floods, earthquakes, and landslides. Much of Assam lies in the Brahmaputra river valley, except for a few southern districts. The natural calamities have thereby affected the lives and livelihoods of the towns and cities where the growth has been haphazard and uncontrolled. There is a heartwarming scene portrayed of the efforts of the young police officer 'Debu Kaku' in saving a friend. Kaku did not have any formal training in swimming but being born and brought up in the land of Brahmaputra, swimming came naturally to him. He mentions how as children they played in the shallow waters because they knew it was safe, but there were areas in the ponds, lakes and tanks that were very deep and dangerous. The experience narrates his courage through swimming in the raging Brahmaputra, which finally culminated in his friend and himself being saved by a boatman and brought to the shore! The episode demonstrated if one wants to dare, one can – just as Debu Kaku dared and chose to save his friend, and that was the biggest lesson learned - to never be a spectator, and in the hour of need to get up and make a difference!

The book also gives the reader a fundamental understanding of how the human mindset operated across people (victims, accused and law makers) in life and death situations, theft and burglary incidents, vandalism, deaths, student and youth unrest, 'bandhs', illicit liquor trade and illegal prostitution three and half decades ago. In terms of facilities and institutional structures, the police systems then had to cope with poor security, inadequate safety and protection arrangements and minimal preventive maintenance. Preventive maintenance is an important part of successful facility management, and it helps efficient operations, increases the safety of employees, and helps mitigate costs and losses of human lives. Sadly, these were not in place at that time, and the book traces the complexities and difficulties encountered. Alongside, the experiences also highlight the camaraderie and friendship with colleagues and the sense of trust that was imbued by Debu Kaku and that which he elicited. The book captures some of his emotions and sincerity of expression which helped others understand him, much to the larger benefit of the police force.

There are some episodes on interactions with the ethnic tribes, indigenous peoples across Assam, the hilly adjacent regions and Nagaland to its east. Understanding the nature and cultural characteristics of the locals is something one must enjoy. One needs to accept the differences and identify with the commonalities of communities to build trust and communication. The book clearly shows that if you show a sense of compassion and care, and take pride in your tribe's social, political, and historical accomplishments, it will reward you many times over. The book also brings in moments of an era when values such as these were upheld by people.

It is philosophical to point out that we humans are intimately connected with the rest of the universe in a very practical way. By studying the cosmos beyond our own planet, we can understand where we came from, where we are going, and how physics works under conditions which are impossible to recreate on earth[5]. The universe will keep handing you difficult situations until you can learn to be more patient. The universe will keep you on your toes with hard times until you can learn to be kind. This is a message that is conveyed in the book. Each of the postings of Debu Kaku's tells a story and it provides a lesson to learn and share. Without clinging to emotions, but

5 spiritsoul.me

with a sense of detachment and determination of duty, Debu Kaku moved ahead and delivered in each of his police missions.

The book delves into the mind of a Police officer, his merits, and memoirs of his career. The events and stories collected are fragile and valuable. The reader is also reminded that we only have the right to perform our 'karma' and not the results these actions bear. Debu Kaku ties together the 'then' existing career concepts, political concepts, and his own concepts in a story form, which helps one reflect, test, and verify his or her own comparative journeys.

Lalita Iyer Bhattacharjee
Nutrition Advisor,
Nutrition Development FoundationThailand
Senior Nutritionist (retd.)
Food and Agriculture Organization of the United Nations
Phone : +669- 24973785
Email: lalita462001@yahoo.co.in

PROLOGUE

There is nothing unusual in certain events manifesting suddenly in one's life. In my life, however, most events have been sudden and unpredictable – writing this book included. A significant part of my life has been dedicated to my career as a police officer. Like most officers, I have borne witness to several incidents, some of which were instructive, intriguing and interesting. I had never thought that I would be recollecting and recording these incidents and that these writings would take the shape of a book. But that is exactly the task that I had to undertake, and the inspiration behind this assignment was 'Ma'.

Nine years after my retirement, I suddenly received Kriya Yoga initiation (deeksha), primarily due to the encouragement of Dr Nagendra Prakash and the compassionate blessings of my Parampoojya Gurudev, Paramhamsa Atmananda Giri ji. 'Sudden,' because I had taken the initiation without any prior knowledge or understanding of what Kriya Yoga was all about. I learnt later that Kriya Yoga was Jagat Guru Bhagawan Sri Krishna's gift to the world, which was lost over the ages. The great yogi, Sri Sri Mahavatar Babaji later revived the lost science and passed it on to his householder disciple, Yogiraj Shyamacharan Lahiri Mahasaya, who was instrumental in its propagation, especially among the householder disciples.

About two-and-a-half years after my initiation, Dr Prakash took me to Ma's ashram (Tapasthali Vatika) in Haridwar. He told me that Ma, who was over a hundred years old, had the blessings of Sri Sri Lahiri Mahasaya. That evening, I could only bow at Ma's feet but did not have the opportunity to speak with her. The brief darshan, however, filled me with an inexplicable bliss and peace. I had the urge to meet her again but learnt that Ma met visitors only on certain days. About a month later, I had the blessed opportunity to visit Ma's ashram on two consecutive days. On the evening of the second day, I sat at a short distance from Ma, listening to her instructive words about the purpose of life and the Supreme Truth. Suddenly, Ma gave me a piercing look and said, "You were with the Police, weren't you?" I was taken aback at the question. I had been barely introduced to Ma and we had hardly had any conversations. How then, did she know that I had been a Police Officer? I somehow collected myself and reverentially responded, "Yes." Ma said, "During your career, you have faced many incidents; why don't you write about those?" "Ma, many of these incidents are surreal; no one would believe my words. People will take it as an attempt to blow my own trumpet by unnecessarily dramatizing things," I said. With an other-worldly look, Ma said reassuringly, "Write, even if people don't believe you. How else will people get to know how demanding the task of policing is? How will they appreciate the complexities, the struggles and the superhuman effort involved in surmounting the various obstacles that arise in the course of police work? Besides, what role did you have in whatever happened? You were a mere pawn (nimitta matra) in the hands of the Supreme. So, pen your thoughts objectively, without letting your ego show through."

Ma's words touched a chord deep within and forced me to mull over the idea, for over a year. I then realised how true she was – I had truly been a pawn in the hands of the Divine. I really had no control over the flow of events in many of the incidents I could recollect. However, since I had no experience in writing, I had still not firmed up my mind. Thereafter, I had the good fortune of receiving Ma's darshan on quite a few occasions and had the opportunity to speak with her as well. During those meetings, I realised that Ma was a river of compassion who bestowed her divine blessings on everyone, without any discrimination. Clearly, she wanted me to write about my experiences so that people who are unaware about the complexities involved in policing can get a perspective.

I could not ignore Ma's command, and hence commenced writing a letter to her, detailing some of my experiences. That letter is now taking the shape of this book. Keeping the readers in mind, I have tried to narrate the incidents and experiences as serialised stories, maintaining a chronological order to the extent possible. Since I was an officer of the Assam Police, the epicentre of my stories is Assam. Due to obvious reasons, the identities of certain people and names of certain places have been changed. Readers may or may not agree with some of my conclusions and opinions, and I leave it entirely up to their judgement.

The book highlights, in the context of true incidents, some of the complexities, difficulties and dangers that I faced during my career, and is perhaps no different from what all other police personnel have to deal with, every day. In spite of having innumerable selfless, efficient and brave officers and men, the Police Department is largely viewed suspiciously as a corrupt organisation by the public. Undeniably, corruption is a sad reality of our lives. Unfortunately however, corruption in the Police Department receives disproportionately more public attention than in any other department or organisation. Even those who have never had a brush with the police, hold similar views about the Police Department. Ask them about the reason for their scepticism and they would cite the corrupt traffic policeman as an example. The entire department thus has to bear the burden of the corrupt traffic policeman's misdemeanour. While corruption in any manner is unpardonable, it is equally true that as per the statistics provided by the National Crime Records Bureau, 24 police personnel died and 117 were injured in the course of their duty in Delhi alone in just one year (2013). Most of the deceased were traffic policemen.

While it is impossible to silence all criticism with mere statistics, it should be borne in mind that police work is unlike that of any other department. The job is not only demanding and challenging, it is also physically and emotionally taxing. There are no weekends or festival holidays for police personnel. Barring those posted in metropolitan areas, police personnel often have to stay away from their families. They also have to face many other challenges and hence, the vehement criticism is often unwarranted and demoralising. Having said that, it is also true that the society needs efficient policing and the police need to be one step ahead of the ever-evolving criminals. Appropriate training and motivation are among the potent tools towards achieving that goal. But how can police personnel feel motivated when the criminals, who are nabbed after much effort, are let off by the courts without appropriate punishment? Our cumbersome criminal justice system is squarely responsible for this serious lacuna. According to a report published in a prominent media house on 27.10.2015, "...verdict raised extremely serious questions the way criminal justice is delivered" in our country. This is a significant statement and I personally feel that just as our economic well-being cannot be ensured without controlling population, expecting better policing will remain a dream till our judicial system undergoes an overhaul. And for that to happen, there is need for political will and consensus. The faster we achieve this, the better it will be.

I had joined the Police without putting in too much thought about the pros and cons of my decision and by ignoring the suggestion of my guardian (Kaka), who had warned, "Policing is a notorious job." Today, after having been through the journey, I feel providence made me do what I was fittest to do. I am grateful for all that I have gone through and received in the process. Though policing is a difficult and often punishing calling, the job offers an opportunity to do 'seva' (selfless service). Police work, after all, is for the people and with the people, and only those who take it as a seva derive real job satisfaction. From my experience, I can unflinchingly vouch that policing is unlike any other job; it is a mission. And that is why, had Kaka been alive, I would have confidently told him, "Yes you were partly right, but policing is a serious job, it is not a joke." Looking back, I feel joining the police force was perhaps the best decision of my life.

Debdas Chakraborty

Commadant (Retd)

AUTHOR'S NOTE

Ma,

I am writing this long letter to you after overcoming many mental obstacles and hesitation, which have kept me from undertaking this task for over a year. I find courage in doing so now, as I am convinced that you are antaryami (omniscient) and therefore, will understand my intent in spite of my limited capacity to express myself through language.

Upon hearing about some incidents of my life (and especially those relating to my career as a police officer) during casual conversations, many have been overwhelmed and have marvelled at what appeared as lucky coincidences. These well-wishers have often asked me to record my experiences in writing. I had felt always hesitant to do so as I am no writer. Besides, would I be able to do justice to these incredible incidents, many of which took place 40-50 years ago, based solely on my memory? Also, many of these incidents involve people with whom I have had a close association. To uphold the truth, I would have to reveal details of their acts of omission and commission, which may portray these individuals in poor light. Wouldn't such revelations put these people or their relatives in an awkward situation?

Some of the incidents of my life are not just dramatic but perhaps fall into the category of the surreal. Readers may not believe these claims and dismiss these either as fiction or figments of my imagination. These thoughts had prevented me from writing anything even after my retirement about 13-14 years ago. I always felt, "What will I achieve by writing about my memories and experiences? These will be of no use to anyone after all." Besides, my experiences are perhaps no different than those of other police officers. So, what's unique about my story?

But on that glorious day (April 15, 2012; Haridwar), I received your divine command as you said, "Write, even if people don't believe you. How else will people get to know how demanding the task of policing is? How will they appreciate the complexities, the struggles and the superhuman effort involved in surmounting the various obstacles that arise in the course of police work? Besides, what role did you have in whatever happened? You were a mere pawn (nimitta matra) in the hands of the Supreme. So, pen your thoughts objectively, without letting your ego show through."

O Holy Mother, your divine assurance is the inspiration behind this work. If my ego has inadvertently crept in anywhere, I seek your – and the reader's – forgiveness.

As I try to recollect the dim memories of many an incident of which I was a part, and try to give them a new lease of life through words, I find to my amazement a strikingly common phenomenon: Whenever I took up an assignment driven by a sense of responsibility and tried to accomplish it without any self-interest, I had always received assistance from an unknown power.

I can now see that in many such cases, a quick observation, an instant decision, a wise counsel, a critical analysis or a direct or indirect remark by someone proved crucial or provided a valuable clue to solving a vexing problem. A new realisation thus dawns on me, as you pointed out, that perhaps I had in fact no control over those happenings – I was a 'nimitta matra' and had merely played my role in a drama already scripted. Understandably, such phenomenon is beyond the comprehension of most common human beings.

I was witness to such a game plan of the invisible hand when I embarked on a very important mission of my career – the rescue operation of two tea garden managers abducted by extremist militants, ostensibly for ransom.

Whilst the mission was poised for failure because of three tactical mistakes committed by those accompanying me, success came unexpectedly at our doorstep. Strangely, those three blunders turned out to be the cornerstones of our success. It was as though someone from behind the scene had playfully made us commit those blunders and finally had His last laugh. Let me begin with that story.

CHAPTER

1 A Near-Impossible Rescue Mission

The gist of this mission was presented in a Bengali book titled 'Jiboner Pathe Prantarey' in the following manner:

There is no dearth of instances where people taken hostage by the hardcore militant groups in the North-Eastern region of the country were set free in lieu of a hefty ransom. But the exemplary courage shown by the Additional Superintendent of Police (ASP) of Hojai, Shri Debdas Chakraborty, in rescuing the two abducted managers of Tata Tea Company within 40 hours is rare in the history of militancy in the North-East.

On October 17, 1995, at about 8 in the morning, Police received information that two executives of the Tata Tea Company, Shri Digvijay Singh and Shri Arindam Dutta (son of a retired Inspector General of Police (IGP) of West Bengal Police) had been kidnapped by militants from Nonoi Tea Estate in Nagaon district of Assam. The victims, it was learnt, had received several threats earlier also. The militants abandoned the car in which the abduction was carried out at Kacharigaon before disappearing into the deep forests of Karbi Anglong. There were only five routes for the militants to escape from this dense forest. One of these routes was through Dokmoka near Hojai. From Dokmoka, one could travel only on a four wheeler truck to Bhelughat forest, a route commonly used by the timber merchants.

This urgent message was sent to the Additional SP, Shri Debdas Chakraborty, asking him to take all possible measures to rescue the kidnapped. A difficult assignment indeed, for no one could predict with any amount of certainty the route the militants would take to escape. Debdas was lost in his thoughts. He suddenly remembered an incident. A few days earlier, three timber merchants of Hojai were abducted by a group of Karbi Anglong militants and were later released for a hefty ransom. Although the crime was committed outside of his jurisdiction, he happened to collect, out of curiosity, some information about the movement of the militants from the timber merchants.

Without wasting any time, Debdas pored over the map of Karbi Anglong district and studied it thoroughly. After a carefully scrutiny, he concluded that it was highly probable that the militants were camping somewhere in between Bhelughat and Dokmoka. If the militants along with the hostages were indeed in that area, it would be better to capture them in the Bhelughat forest itself. A 20 km stretch of dilapidated road connected Dokmoka and Bhelughat. Since the exact location of the militants was unknown and the road was treacherous, the only option left was to travel on foot. He also realised that if the rescue mission was not accomplished by that night, the chances of finding the hostages would be negligible.

Once the mission's objective was decided, Debdas swiftly moved towards Karbi Anglong with a platoon of CRPF. At Dokmoka, he took the help of the local police to block all the possible escape routes and then started for Bhelughat on foot through the 20 km stretch of jungle.

It was past evening. There was no sound except for the occasional cries of wild animals. The team decided not to use a search lights as that would be very unsafe. This, however, impeded the speed of the group's movement. Whilst every one trudged on, no one really believed that they would be successful in the mission. After all, there was no certainty that the militants would come that way. After a while, the CRPF men became restless and tired. They were also hungry and thirsty. However, Debdas remained firm in his resolve. He would have to reach Bhelughat at any cost and make an all-out attempt.

To accomplish any task perfectly, one should not miss any opportunity that comes one's way was Debdas's principle. In an exemplary display of leadership, Debdas calmed the agitated jawans and moved ahead fearlessly towards Bhelughat. Arriving at Bhelughat, he watched around carefully and lay in wait to nab the militants. There was no way out except for waiting, if necessary for the whole night, for the plan of this operation was not based on any advance information but solely on Debdas's intuition, rooted in his intensive training and his extraordinary intuitive faculty.

After a wait of over two hours, suddenly the sound of a truck's engine was heard. The sound appeared to get closer and closer to the police team. As soon as the truck came within their range, the police signalled it to stop. As the truck driver tried to ignore the signal, the police fired a volley of shots. The militants had been caught completely unawares. It was beyond their wildest imagination that the police would dare to confront them in this dense forest, that too at night. Unable to stand against the sudden assault, they escaped into the forest, leaving behind their weapons.

After a brief lull, Debdas moved towards the truck to discover that two persons were lying prone on the vehicle's floor and were trembling all over. To his relief, the two persons were identified as Shri Digvijay Singh and Shri Arindam Dutta, the abducted managers of Tata Tea.

The real story of the rescue operation

The two managers were abducted from a place 150 kilometres away from my jurisdiction. So, I really had nothing to do in particular in this matter. Like many of my colleagues, I had assumed that perhaps this was the handiwork of United Liberation Front of Asom (ULFA) militants. This abduction took place when militancy in Assam was at its peak.

Almost 24 hours after the abduction, the DIG (CWR) flashed a message on October 17, 1995, that the abductors had crossed over to the Nagaon district the night before and had entered the hilly regions of Karbi Anglong district on foot. The leads available at that point indicated that the abductors were expected to come down somewhere within the jurisdiction of Dokmoka Police Station. Although Dokmoka was under the jurisdiction of Karbi Anglong District Police, the top brass assigned me the task of mounting a rescue operation.

On receiving the message, my first thought was that the abduction must have been carried out by some tribal militant outfit and not the ULFA, as in those days a good number of Karbi tribal groups were active in Dokmoka and its adjacent areas, apart from the Bodo Security Force, a dreaded group of ultras. Dokmoka, under Karbi Anglong district, was close to the Hojai and Doboka police stations.

These militant outfits funded themselves by fleecing the local timber merchants, abducting them at will and releasing them in exchange of hefty sums. As most of these merchants were involved in unlawful timber trade, the abductions would deliberately be kept a secret and thus remained unreported. Once, one such victim had related his agony to me. The militants had abducted his minor son and kept on increasing the ransom amount. The child was finally released from captivity after three months of hectic negotiations. During his son's detention, the merchant had visited the militant camps several times for negotiations and therefore had an opportunity to see their hideouts – about half a dozen or so, and of various sizes.

Whatever information I had then gathered from this merchant gave me only a broad idea about the probable location of these camps. But venturing into a hilly forest to conduct a full-scale search and rescue operation on the basis of such scanty information was as good as searching for the proverbial needle in a hay stack. However, I could ill afford to sit idle.

As I did not have enough forces at my disposal, I went about contacting the adjoining police stations to arrange for the necessary troops. An Inspector of the CRPF detachment posted at Hojai informed me that he would be able to spare about 20 to 25 jawans in an hour or two. The Officer in Charge of Doboka Station chipped in and added that he had a platoon of Central Reserve Police Force (CRPF) at his disposal. Though they were on routine town patrol duty, they could be withdrawn in case of exigencies.

So, without wasting any more time for reinforcements to arrive from Hojai, I along with two of my sten-gun wielding Personal Security Officers, started off for Doboka.

On reaching Doboka, I instructed the Circle Inspector to assemble a team of suitable officers and constables from Morajhar and Jamunamukh Police Stations and report to me as early as possible, at Dokmoka. I took with me a platoon of CRPF jawans, a few constables and two officers from Doboka, and set off for Dokmoka. After a stretch of four or five kilometres we arrived at a zigzag hilly road. Highway robberies were rampant on this stretch. In order to supervise the investigation of cases, I often used to visit Parakhowa in Karbi Anglong district. On one such occasion, I had met an Assistant Sub Inspector (ASI) of the Intelligence Branch. Though highly efficient, this man kept a low profile and never sought the limelight. I had great regard for him and believed that by virtue of his long posting there, he would have access to a wealth of information.

As soon as I reached Parakhowa, I enquired about this officer and was fortunately able to meet him. I quickly briefed him about the case and told him that the abductors had already crossed Nagaon district and were now, in all probability, on the hill tract. The officer heard me with rapt attention and then suggested that the abductors would most probably climb down from the hills at Bhelughat, from where they could move on motorcycles or some other vehicle.

On further enquiry about the state of police surveillance or the possibility of receiving reinforcements at Bhelughat or its adjoining areas,

I gathered that it would be futile to expect any help. Search operations against the militants had been conducted a year ago and had failed to yield anything worthwhile. The militants had a solid network of informers who alerted them of any impending operation well in advance and even helped them escape in good time.

The officer further added that some of the remote locations had virtually become a liberated zone for these extremists now. Inside the jungle, one would find valuable logs scattered all over the place as the ultras would not allow the timber merchants to lift these till they got their share of the booty. Tackling these issues was beyond the capacity of the Dokmoka Police as it hardly had enough men to guard the police station itself.

Having collected some more relevant information, I started off for Dokmoka Police Station and reached there by high noon. My visit to the station was quite unexpected. As soon as the Officer in Charge (OC) saw me, he hurriedly went about making arrangements for entertaining his guest. I cut him short. "Let us talk work first. Show me your area map," I demanded. I examined the map thoroughly, pointed at a location on the map and said, "Let us go for a round of this area."

Taken aback, the OC muttered, "Sir, is it very urgent? No vehicle can drive up to that point and you may have to walk a long distance to get there," he said, in an effort to dissuade me.

I instructed him firmly to get ready as quickly as he could as the militants were expected to descend from the hills and reach Bhelughat with the abducted managers at any time now. The poor fellow looked miserable at the prospect of foregoing his leisurely post-lunch siesta. This is one of the many occupational hazards of being a policeman. One cannot follow regular meal or rest timings. That is why, during our training, our master trainer used to say, "*Tab bhi mauka miley, letney ka aur latrine jane ka aadat daalo. Nahin toh kaun jaaney, dobara iska mauka kab miley.* (Learn to rest or relieve yourselves at any time, lest you may not get a chance in a long while.)"

After travelling some distance from Dokmoka, we noticed heaps of logs strewn alongside the road. We were on the right track, I sensed. The area was almost deserted. Far from the road were some settlements scattered here and there. After travelling a short distance, we arrived at a point beyond which the road was too marshy for the vehicles to proceed.

The team members got off the vehicles and assembled around me. I quickly briefed them about our mission. "Our destination is Bhelughat. We will have to go on foot hereafter. The abductors may be armed with sophisticated weapons and it is highly likely that they may also have grenades. So, in case of a face-to-face confrontation, keep a safe distance. Stay alert and be on your guard at all times. While a single mistake committed by any one of us may be calamitous for the entire team, courage displayed by even one member may lead to the mission's success. Remember, the rescue of the abducted managers is the one and only aim of this mission," I told them.

Just then, a thought flashed through my mind. We had scrambled on the mission in great haste. But it now appeared that we would have to spend the whole night in the jungle. As no food would be available inside the woods, I thought it would be prudent to carry some eatables with us. Just as I was mulling over the thought, the In-charge of Dokmoka requested me to spare him for an hour as he wanted to attend to a very urgent work that he had left unfinished.

I became very critical at this. "Isn't he trying to evade the mission fearing the hard work and the probable risks?" I thought. But I could do little as Bhelughat was outside of my jurisdiction and the roads here were unfamiliar to me. If anything untoward happened and I had no local police with me, I would not only be answerable, but my service might also be at stake.

So, I said, "I too have some urgent work at Dokmoka. Let us go and return together." Before proceeding to Dokmoka, the team was asked to be careful and ensure their safety while waiting for us to return. Officers in the team were specifically instructed not to allow anybody to go towards Bhelughat. The purpose was obviously to keep the police movement a secret.

As we arrived at Dokmoka, I was surprised at the sight of some curious local youths crowding the wayside. Many of them were on motorcycles. Since the presence of some extremist elements or their supporters among the crowd could not be ruled out, I thought of engaging an experienced officer to take care of these boys. Fortunately, after a short while, the Circle Inspector and the Officer In-charge of Morajhar, accompanied by a few officers and constables turned up. With their help, three probable routes by which any vehicle or other supplies could reach the militants inside were identified and sealed.

We then bought some snacks and other eatables available in the local market and returned along with the Dokmoka In-Charge to the spot where our team was waiting. We took with us some more constables from Dokmoka as they were quite familiar with the area.

"From now onwards, you are my ears and eyes. Always be by my side," I told the constables. This really motivated and energised them. It was dusk by the time we returned. While I mentally regretted the loss of valuable time in travelling all the way to Dokmoka for fetching food, the invisible power might have been amused at my predicament. Then the whole team set out for our destination on foot. A while later, a constable whispered in my ears, "Sir, we have made a great mistake."

"Why? What happened?" I was taken aback.

"Sir, a log carrier truck has already gone inside. It was carrying a wedding party with many tribal people. When they were asked not to move inside, they got agitated. So…"

"Who let them go?"

"Sir, our Junior S.I. ...out of fear"

"Where was the OC then?"

"He might have gone for tea."

Disgusted, I grumbled to myself. "These people are so irresponsible. They are behaving as if we are here on a picnic."

I started brooding over the blunder. The people on the truck must have noticed the armed police contingent. If the abductors come via Bhelughat as we were hoping, they would obviously get the information about the police presence from the people in the truck. Therefore, they will either take cover or take a different route to escape. "We are doomed to fail now. How can one commit a mistake like this?" I rued.

While I was cribbing mentally, the omnipresent Almighty must have smiled again.

Under normal circumstances, I wouldn't have let such mistakes go unpunished. I would have taken those guilty to task and chastised them. But in this case, considering the gravity of the situation we were in, I did not utter a word and walked on as if nothing had happened.

Soon, it was dark all over. Suddenly, my attention was drawn to a peculiar sound.

"What is that?" I asked a constable.

"Sir, don't you know, our officer is a patient of high blood pressure," he replied. I couldn't see any reason why this officer's blood pressure had shot up, since nothing stressful had happened till then.

I knew from personal experience that even trained men can be assailed by panic attacks in the face of adversity. I had had this experience right at the beginning of my career. Let me digress briefly to relate that story.

It was in the latter part of the year 1968. A major anti-encroachment drive was being conducted in the Kakodonga forest located in the then Sivasagar district of Assam to evict encroachers occupying forest land. An armed contingent was considered necessary to accompany the Forest Department officials as the Naga extremists were opposed to the move. As the In-Charge of the local police station, I had accompanied the team that carried out the drive.

It was the third day of the campaign. At noon, we gave ourselves a break for lunch near a stream inside the deep forest. Just as we were getting ready for a meal, some of our men began fleeing and yelling, "The Nagas have opened fire! The Nagas are shooting!"

Although we did not hear any gun shots, many members of the team became very agitated and panicky. A magistrate, a burly fat man, and the District Forest Officer (DFO) rushed towards the stream to save themselves. One of them slipped into the water while another was almost dying, gasping for breath. And one Thagiram Mandal, a highly revered strongman who was known to 'squeeze blood out of stone,' ran for his life and stopped only at the base camp that was located several miles away. Mandal spread a rumour that heavy exchange of fire was going on and many had died or were wounded. The most damaging rumour was that the DFO had been captured by the Nagas.

Meanwhile, there was utter chaos at the site of our lunch. The civilian members of the party notwithstanding, even the new and inexperienced jawans accompanying the team forgot their drills and discipline, and ran helter-skelter for their lives.

The fact, however, was that there was no firing. The advanced party of our team had actually confronted a team of the armed wing of Nagaland Police, who signalled them to stop and forbade them from proceeding any further into their territory. This had triggered the pandemonium.

But, in the present campaign, the CRPF jawans had returned a few months ago from their duty in Kashmir. They were well experienced and trained, and I was fully confident of their capability. They had been on duty since early morning, which made them a little edgy. Otherwise they were steady enough.

Bhelughat was not very far. We expected to reach

there in the next hour or hour-and-a-half. Suddenly, gun shots were heard. As the guns fell silent, I rushed to meet the advance party and learnt that they had fired the shots. When questioned, one of the jawans said, "We thought the enemy was ahead, Sir."

"How did you know it was the enemy?" I asked.

But nobody could give me a convincing reply. Some of them even contradicted one another. However, I gathered that they had acted out of fear, anxiety and panic. Alas! The team was committing one blunder after another, I thought. My intent of making a surprise swoop instead of engaging in a direct encounter was in jeopardy. Here we were, drumming our presence and position to the enemy. As my heart sank in frustration, the omniscient entity must have chuckled again. The possibility of rescuing the abducted was getting slimmer by the minute. 10 to 12 hours of hard work was all set to go down the drain.

This time, I failed to restrain myself and severely reprimanded the advance party and even threatened to suspend the whole platoon. This worked well. The party admitted their mistake and promised not to repeat it in future.

After this incident of reckless firing, I decided not to move any further for this might invite danger for the whole team. If the advance party had really fired at the militants, they would surely plan a counter-attack under the cover of darkness. This would give them an opportunity to not only inflict casualties but also snatch arms and ammunition. "What next?" I mulled. Calling off the operation at this stage was, of course, not an option.

So, before making any further move, I decided to go back to the drawing board and look at the problem afresh. The team was therefore given a break for some time for resting in a comparatively safer place. Most men in my team were anticipating that I would call off the operation after this undesirable incident. But when they noticed that I had no such intention, they started putting direct pressure on me. I brushed aside their requests and asked them to be patient.

Meanwhile, I tried to reckon within myself the next possible move of the abductors after arriving at Bhelughat, covering a long distance through hilly terrains from Nonoi.

If they had any plan to go to Dokmoka from Bhelughat, they could do so only by taking this motorable road. From Bhelughat, they would have to move further up a steep hill to reach their camp. It would be impossible for the managers to stand this continuous long walk for more than 36 hours and then again climb the steep hill.

In any case, the militants would have to cross Bhelughat. Now, the question was whether they had already arrived at Bhelughat? If so, there was every possibility that they would spend the night at Bhelughat or somewhere close by as finding a vehicle to cross the forest was remote.

So, what should be our next move? As I was weighing on the various possibilities, it suddenly occurred to me that the truck carrying the wedding party had not yet returned. Since there was no other motorable road nearby, where was the truck? I decided to check its whereabouts.

As soon as I popped the question, a senior constable of Dokmoka informed me about a person, a village headman of sorts, who resided in a nearby village. “Perhaps, he can help us with this, Sir,” he proffered. Without any delay, I proceeded to the headman’s village with a small group, including the constable, and succeeded in tracking him down. This man informed us that the driver of the truck was a Muslim youngster who lived in a village down the Bhelughat hills. The truck was also usually parked overnight in the village itself. Having learnt about this, I sighed in respite. “Even if nothing works in our favour, we can at least use this truck to return and spare ourselves of the rigorous 14-15-kms walk,” I mused.

As we returned to rejoin the larger group, I noticed a hot discussion going on amongst a few team members. Some of my officers were highly critical of the manner in which the team had been pushed into a jungle in the dark night and that too on an uncertain and dangerous mission. Some of them even concluded aloud that this was nothing but sheer madness on the part of the group leader. Interestingly, one of these officers often used to brag about his bravado and how he dominated his area by keeping robbers, hooligans and other anti-socials on a tight leash. I too used to regard him as a very brave officer. But now he appeared to be quite an antithesis of what I had believed him to be.

As soon as the officer saw me, he broke down and blurted, “Sir, see what you gotten us into. You have brought us here to get butchered. Last night, an ASP from Nagaon had also come in search of the abducted managers but he did not move a single step inside the jungle and returned from the main road itself. But ever since you have entered the jungle, you seem to have no intention of returning.”

“He is frightened and has panicked,” I thought. But fear is often infectious. His rants could have affected the morale of the other team members. So, I had to be tough with him. I tried to calm him down. However, he remained unnerved. He pulled out a cigarette and began puffing as if this was his last smoke. The poor fellow had completely forgotten that smoking in front of his superior was a serious breach of discipline. I had never ever seen him behave so desperately. Perhaps fear and the thought of possible death overcame his professional discipline.

The primary tasks of Police are to maintain Law & Order and keep crime under control. Ensuring the internal security of the State is also another key duty. Moreover, police these days have to shoulder two additional responsibilities – they have to act as the first line of defence against extremists and they also have to ensure security for the VIPs.

To discharge these responsibilities, policemen need not be as strong as Veerbhadra, the fearsome avatar of Lord Shiva, but they certainly need to be brave and courageous. People expect policemen to be gutsy. A police officer in panic in the course of a difficult mission can be a huge liability, to put it mildly. However, in this case, the attitude of some officers of my team was not only uncalled for but also disgusting. I was really very upset. I could not even connect with the problem at hand for some time. When the commotion subsided, I started thinking afresh about our future course of action.

Suddenly, I recalled that the headman had said something about the location of the truck. A thought flashed like a lightning in my mind, illuminating a possible move on the part of the militants. "The abductors, after descending from the Bhelughat hills, may not find any vehicle. They may then possibly go straight to the truck driver's house, pack the mangers in the truck and head for Dokmoka," I thought.

It was a Eureka moment for me. The thought of the faint possibility gave me a burst of fresh energy, boosting my body and spirit. I became very alert but said nothing as no one would have possibly believed me.

Time slipped away in silence and suspense. After what seemed like eternity, I heard something that sent a chill through my spine. It was a distant but unmistakable roar of a motor vehicle's engine.

"Am I hallucinating?" I asked myself. I concentrated on the sound more intensely for some more time. After a while, I was sure that a heavy vehicle was coming down from Bhelughat towards us. "A truck is moving at this hour of the night. Is my guess correct then? Who else would drive a truck through a thick forest at the dead of the night?" I asked myself.

To be doubly sure, I asked some of my team members if they could hear something. Now, the whole team became alert. "Yes, Sir," volunteered one of them. "It sounds like a heavy vehicle hurtling towards us." I was then quite sure that this was the same log carrier that was allowed to enter the forest.

The truck appeared to be at a distance of 5 to 7 minutes' drive from our position. I alerted the team at once. We would have to stop it by any means as it was possible that the militants along with the tea garden managers were in this truck.

The CRPF platoon was already divided into three groups, each of which took up positions at three different places on the route. The local police also joined them. The Sub-Inspector in-charge of CRPF led one section whilst another Sub-Inspector took charge of the other two sections. I took with me a Havildar from the CRPF, armed with a Self-Loading Rifle (SLR), and two sten-gun wielding Personal Security Officers (PSOs), and took up a position between the second and the third sections.

The first section was instructed to signal the vehicle to stop. In case the vehicle ignored the signal, they were to follow the vehicle at a safe distance, to avoid a grenade attack.

In case the vehicle ignored the second section's signal too, the troops were instructed to shoot at the tyres and forcibly stop the vehicle.

The third section was asked to be ready to extend any support, based on the situational contingency. In any case, the truck was not to be allowed to move beyond our range of fire.

Everyone took up the assigned positions and lay in wait for the vehicle to arrive. The tension grew palpably with each passing moment and so did the engine's roar. Soon, the truck entered within our range.

A brief moment later, I noticed that the vehicle had crossed the first section. "But why didn't it stop? Did they signal on time? Did the driver overlook it?" I wondered worriedly.

I could now see the glare of the headlights and a clear signal from the second section, but to my dismay, the vehicle arrogantly passed by the second section. The vehicle now moved towards the point where we were lying in wait.

"My God! Any more delay and we are ruined!" I was tense. Wasting no time, I commanded the CRPF Havildar to open fire. The man raised his SLR and aimed at the truck but did not fire. He stood still with the gun. Puzzled, I looked at him. He was trembling all over as his finger clinched around the trigger, but he hesitated to shoot for some inexplicable reason. I flew into a rage and shouted at him again, "Fire!"

As soon as I gave the second command, the vehicle screeched to a halt. The Havildar, too, refrained from firing. The truck stopped 30-40 meters away from us. Suddenly, several gun shots were heard from the rear of the truck.

"Who's that?" I was perplexed and at the same time anxious. Just then, I saw against the backdrop of the truck lights the silhouettes of two human figures with their hands raised above their heads, advancing towards us. They seemed unarmed.

"Who are they? Surely not the miscreants?" I thought.

As they came nearer, the contours of their shabby appearance and unshaved faces were apparent. "Must be tea garden labourers," I thought dismissingly.

"Who are you?" I asked them nonetheless in Hindi as they came close. *"Hum garden kay aadmi hain,"* (we're from the tea garden) came the reply.

So, I was right. "But what the hell are they doing here at this unearthly hour?" I thought.

Just then, the man with a moustache uttered an English word.

"Are you the Garden Manager?" I asked, almost in disbelief.

"Yes, I am Senior Manager Digvijay Singh," he replied and motioned me to look at my feet even as I struggled to recover from the bewilderment.

I saw a sturdy young man kneeling by my side, shivering all over. I had not noticed how he got there. I deduced that he must be the other manager, Arindam Dutta. Readers can well imagine my condition at this point.

We quickly threw a protective cordon around the two. Later, asked about how it all had unfolded, the two managers narrated in brief: After the abduction, Arindam had made a desperate attempt to free himself but was overpowered after a scuffle. The abductors outnumbered them and were well armed, too. The duo was then made to trudge continuously over the inhospitable hilly terrain for two days, which totally exhausted them. As a result, the group's pace slowed and by the time they came down to Bhelughat, it was already late at night.

Meanwhile, the abductors had sent two of their men in advance to arrange for a vehicle. When the group, along with the abductees, reached Bhelughat, they could neither find a vehicle waiting for them, nor the persons who had come earlier in the day. In desperation, the abductors then woke up the truck driver and forced him to take them to Dokmoka. The militants appeared very happy at the success of their mission while they were travelling in the truck and did not anticipate anything untoward. But as soon as the truck was challenged by the police, the abductors became agitated. Pointing a gun at the driver, they instructed him not to stop. The managers also mentioned that they were seated on the front seats besides the driver in the truck's cabin. A silent prayer escaped my lips and I mentally thanked the Havildar for not opening fire. Had he done so, the two managers could have either been killed or severely wounded, bringing the purpose of the whole operation to naught.

Much later, I asked the Havildar why he had hesitated to fire at my command. With a wry smile, he said, "Sir, the severe dressing down you had handed us when we had opened fire recklessly earlier was fresh in my mind. *Iss liye soch raha tha iss baar kuch chook na ho jaye.* You had threatened us with suspension and that really leashed me."

"What a game plan!" I thought in silent appreciation as the pieces began to fall in place.

The first move was to separate me from my team for some time. Had I not been compelled to go back to Dokmoka for buying food, the truck would not have been allowed to move towards Bhelughat. And in that case the abductors would not have had the opportunity to use the vehicle to execute their movement.

Secondly, if the advanced section had not opened fire, I would not have hollered at them. And in that case, the Havildar would not have hesitated to fire at the truck at my first command. The outcome, in such a situation, would have been gravely different.

I humbly prayed, "O God! Thousands of salutations to you. You have saved us from a great disaster. Had the managers been harmed, I could never have forgiven myself for the rest of my life."

Like any other fiction, I could have put an end to the story here. But facts are often stranger than fiction. Such stories do not always end with "...and they lived happily thereafter."

So, I cannot help sharing the remainder of the episode, which was obviously not so sweet, as my readers may guess. I am narrating the farce that was played with me later, purely to make readers aware of the peculiar problems police personnel have to face as part of their duties.

With the managers safely huddled by our side, we arrived at Dokmoka Police Station. 'Mission Accomplished' was a terse Wireless Transmission (WT) message dispatched to the DIG, then stationed at Nonoi. The WT operator was instructed not to disclose anything more than this. The purpose was to keep the details a secret so that the militants did not get an opportunity to launch a counter-offensive even if they intercepted the cryptic message. At around midnight, with enough precautions, we set off for the District Headquarters at Nagaon. The two mangers, tired and weary as they were, expressed their desire to have a cup of tea. We halted briefly at Doboka, but not a single tea stall was open. Due to the prevailing disturbed situation, traffic movement at night was curtailed. The bustling town wore a deserted look. We had to abandon the idea of having refreshments.

As I was about to move back to my vehicle, the officer who was very critical about the mission and had spoken all nonsense out of fear, came forward, saluted me and stood silently like a guilty school student. The quick succession of events might have swept off his tipsiness by then. He looked repentant for his behaviour. He fumbled for words to express his regret. I took pity on him and said, "You need not go to Nagaon. Better take rest, here."

It was past midnight then. We were heading towards Nagaon, about 10-12 kilometres away, when another problem came up. A convoy with red beacon was spotted on the opposite direction. "Whose convoy might it be? Surely not a minister's?" I thought. The movement of ministers was prohibited at night in the militancy hit areas. Moreover, the DIG and the SP were at Nonoi till 12 a.m. They were not supposed to return so early and even if they did so, why should they come by the opposite route? Was it then a ploy of the militants to wrest the managers from us? Not unlikely, for they had lost a prize catch.

I was at once on my toes. I instructed the driver to stop the car and also asked others to do so. As we stopped, the convoy at the other side stopped too. No one moved for about five minutes. Then, a few men from the opposite side began walking towards us. Some of our men also went ahead, while the rest took up positions. When the men from both the sides came face to face and nothing happened, I was assured that there was nothing to fear. "But who is the person in the red beaconed car?" I tried to guess.

A short while later, an SI of the armed branch came to me, and identified himself as the security officer of the Deputy Commissioner (DC), Nagon District.

"The DC is in his car, Sir. He wants to speak to you," he said courteously, adding, "He has come all the way only to meet you, Sir."

I was a little surprised as to why the DC should come to meet me midway.

"He might have come to know the condition of the managers," I thought while I went up to the DC's car. As the DC saw me, he alighted from his car and profusely congratulated me. "You have done a wonderful job. This abduction case has been a cause of the Government's headache and embarrassment," he said, adding, "Bring the managers to the Circuit House. All arrangements have been made for a meeting there."

In fact, I had planned to go to Nagaon Police Station first. But now the DC himself had ordered otherwise, so I replied, "Alright, Sir."

The DC's convoy then turned towards Nagaon. I came back to my team and asked them to move towards the Circuit House.

At Nagaon, our convoy moved past the Police Station and hurtled towards the Circuit House. We were being escorted by the CRPF vehicle, which was being followed by the managers' car. A few other vehicles with armed guards were behind it. Suddenly, my attention was drawn to the standing-in Additonal SP, who was himself standing at the traffic point and directing our convoy to take a turn. But the Circuit House was straight ahead. I was a bit surprised and asked the Additional SP, what the matter was. He motioned towards the Police Officers' Guest House, saying that this was the DIG's instruction. I was caught between two different orders. Was it then an ego clash between the heads of two departments of the administration or something else?

I was worried about disobeying the DC as I might be answerable to him in the future.

When we reached the Police Guest House, we found that all the senior police officers had already arrived by then. I received some high praise, although some of the officers looked a bit worried. I could almost hear them mutter under their breath, "The Additional SP of Hojai is going to get another elevation. He is really lucky." A newly inducted DySP put it this way: "Sir, a sure gallantry award awaits you."

I said nothing, but thought to myself, "Brother, you are a newbie and are yet to learn that good work alone does not fetch a medal. You need lobbying and clever scheming. Above all, your personal chemistry with your boss will determine whether you get a recommendation for a medal or not."

After two and a half hour's wait, the DIG and SP arrived. Both of them embraced and profusely congratulated me. Needless to say, I felt elated.

After the arrival of the DIG and the SP came about a dozen executives of the Tata Tea Company and their families. Just as the senior-most among them started thanking the Police department for rescuing the two managers, the DIG cut him short abruptly and gave them a severe tongue-lashing, the viciousness of which took everyone aback. I myself felt quite ashamed and uncomfortable. Everybody present, especially the ladies, were stunned to silence. They might have thought, "Oh God, are police officers always so rude?" The DIG's demeanour perplexed me. Later, I learnt that someone from the Tata group had made adverse comments alleging police inaction and had questioned the SP's role. The comments had come to the notice of the Government higher-ups. Now, armed with the success of the police, the DIG took the opportunity to lash out at them.

But I felt a generous gesture by the DIG as a victor could have put his critics to shame and regret whereas his out outright firing immediately lowered the image of Police in the eyes of the public.

This unpleasant situation thankfully came to an end when the head of Central Intelligence Bureau from Delhi accompanied by Arindam's father arrived at the scene. Arindam's father (a retired IG) embraced me and said, "Officer, I assure you at least a gallantry medal."

"Again a promise of gallantry medal? Oh, how many times have I heard these empty words!" I thought. Yet, for courtesy's sake, I replied, "Thank you."

Then, as the ambient mood eased, all of us had tea and snacks. My job was now over. I had to go back to Hojai. While taking leave of my senior officers, one of them asked, "Couldn't you get some dead bodies as well?"

I was completely unprepared for this. "Where would I get those, Sir?" I humbly submitted, "The abductors had fled under the cover of darkness."

"So what?" the officer retorted. "If I were you, I would have picked a few locals from the neighbouring villages, and then..."

The remark left a bitter taste in my mouth.

I thought resolutely, "I refuse to belong to this wretched breed that needs corpses of the innocent to prove its gallantry." The bitter feeling haunted me all the way back to Hojai. 'Mission Accomplished' was a wrong message, I thought in disgust. To many, a mission without a kill was only half accomplished.

NOTE: The State Government and the Police Chief declared a reward of Rs 5 Lakhs for the success of the mission. But how the reward money was distributed later remained a mystery for me. In my career spanning over 36 years, I have come across many such instances of injustice. I look forward to writing more about these in future.

CHAPTER

2 Policing is A Notorious Job...

Destiny works in strange but methodical ways. As I recall the incidents of my life, I can now clearly see that life meticulously paints the backdrop of an event, often over a long period, much before the event actually unfolds. This happens without one's knowledge and the events manifest just as the invisible power wills.

Recounting a few incidents from my boyhood would not be out of place here. In 1952, I had joined Class 5 at the Dibrugarh Bengali High School, which was located 8 kms away from our home. Classes began at 6 a.m. and finished at 9:30 a.m. I used to get up at 4, gulp down a meagre breakfast and rush out. The crisp and cold morning air would wake me up. I would walk 2 kms to reach the railway station and take a train to reach Dibrugarh. But after a few months, the train's timing changed, which brought an abrupt halt to my everyday routine. Hariya, a local youth, was then hired to pedal me to school on a bicycle. I learnt to sit on the crossbar (the rod between the handle and the seat of the bicycle) and balance myself. Hariya was paid Rs 15 a month for his services. I used to get a daily pocket money of chaar anna (25 paise) as my return bus fare and an equal amount for my tiffin. From my tiffin allowance, I would give Hariya 2 annas as it pleased the poor fellow. He would make me promise not to tell anyone.

Soon, I learnt to ride half-pedal bicycle, which is quite a balancing act. My newly acquired knowledge had an entirely unintended consequence – the dismissal of Hariya. I then began riding to school on my own. Dibrugarh is quite chilly during the winters. The wintry air would make my eyes well up while cycling. As tears would flow down my cheeks, passers-by would remark: "Poor boy, he must be in great pain." I would secretly rejoice at their predicament. Thus was the laid the foundation for a life full of struggle.

I learnt the importance of struggling for life – literally – quite early. I was then a student of pratham bhag (elementary school). The school, a dilapidated structure, was about a mile away from our home. One day, soon after the school had assembled, an ugly thunderstorm (kalbaishakhi jhor) welled up. As the sky darkened and the wind began howling, the school master asked all the students to take shelter in the veranda of a large pucca house near the school. Everyone ran to safety. I, however, decided to return home. I had witnessed an unsavoury incident in that house some time ago and was reluctant to go there.

Soon, the wind turned into a storm and it began raining. To reach home quickly, I took a shortcut by running through the paddy fields. All of sudden, it became very dark. Powerful gusts tossed my little body and at times, I felt that I was being lifted up. This was my first encounter with nature's fury and it made me realise how powerful a force the unassuming wind can be. With dogged determination to survive and all the strength at my disposal, I managed to reach a pond near our house, where I could see some people.

I yelled for help, but no sound escaped my throat. My little frame could not take it any more. My breathing became shallow and soon, I passed out. I don't remember what happened next but was lucky to find myself alive. Someone had found me and carried me home. Once I regained consciousness, I could see and recognise everyone, but could not speak. That was an extraordinarily helpless feeling. But at that tender age, I had learnt that one has to struggle in order to survive in this harsh world.

When I was in Class 6, we shifted residence to Dibrugarh town. Our locality had lots of children and we played a lot. By then, I had developed a distaste for academics but dreamt of becoming a sportsman some day. My sporting fantasy received a rude jolt very soon, as I broke my ankle while playing football, barefooted of course. After about an agonising year, I was back on the field. Apart from sports, we also fancied adventure. Unlike kids today, we had no access to the Internet, television or video games. So, we became experts in raiding neighbourhood trees laden with fruits or fields with ripe, juicy sugarcane. Soon, we had graduated to 'stealing' coconuts.

Our ring leader for such activities was Shibu, an expert in running, swimming and climbing trees. Our den was a quiet corner in the house of Dilu, a cousin of Shibu. I still vividly remember our first coconut stealing expedition. In our locality lived a rich man named Singh. He lived in a sprawling mansion surrounded by several bighas of orchards. A posse of domestic helps and servants guarded the mansion. Singh's backyard had many trees including coconut palms. Soon, our eyes fell on the coconut-laden grove. All we needed now was a good reason to raid the place. "Arrey, the Singhs do not pick the coconuts," it occurred one day. "That's sheer wastage. So, if we hungry kids savour a few of those coconuts, wouldn't the coconuts be really obliged?" There was no stopping after this incontrovertible 'reason' dawned upon us. Planning for the assault commenced forthwith. It was decided that the raid would be conducted on a monsoon night with some background music support from the thunders. Else, if the coconuts fell with a thud, Singh's almost dozen and a half helpers and pehalwans would be after us. And, if they laid their hands on us...

Soon, the night we were waiting for arrived. The group overcame a mixture of fear, caution and excitement to execute the operation with perfect finesse. The success made our confidence soar. Thereafter, the raids became easy and quite frequent. Whenever someone felt like feasting on coconuts, a raid on Singh's orchard would be organised.

Soon, the news spread at school. Shanti, Shibu's classmate, who lived in a different locality, begged to join the gang. He pestered us so much that we could not refuse. After a lot of deliberations, it was decided that the Constitution would be amended to accommodate Shanti. Shanti was then formally inducted. The rules and regulations were explained and he was asked to report on a night when the thunderstorm struck.

Accordingly, he turned up one night. Under Shibu's leadership, we took Shanti and entered the coconut grove. It was Shanti's first expedition and he was shivering with excitement. He was very cautious and alert too. Shanti's overcautiousness resulted in a peculiar situation. As mentioned earlier, the landlord had a large number of helps. Two series of restrooms with brick walls and tin roofs had been constructed in the orchard for their use. We had never bothered to check those during our earlier expeditions. But overcautious Shanti wanted to be doubly sure. Thought we forbade him, Shanti did not heed. "What will you do if you find someone?" we demanded. Shanti whipped out something. "See this?" he said. It was a dagger.

As soon as he opened the second door, a weak, wailing voice was heard, "Chor…chor (thief, thief)!" Alas! Wasn't that Pulin's grandfather? Our neighbour Pulin's grandfather was a supervisor in Singh's estate and he would sometimes stay the night. But who knew that he would come out to answer nature's call at that very moment? By then, Shibu had already climbed up a palm. If we escaped without him, he would be in danger. On the other side, Dadu's (that's how the elderly gentleman was reverentially addressed) trembling voice began to weaken further. Somehow, we got Shibu to slither down and all of us ran as fast as we could. Shibu was livid as he couldn't quite fathom why the expedition had been called off all of a sudden. We did not stop till all of us were back in the safety of our den. Everything was then explained to Shibu.

While we had all escaped without being caught, we were now worried about Dadu. The poor old man suffered from asthma. Nantu, the poet, commented ominously, "I hope he does not breathe his last tonight." Though we felt even more miserable at this, there was little we could do till the day broke. At the first rays of dawn, we ran up to check on Dadu. We found him standing tall at the crossroads, wrapped in a chador (a sheet worn as a shawl), excitedly bragging about how he had single-handedly saved Singh's estate from dacoits the night before. The moment he spotted me, he said, "Hey Debu, where were you boys all this while? Do you know that but for me, there would have been a dacoity last night? Tall dacoits with swords had burgled in." It didn't take long to figure out that Shanti's dagger had, in a matter of few hours, grown into a sword and at 5.5 ft, we had become the "very tall dacoits." Whilst Dadu regaled everyone with his 'heroic exploit,' we could barely stay still and contain our giggle, but all of us feigned to be in awe and admiration of his bravado. Dadu was very happy. We too sighed a relief, as Nantu's prediction had failed. Else, if Dadu had really died that night, then we would have had to carry his body to the cremation ground, which would have ruined the day.

With that episode, however, curtains fell on our coconut expeditions. While one might credit Dadu or Shanti for this, I believe that this was preordained by the Almighty. Otherwise, Abhay would not have become a Doctor, Shanti would not have joined the Army or Shibu would not have become a pious, spiritually inclined person. Else, the way the wind was blowing, who knows, some of us may have ended up in prison.

It is said that whatever the Lord wills, one has to do. My father wanted me to study Sanskrit and become a pundit (priest). Later, my guardian and youngest uncle, Shri Rashamoy Chakraborty, wanted me to study law and become a lawyer like him. But providence had planned it otherwise. I had just passed my BA examinations when the proposal to study Law was mooted. I had no interest in further studies. Hence, I desperately started searching for a job as that was the only way I could escape the dreadful books. Things happened rather swiftly thereafter – from filing an application to appearing in an interview – almost like a pre-scripted play and without the knowledge of anyone in the household. On March 11, 1964, I returned home at about 9 p.m. after hanging out with my friends, to find a gentleman sitting with Kaka (uncle). Kaka saw me and asked, "Do you know him?" "No," I said, hesitatingly. "He is the DySP Special Branch." Perplexed at the unannounced visit of a police officer at that hour, I greeted him. The officer explained that the Assam Police headquarters had sent a message that I should report at the Dergaon Police Training College the next morning. He added that all the other selected cadets had already joined the training and due to some reason, my selection and joining order had not been mailed.

As soon as the officer left, Kaka asked if I was really interested in joining the Police. I replied in the affirmative. Kaka spent a long time dissuading me. "Police work is very arduous and physically taxing. Danger and disrepute are constant companions. You will never know where you will be posted. You may not get leaves even if you need them." And so on. I listened to his tirade, but stood firm on my resolve and began preparing for my journey to the training college. Grudgingly, he consented. "Go, but remember, policing is a notorious job." I respected my uncle and listened to all his comments. I however disregarded his advice as I thought that he was only trying to test me. I joined the training the very next day.

CHAPTER

3 First Year of Service (1965)

After completing my training at Dergaon Police Training College, my first posting was at Gauhati (now Guwahati) Sadar thana (city police station) as a probationary sub-inspector. Recently, there was a news on TV that a fourth grade employee in an Uttar Pradesh hospital was conducting a surgery instead of a doctor. The news triggered memories of an incident on of the first day of my career.

I reported to the senior officer on the first day of joining the Guwahati Police Station. He asked me to learn how to record the general diary and other such works from the Sheristadar, ASI Paresh Sarmah. After an introduction, he said, “Please wait till I finish off the pending work.” I kept waiting for the next four hours, while Paresh babu continued with his work.

At about 1 p.m., an information was received that an unidentified dead body was lying at the MM Hospital, adjacent to the Police Station. The deceased’s finger prints had to be collected. Such activities are usually handled by the Court Inspector. But finding me idle, Paresh babu did not think twice. “Please go and get the work done,” he instructed.

I had never imagined that I would have to do this on my first day at work. A string of thoughts ran in my mind. "What if the dead body is rotten? Wouldn't it stink? If I have to touch the dead body, I would have to take a bath. I would also have to wash my uniform." Now, that was a dreadful thought, as I had only one pair of uniform made of cotton fabric. In those days, terrycot clothes were not available and cotton clothes took a long time to dry. My worry was probably apparent. Paresh babu read my mind and said, "Don't worry, you won't have to touch the body or take a bath. The constable accompanying you will do the needful. Do you have some money with you?" I replied in the affirmative. "Good. Then off you go, no worries."

In spite of Paresh babu's assurance, I was not sure how the fingerprint of a dead man could be taken without touching it. In a few moments, things became clear.

On reaching the morgue, the accompanying constable said, "Please wait, I will go and call the Sardar." I thought that he must have gone to bring the head sweeper to help move the body. But after waiting for a long time, no one turned up. I wondered why he was taking so long. Then, I saw something that was beyond even my wildest dream. A short, betel nut chewing man walked behind the constable. He was bare bodied, wearing only a short dhoti. On his left hand dangled two blood stained leather glove like objects. As the man came closer, I realised that the 'gloves' were actually severed hands, freshly chopped off above the wrist. It was a repulsive sight and I thought it was quite disrespectful to mutilate a dead body. But this was Sardar's everyday work. In a few minutes, the finger printing activity was completed. As Paresh babu had said, I did not have to take a bath.

In those days, there was only one Police Station for a big city like Guwahati, though there were 6-7 outposts. From 10 p.m. to 8 a.m., only one Sub Inspector – the Night Duty Officer – used to be effectively in charge of the entire city. My first few months included night duties, investigating petty offences and raiding drinking and gambling dens, and the like. There was a lot of work but I was brimming with enthusiasm.

Then came the 1965 Indo-Pak war. The present Bangladesh, which was then East Pakistan, allowed the enemy a front to attack to North-east India, particularly Assam, making it vulnerable. Everyone apprehended that the newly constructed Saraighat bridge over River Brahmaputra would be targeted. The tension was apparent everywhere.

One evening, we received information that Pak paratroopers were landing near the Jorabat hills. A senior officer of the Police Station was entrusted with the task of finding the paratroopers. I was sent to assist him. We started off with a truck full of jawans and guards. At about 11 p.m., when our convoy reached Jorabat, the leader ordered a halt. Then there was no movement. The point from where the paratroopers had allegedly landed was another 10-12 kms ahead. At first, I thought that the leader was planning some action against the paratroopers. But why was he taking so long? I became impatient and asked, "Sir, why are we not advancing?"

“Why hurry?” the leader replied nonchalantly. “Enjoy the beautiful moonlit night. Here, listen to a poem.” In spite of my unwillingness, I had to endure a couple of poems. He then said, these are my compositions, expecting some appreciation. But I did not oblige. My mind was engrossed with only one thought - getting face-to-face with the enemy. The leader’s poetic outpouring was therefore unbearable at that moment. But I had no way to escape. Later, I understood that the experienced and smart leader had adopted the safety-first tactic of ‘ashubahsya kalaharanam’ (let the inauspicious time pass). With such a leader at the helm, readers can well imagine what the outcome of the operation would have been.

Early next morning, soon after returning from the operation, we received instructions to check all the steamers in Brahmaputra as information was received that Pak saboteurs were hiding in those vessels. The search operation continued unabated for over 20-22 hours. As probationers, there was no rest for us. However, there were some interesting moments that gave some respite.

One of our seniors used to blame India whenever there was a discussion about the war. While we never supported his ideas but considering his age, we did not oppose him either. A few days after the war broke out, while we were in the office one night, there was sound of shells exploding all around. We came out and saw the sky was literally red. Thousands of firefly like glowing fire balls were descending slowly from the sky. Like others many others, our senior colleague too thought that Pak fighter aircrafts were raining bombs. He swore against Pakistan and darted under the Sheristadar's table to save his life. We too rushed to take cover in the freshly dug trenches in the Police Station compound. We pleaded with him to join us in the trenches, but he refused and continued to yell at the Pakistani pilots: "The dogs are going to finish my children" Another colleague chuckled at this sudden turn of heart.

In reality, the Indian radars had detected two enemy aircraft in the airspace around Guwahati. Immediately, the anti-aircraft guns around the bridge and the hills opened rapid fire in the direction of the aircraft. The firefly-like glowing balls we had observed were nothing but the tracers of the shells. As no one knew about tracers, we thought these were bombs. Another outcome of the event was that our senior colleague was disenchanted with Pakistan.

A few days later, we received instruction that all the beggars and mendicants roaming the city streets were to be screened. There was a possibility that the Pak spies were roaming the streets in camouflage. Then began the verification drive of the beggars. Hundreds of beggars were apprehended. The large Police Station lock-up was insufficient, so we had to vacate the large room that we used to sit in. As expected, the verification duty was entrusted on a few of us probationers – Jayanta, Asanullah and me. We were on the job throughout the day and night, patrolling the streets, conducting verifications and running around endlessly. In spite of the tremendous work pressure, we still had some moments of fun.

Though the investigation room had been vacated for the 'guests', only those who were of higher standard had the privileged of finding accommodation in that room. One day, we saw the room had been filled with a large number of religious mendicants of various denominations. Vaishnavas, shaktas, hanu-bhaktas and peer-farkirs of all sorts occupied the room. We thought of having a little fun at their expense. That afternoon, we began deliberately discussing loudly amongst ourselves near the room, so that the inmates could overhear. "Looks like there are a few false sadhus amongst these. Some of them may be spies too. We must watch them carefully in the evening to separate the grain from the chaff." We then quietly moved away.

Our other colleagues also learnt about the ploy and ventured towards the aforementioned room to find out what would happen. Meanwhile, our words had the intended effect. As soon as it was dusk, each one of the inmates got ready to prove he was the greatest devotee of his ishta (Deity). Soon, loud naam, gaan, paath and azan could be heard. It was a hilarious. No one had any sense of time. But when the prayers grew louder, we became a bit nervous. Our eyes were then at the HQ DySP's room. We did the vanishing act as soon as we sighted him. The officer had no clue about what was happening and was infuriated. The fervent prayers were brought to a rude and abrupt halt with the DySP's blood-curdling yell.

CHAPTER

4 A Sensational Burglary

I had just about completed my first year in service when I was given the investigation of a sensational burglary case in a rather unexpected manner. During the investigation, I had to face a lot of problems but the case was eventually solved in a miraculous manner.

I was on night duty. At about 3:30 a.m., the Paltan Bazar outpost reported that a major burglary had happened in the newly constructed RCC building of a doctor couple in Lachit Nagar. The thieves had taken a large amount of gold ornaments and cash. As the Night Duty Officer of the biggest Police Station, I had to respond to any incident that took place during the night anywhere in Guwahati. On reaching the spot, I spoke to the owner of the house and learnt that the criminals had broken into the house and taken away 14 sets of gold ornaments and a substantial amount of cash. They believed that the burglary had happened at about 2-2:30 a.m. But they were at a loss to understand how the burglars had entered the house as no door, window or door latch had been broken.

Listening to the description, we tried our best to find the entry point by looking around with the help of a torch. The exercise yielded nothing. So we waited for day break. Meanwhile, the constable of Paltan Bazar reported that the teams I had sent to patrol the local area in an effort to locate the burglars had returned empty handed and no suspicious persons were found.

Considering the gravity of the case, I sent an urgent message to the In-Charge of Paltan Bazar and the Circle Inspector (CI), requesting them to come to the spot. The CI and two senior sub inspectors of Guwahati Police Station came to the spot in response. They tried their best to locate the entry point but were unsuccessful. While we were perplexed with the issue of entry point, we noticed some dirt patches on a curtain at about 7 – 8 ft height. On observing closely, it was identified as soil. On finding this spots, we thought did the thieves may have entered the house through the ventilator above it. The ventilator was secured by a grill, which appeared to be intact. No sign of any other breach could be found.

In all cases of theft and especially in case of burglary, it is important to establish the veracity of the complaint, and for that it is essential to find out the entry point. This information is also useful in identifying the criminals as they usually use the same modus operandi to break in. In this case, the doctor's allegation was true was without a doubt as the parents of the doctors were owners of tea estates and the newly married couple could easily have 14 sets of ornaments.

We were still mulling over the point of entry but nothing could be found inside. We came out of the house and observed the grill over a particular ventilator was slightly bent. But the opening was too small for an adult to pass through. In absence of any other entry point, we assumed that that was the likely point of entry of the burglars. Then, I observed a faint footprint on the soil below the window. Even though the entire foot was not visible, the front part of the print was visible prominently. On seeing this, I enthusiastically called a senior officer and show him the print. He tried to wipe it off with his feet but I prevented him from doing so. The officer was a little taken aback but he did not show his displeasure. "Why are you taking this pain," he said under his breath, "It will only increase the workload." He was trying to tell me that his action was directed at lessening my burden. But with the help of an enthusiastic youth nearby, I managed to collect a plaster of paris cast of the footprint. Without having found any other clue, the CI and other officers left the spot at around 10 a.m. I returned to the police station with the cast at around 1 p.m.

That evening, I came to know that that I had been entrusted as the investigating officer of the case. The crime had been committed under the jurisdiction of the Paltan Bazar outpost and the case should have been entrusted to an officer of that outpost. So, I was surprised at the move. Usually, no probationary officer is given charge of such a big burglary case. Seeing me worried, a colleague teased me and said "Serves you right. What was the need to show so much enthusiasm and take that foot print cast? Now feel the heat." Others too cautioned me and said that since the case is related to a well-to-do family it is possible that they are well connected to ministers or high ranking officials, who could put pressure. "Investigate very carefully and keep the case diary up-to-date, as you never know who will come down to supervise," I was advised. This added a bit to my worry.

I was inexperienced and had little knowledge about burglars in Guwahati, so I used the opportunity to learn as much as possible from anyone who cared to share anything and took suggestions from everyone, including senior officers, junior constables and the old hands. Everyone gave plenty of advice but no clear instruction. Within 48 hours, pressure for the detection of the case began mounting from various quarters. By then a few random searches and a few arrests had been made, but there was no real progress in the investigation. I was told that Shri Sricharan Barua, Senior Superintendent of Police would arrive in a day or two from the Police Head Quarters in Shillong to take stock of the case. I had never met him till then but had heard how even experienced officers broke into a sweat on hearing his name. Besides, in those days, the SSP CID did not supervise any ordinary case. I understood that though the case was not of 'Serious Case' category it had assumed such status.

Panic spread along with the news of the SSP's arrival for supervision of the case. Till then, there was no clue other than the foot print. Therefore, the higher ups of the Guwahati Police Station sent an instruction that all the A and B class History Sheeters of the Police Station be rounded up and their foot prints be taken. An arrest was to be made if there was a match.

Receiving the instruction, I began going after the history sheeters every night. Evidently, the Police Station records had not been updated as many of the history sheeters had died, some were physically incapable and some were too old or ill. A few others had moved on and now owned illegal drinking and gambling dens.

Those that were physically capable or possible suspects were rounded up and their foot prints were taken. Every night, a couple of such characters were brought to the Police Station for foot prints. In about four or five days, this activity became a matter of joke. Initially the constable and havildars in the Police Station barrack were quite inquisitive, but later they too began making fun. Some commented that this 'Poali Babu' (kid officer) has lost his mind. As I was the youngest amongst the Sub Inspectors, I was often addressed as Poali Babu behind my back. My colleagues passed various remarks as they thought it was impossible to make a detection on the basis of just a footprint? Truly speaking, even I used to be assailed by self-doubt at times. But my mind refused to let go of the case till I had seen the end of it.

I disregarded the Malkhana (store-room) in-charge, Miri babu's grumbling complaint that I was filling up his store room with footprint casts, and continued with the activity diligently. One day, the SSP finally arrived from Shillong for the inspection. He was known as Durvasa for his sharp tongue, so I faced him with a beating heart. With me was the Circle Inspector, who introduced me as the investigating officer of the case. The SSP stared at me for a long time. Then he asked, "How much investigating experience do you have? How many burglary cases have you investigated prior to this?" I answered the queries truthfully. After listening to me, he thundered at the CI, "Does Guwahati Police Station not have any other investigating officer?" Before CI could answer, the SSP asked me to leave the room. I too felt relieved. After a long while, the CI came out with grim face. I enquired if the SSP had any special instruction regarding the case, but received no reply. The CI said, "Keep doing whatever you have been instructed to do." Thus, my tryst with history sheeters and bad characters continued.

But even after 10-12 days of the incident, when there was no new breakthrough, everyone thought that the case would remain unsolved. The reason for the assumption was that cash and ornaments had been stolen. The possibility of recovering cash is always negligible and the ornaments would have been melted by now. Still, my enthusiasm was undiminished. The case continued to buzz in my head during every second of the day and night.

And perhaps that is why the Almighty effected a sudden turn of events, eventually leading to a miraculous detection.

I was on night duty when, at around 10 p.m., a message was received that a law and order problem had erupted at the Guwahati indoor stadium where a Japanese table tennis team was playing an exhibition match. I rushed to the spot. In a short while, the situation brought under control. I then learnt that the Paltan Bazar Police had caught a few bicycle thieves. I decided to check and headed towards the Paltan Bazar outpost. The outpost constable confirmed that a gang of 5-6 bicycle thieves had been captured. The group included a young fellow from a decent family. “If interrogated properly, he could spill the beans about many other bicycle thefts,” the constable suggested. I asked him to bring the youngster.

The havildar presented a healthy and handsome young fellow. Evidently, he was from a decent family. But his gangster-like hairdo and cigarette burnt dark lips gave away the fact that he had gone astray due to bad company. The boy admitted that he was the son of a Gazetted Officer. In those days, the number of Gazetted Officers could be counted on finger tips and they were highly respected. A tinge of anger rose within me as I thought that the boy had no regard for his father’s dignity. I gave him a dressing down, advising him to shun bad company and concentrate on his studies instead. The youngster, whose surname name was Kalita, nodded like a good boy and promised to reform.

I melted at Kalita's childlike-face and felt that since he is new to this profession, he may not have any worthwhile information. I discontinued his interrogation asked the constable to bring the others who had been caught along with him. Their faces gave away that they were old hands in the trade. On interrogation, they admitted their involvement in several cases of cycle theft.

It was almost time for me to leave for city patrolling. So, I instructed the constable to inform the outpost in-charge early in the morning so that he can further interrogate the suspects and recover the stolen cycles. As soon as I prepared to leave, the battle-scarred constable whispered some sage counsel in my ears... "Sir, the boy from the decent family is not as clean as you are assuming. He is as venomous as a black cobra. If he is firmly interrogated, he may give information about many other bicycle thefts. This is the right time. He many not confess later."

As I was new and inexperienced, everyone used to unhesitatingly share suggestions and advice. But this day, I heeded to the advice and called the boy again. He was fearful and anxious, as he had witnessed the plight of his 'seniors' who had had to confess to their crimes. His emotional state did not escape my eyes and I took full advantage of the situation. I gave him a verbal lashing and firmly asked, "Who has committed that theft?" Actually, I wanted to know about other cases of bicycle thefts, but since the burglary at the doctor couple's house was in my mind, I inadvertently said, "that theft." As soon as the question escaped my mouth, I realised my mistake. "What did I ask? This was not the right question." But my unintended simple question worked like magic. The boy was taken aback and said, "Sir, which theft are you referring to." I thought, "What is the kid saying? He wants to know which theft I am referring to? That means he knows about many thefts." I screamed at him again and said, "What do you mean by 'which theft?' That theft."

"Oh, the Lachit Nagar theft?"

As soon as I heard 'Lachit Nagar' a faint ray of hope rose in my mind. But the next moment, I thought the boy was probably referring to some bicycle thefts in Lachit Nagar and not the burglary case. Thus, hanging between hope and despair, I gave another yell and said, "Yes, the one in Lachit Nagar."

"Sir, you mean the burglary at the doctor couple's house, right? Isn't that what you are asking about?"

"Yes, Yes."

"Sir, I did not do that."

"So who was it?"

"Sir, Mustakim did it."

"How do you know?"

"Sir, I was with him."

Listening to the boys words, I felt as if I was dreaming. "The fellow looks like a kid. He has been caught on suspicion of bicycle theft. It now turns out that he is involved in such a big burglary and he is confessing that too," I thought.

But even though the boy mentioned the doctor's house, it was important to know which doctor. I hesitated to ask that question to Kalita, fearing that he may backtrack. So, with a lot of effort I refrained from asking any leading question. I assured myself that the bird was in the cage so how could he escape? His role in the burglary can be ascertained later. But right now it is most critical to confirm that the boy was referring to the doctor couple's house.

I intuitively changed my style of interrogation and gave him a sense of softness. I gave him the impression that knowing about the theft and not revealing it is a smaller crime than actually committing it. Kalita was now at ease. I had tea and biscuits with him and he agreed to lead us to the crime spot.

With great hope and with the havildar and a few constables in tow, I headed towards Lachit Nagar along with Kalita. I made the boy sit with me in the front of the vehicle. This gave him a lot of confidence and he guided us straight to the doctor couple's home. Kalita showed the window under which the footprint was found and said Mustakim had climbed the window, bent the grill of the ventilator and entered the house. The couple also identified Kalita. The boy's family was known to them and the boy used to visit them, even though Kalita's family stayed in another part of the city. This made me sure of the fact that Kalita and Mustakim had burgled the house.

If Mustakim learns that Kalita has been captured by the police, he will definitely try to escape. So, I immediately headed towards Navagraha via Zoo Road to catch him. Kalita led us to the dilapidated house where Mustakim lived as a tenant. I arrested him and searched his residence. Nothing suspicious was found. Mustakim feigned ignorance and pleaded that he was only a poor daily labourer, adding that he was not involved in any crime. He also refused to recognise Kalita. I sensed that Mustakim was made of tougher material and to break him, an experienced officer would be required. I thought of taking him to the Main Police Station at Guwahati. The objective was to inform the OC about the arrest. It was soon going to be dawn soon, so I had to hurry. Instead of taking the main road, I took a by-lane. Kalita was still with me, sitting on the front seat of the vehicle. I commended him for helping arrest Mustakim. He was quite pleased and enthused with this. We were then near Gauhati Club in a by-lane when Kalita suddenly asked us to stop. He then disclosed that other than Mustakim, Padam Bahadur from Nepal was also involved in the burglary. Padam Bahadur used to live in an abandoned garage close by. Kalita then took us to the spot on foot. Padam Bahadur was then in deep slumber. He was woken up and questioned, but he flatly refused any involvement in the burglary or any connection with Kalita. However, I arrested him on suspicion.

As soon as I reached Guwahati Police Station with the suspects, I sent a word to the OC through the Police Station sentry. But the sentry returned with the OC's terse instructions: Investigate the case properly and if successful, you will be rewarded. I surmised that the OC was not willing to leave his comfortable bed so early and come to the Police Station. Then I thought of informing the Circle Inspector. But the havildar objected. "Sir, there is no point in waiting for senior officers. It is early morning, and if word of Mustakim's arrest spreads, the stolen property may never be recovered. So, we have to interrogate the criminals and do the needful ourselves," the old hand said.

I reflected on his advice and felt that it could not be dismissed summarily. At that point, time was of essence. So, I decided to proceed with the interrogation and do whatever was necessary.

On interrogation, Mustakim and Padam Bahadur denied any involvement in the burglary. Then Kalita was brought in and face to face interrogation was done, Mustakim finally admitted that he had committed the burglary and added that some of the stolen ornaments were sold to the recidents of Silphukuri area at throw-away price. He also confessed that he had entered the house by standing on the shoulder of Padam Bahadur and that Kalita had suggested them to commit burglary in that house. As Kalita used to visit the house, he knew very well where the almirah in which the ornaments were kept. Padam Bahadur stuck to his guns and denied any involvement.

On the basis of Mustakim confession, he was taken to Silpukuri. He took us to some four-five houses in that area. The people who had purchased the ornaments from him, produced the ornaments. The ornaments were seized as suspected stolen property. The hapless buyers disclosed that Mustakim had claimed that the ornaments belonged to his wife and he needed money for her treatment. As the seized ornaments were only a fraction of the stolen property, Mustakim was interrogated again. He then confessed that the major portion of the stolen ornaments were sold off to a jewellers in Chandmari.

Then with Mustakim in tow, I sped to Chandmari. He took us to the jeweller's house. A search was conducted on suspicion but the stolen property was not recovered. The jeweller was arrested on suspicion. Then, I took the jeweller to his shop and searched the premises. However, nothing came out of it either. It was about 12 noon. Till then, no senior officer or additional help was available. But a large number of onlookers had gathered behind us.

Right at that moment, the Deputy Inspector General of Police was passing through the Silphukuri fish market. On seeing us, he stopped his vehicle and enquired which case we were investigating. I told him that this was the Lachit Nagar doctor's house burglary and told him that last night I had arrested three suspects and some stolen ornaments had also been recovered. The DIGP mentioned that he had seen our team during his morning walk. He expressed his displeasure as no other senior police officer had turned up to help with the investigation.

I told the DIG that my next destination was Kalita's house. As he left, the DIG opined that I should conduct a search only in the presence of a senior officer. Then I understood that he would arrange for a senior officer to supervise the case.

At about 1 p.m., we reached Kalita's house. By then news had spread that Kalita had been arrested by the police. A large agitated crowd had gathered and was ready to challenge the police. The Circle Inspector and Paltan Bazar in-charge too reached the spot and pacified the crowd. Kalita's room was then searched but nothing suspicious was recovered. This was not surprising as Kalita had already disclosed in his statement that he had not taken any ornament and Musthakim had given him some cash only. Mustakim had assured him that he would sell off the ornaments and give him his portion of the booty in cash, which he didn't. He had not estimated that Mustakim would cheat him, else he would not have advised Mustakm to commit the burglary at the doctor's house.

The Circle Inspector, who was usually very affectionate towards me, appeared very annoyed. He demanded to know why had not been informed of the arrests in the morning. I told him that I had informed the OC, but he was not satisfied with my reply. There was no mobile in those days and there were only a few STD booths. The CI's attitude, however, surprised me. I later came to know that the DIG had taken everyone – from the OC to the

SP – to task, saying that a probationer was doing everything all alone since last night and questioning why no support was extended to him. The officers were unable to give a satisfactory reply and were very annoyed with me.

At about 3:30 p.m., I returned to the police station along with the arrested persons. My intention was to interrogate the receiver of stolen property – the jeweller – so that some more stolen property could be recovered. But the moment I stepped into the Police Station, I sensed that the seniors were furious with me. They had only one question: why I had not informed them earlier. No one wanted to recognise the fact that I had informed the OC. Meanwhile, the City DySP hinted that I was trying to keep the stolen gold for myself and that is why I had not informed anyone. I had never thought such an allegation would ever be levelled against me, even in my worst nightmare. This statement hurt my self-respect. The officer had probably got an earful from the DIG and therefore he levelled many other allegations and demanded explanations. I was tired and hungry. I had also probably expected a little appreciation for solving a clueless case. Instead, when I saw that the opposite happening, I could not control my pain and insult. I do not remember what I said to the officer in rage but the two inspectors present there almost physically carried me out of the DySP's room and pacified me. At that point, I remembered Kaka's words. Woefully, disrepute had come to me from within the organisation.

Bitter with the unsavoury experience, I immediately decided that I would not continue as the Investigating Officer of this case and informed the senior officers with all the firmness at my command. In the evening, I handed over the case to the Paltan Bazar Police Station in-charge. But before that, I ensured the footprints of Mustakim, Kalita and Padam Bahadur were taken, as I was unsure if the new investigating officer would do that.

Later, an expert opined that Padam Bahadur's footprint matched with the footprint procured from the crime spot. On this basis, a chargesheet was filed against Padam Bahadur along with Mustakim.

A few days later, the case came up in the court of First Class Magistrate Shrimati Sucheta Ray Chaudhury. The court awarded rigorous imprisonment to both the accused. Shrimati Ray Chaudhury was a well-known person. I remember that she had shielded me from the unnecessary and uncomfortable questions of the defence lawyers, which is very rare. Notably Kalita's case was sent to Juvenile Court.

CHAPTER

5 Nature's Fury: Temblor and Brahmaputra's Undercurrent

A few months after the closure of the burglary case at the doctor couple's house, I faced another similar challenge. These challenges and other such untoward or unfavourable situations never bothered me too much as I had already been steeled after going through some very difficult phases during my early life. Therefore, before narrating the story any further, let me share a few experiences from my student days.

A devastating earthquake that struck Dibrugarh in 1950, on Independence Day, is among one of my earliest recollections that haunts me to this day. In those days, Independence Day was a very pious affair. Everyone would participate in the celebrations with great nationalistic fervour, irrespective of age or gender. The children would participate in sports and get free tiffin. I was then a student of Class 3. I had just sat down for my studies in the evening, after spending the entire day merrily when I felt my chair being pulled from the rear as one of my elder sisters rushed past behind me. I thought that my sister was perhaps teasing me or playing a prank. Still sitting on the chair, I turned around sharply, yelling, "What are you doing?" To my surprise, there was no one in the room. Before I could understand anything, there was another jolt. The shake was so strong that it destabilised the American lantern that stood on the study table (there was no electric lamp in our home back then), which fell on my left hand. This caused a deep burn injury, and the mark kept the memory afresh for many years.

Thereafter, the shaking continued intermittently and every once in a while, there was a massive jolt. The agony seemed unending as the quakes showed no signs of abating. Panic reigned as paranoid people across the neighbourhood rushed out and gathered in the open. I had experienced earthquakes earlier, but those had lasted for a maximum of one minute. But what was this? The shaking continued through the entire night, without respite for even a minute. The situation was unbearable as one could neither sit nor sleep. Standing seemed to be the only option, but how long could one stand? The tremors continued for 8-10 hours after which their frequency reduced gradually. But a big jolt would shake everything up every once in a while. The devastating tremors continued for about a week, causing extensive damage to the city. Fortunately, there were no multi-storied buildings in those days.

The undivided Lakhimpur district, of which Dibrugarh was the headquarters, was the worst hit during that earthquake, resulting in a dramatic change of course of the mighty Brahmaputra that majestically flowed past the city of Dibrugarh. People would watch the river gobble up the land and wonder how long the city could bear the onslaught. The river threatened the famous Peri Park, which stood on its banks. To save the park, huge boulders were piled up to build a strong embankment. We were confident that the river would never breach the embankment and threaten the city beyond. Unfortunately, over the next two years, the beautiful and vast Peri Park submerged in the river.

The then prime minister, Pandit Jawaharlal Nehru, had arrived with an entourage to inspect the damage. I too went to see him - from a distance, of course. As the prime minster stood on the courtyard of the Dibrugarh Main Post Office, inspecting the river, a crack appeared on the ground behind, measuring about 60-70 yards, encircling the Post Office. This was due to the remarkably strong undercurrent of the Brahmaputra. Thankfully, some people noticed it on time and raised an alarm, alerting the prime minster and the officials accompanying him. The officials prevailed upon the prime minister and quickly took him to a safe distance. Soon after the prime minster vacated the spot, the entire land mass and a significant part of the post office submerged in the swirling Brahmaputra waters, right in front of the prime minster and the curious onlookers. Later, the Polo ground, court field and many other office buildings and residential houses were swept away.

Initially, I would feel amused to watch the river dramatically eat up large chunks of land and huge trees. I would watch with wondrous amazement how a massive tree would fall into the water, bob up for a brief while and then disappear under what appeared to be a relatively calm but dirty watery surface. People would say this is the Brahamaputra's undercurrent. I had no idea what an 'undercurrent' was but in about a couple of years, I had a first-hand experience of the deadly undercurrent.

Those who haven't experienced the undercurrent may perhaps not be able to fully appreciate its ferociousness. In 1954, to save the Dibrugarh Town from the river, the government took the initiative of creating a Chinese pattern stone embankment. This required thousands of labourers. But where would one find so many people? So the slightly older students of schools and colleges were enlisted for the work. I was then in Class 7 and was therefore eligible. With great enthusiasm, we started working on the embankment. Every day, after toiling for 2-3 hours, we would be given a refreshment of tea, singara (samosa) or boondi laddoos.

One day, we were throwing stones in the river near what was formerly the DC's bungalow. The river appeared very calm on the surface. At the end of work, with a cup of tea and a singara in hand, I had a sudden curious urge to explore the DC's bungalow. Till a few years ago, the administrator's residence was out of bounds for people. But by now, the river had swallowed much of the bungalow precincts, forcing the government to abandon it. From the surface of the river, the bungalow stood at a height of 15-20 feet, overhanging the river. I entered the bungalow and move towards the river side to see how the river looks from the height. Suddenly, I spotted a few black-hair covered heads bobbing on the river, near bank. Before I could understand what was happening, I spotted another head, a short distance ahead. It didn't take me long to sense that those were perhaps school children who had fallen into the river and were drowning. Without another thought, I spontaneously plunged into the river, aiming for the farthest head.

I had learnt swimming early in my childhood so I had no fear of the water. As I was taking the plunge I quickly worked out a plan for the rescue mission: I would first hit the river bed and then push myself up and then pull the drowning fellow to safety. Accordingly, I loosened my body as soon as I touched the river, so that I could dive deep quickly. The water was colder than I had imagined. But wait, where was the river bed? I had dived pretty deep by then but the river bed was nowhere in sight. I was running out of breath, so instead of diving down any further, I decided to resurface. But alas, I could not move up! My body had turned stiff and heavy like a stone.

I mustered all my strength to push up. Curiously, I was encountering another underwater situation that I had never faced before. My entire body, especially the part below the waist, was being twisted like a wet cloth. With great effort, I managed to reach the surface, gasping for breath. I turned around to see that the person drowning had moved a few feet farther. Summoning all my remaining strength, I swam towards the person and was somehow able to catch his head with my left hand. I turned around and began trying to go towards the bank. But what was this? If I moved one feet ahead, the river pushed me back by two feet. I was perplexed and worn out at the same time. Then survival instinct kicked in as I realised that I would possibly die if I tried to save the drowning boy any further. I tried to free myself from the boy's grip. But the boy was barely conscious and was holding on to my neck. As I tried to free myself, I noticed that it was my neighbour, classmate and bosom friend, Abhay (Abhay Bhawal). I immediately gave up the idea of pushing him away. "We'll die together, if we have to," I resolved.

Struggling in this manner, I estimated that we were now about 40 feet away from the bank. The students on the bank were shouting, but could do nothing. Completely worn out by now, I was trying to somehow survive by keeping the body afloat and swimming with my right hand. The chances of survival was minimal and I gave up the idea of struggling any further. We were floating close to a stationary motor boat, anchored in the river. But due to the undercurrent, I could barely move towards the boat. Every time I tried, the mighty river pushed me back. Reluctantly, I awaited the watery grave.

Suddenly, the boatman arrived like a godsend. He had seen us drowning and jumped from one boat to another to reach his motor boat. "Ghabrao mat," he shouted, as he picked up a long, thick rope and hurled it towards me. I had neither the strength nor the will to catch the rope and therefore missed it at the first attempt. But then, realising a faint opportunity, I somehow found some strength and will to survive. At the next attempt, I caught the rope with my right arm. The Good Samaritan then pulled us to his boat with great effort. By then, a few senior students had joined the boatman and they finally managed to pull us up. With sheer luck, both Abhay and I had survived the ordeal.

Later, I had learnt how the students had fallen into the river. First, Abhay slipped into the river while washing his tea cup. To save him, another boy rushed in. To save these two, two others jumped in. As luck would have it, none of these boys knew how to swim. While the students were busy rescuing the three who fell into the river after Abhay, he had flown quite a bit farther unnoticed and would have certainly been washed away had I not noticed and plunged. All would have been well had the story ended here. However, I crave the reader's indulgence as I would like to relate how I was rewarded handsomely for my heroism.

A few teachers from each school used to accompany us students to supervise our work of dumping stones in the Brahmaputra. After the work, the teachers also used to have tea and refreshments, but not with the students. Obviously, they were oblivious of the goings-ons. After we managed to reach the bank alive due to God's will and the boatman's timely efforts, some over-enthusiastic students said, "Let us take him to the teachers. He will surely get a reward and his pictures will be published in magazines." My clothes were still wet and I was very tired, but the seniors dragged me to the teachers. Meanwhile, the teachers had learnt that some students had fallen in the water. They hurried towards us in great anxiety. Accosting us midway, they found me in wet clothes and thought, "This unmindful child must have fallen in the river. Had he died, we would have been in the dock." The teachers came down on me like a ton of bricks. The senior students, too, were taken aback and could not speak a word. I somehow managed to get away and felt fortunate to not have been caned by the teachers.

Later in my service life, many such unpredictable, unexpected and depressing events happened, especially in the first 4-5 years of my career. But remarkably, my back was saved every time due to some invisible power. I will now relate some of those events in the following pages.

CHAPTER

6 Copper Wire Theft and Blank Cheque

One day, the theft of a large quantity of copper wire worth several lakhs of rupees was reported at the Guwahati Police Station. The theft had been committed at the Post and Telegraph (P&T) department's godown located in the Basistha area, which was then a desolate place, far from the city. Copper wire thefts were very common in those days. But those thefts would usually involve removing relatively small lengths of telegraph lines from desolate stretches of roads. To my knowledge, this was the first case wherein a large quantity of copper wire was stolen from a godown. As the lion's share of all the clueless burglary or theft cases was assigned to me, the investigation of this case too fell on me even though this was a high-value case.

Stolen copper wires were rarely ever recovered, as the wires can be easily melted. Thus, I along with two constables, proceeded towards Baisistha without much expectations. In those days, spotted leopards and other predatory animals were common in those parts and the Sheristadar babu reminded me to return before sunset. The godown, which was located some 18-20 kms away from the city, wore a deserted look. No official was available. A few labourers showed us the place from where the wires had been stolen. The periphery of the godown, where dozens of expensive copper wire bundles were stocked, was secured by a mere barbed wire fencing. There was a 15-16-feet gate at the entrance, but it had no lock. I took a quick look around and surmised that the thieves must have and an eye on this place for a long time. They had an easy day as they had not carried the bundles themselves but had brought in a truck, loaded all the material and drove off merrily, without facing any resistance. This was evident from the clear imprints of truck tyres all over the place.

"We can find the thieves if we can find the truck," I told the accompanying constables, asking them to find some plaster of paris or wax to take a casting of the tyre imprints while I began studying the patterns and making measurements of the marks. However, I noticed that senior constable Surinder Singh was not enthusiastically participating in the investigation and was standing aloof. Questioned about his inactivity, the constable said with considerable sarcasm, *"Chhoriye na Poali Babu. Yeh sab bekar hain, iss se kuch faida honay wala nahin.* (Leave it Sir, all of this is a waste of time and nothing will come out of it.)" I reacted strongly to his defeatist statement. "Why should it be of no use? If we can trace the truck, we can catch the thieves." The experienced Singh taunted, "Even if you find the thieves, you will not be able to do anything." I was taken aback at his unusual demeanour. "What does he mean by 'You can't do anything if you catch the thieves?' Doesn't the law empower me to take action?" I raised my voice and said, "Do you think I am so weak that if I find the thieves I will not be able to bring them to book?" I had a verbal spat with Singh as he adamantly stood by his words. But seeing my seriousness in cracking the case, Singh threw me a challenge, "I will take you to the place where the stolen property has been stored but on condition that you will arrest the receivers of the stolen property."

I pondered for a moment, trying to guess what he was trying to get at. "First show me the stolen property. Then see what I can do," I said. "Then let's not waste any more time here," said Surinder, "let's return to Guwahati." I agreed, as recovering the stolen property was a priority because copper wires hardly take much time to be melted. We could deal with the thieves later.

Returning to the city, Surinder took me to a narrow lane near the place where the Nehru Stadium stands now. He pointed at a long, tin-roofed shed and said, "The stolen copper wires can surely be found if this house is searched." On enquiry, I learnt that three brothers from Bihar, Shambhunath, Vishwanath and Bholanath, had been staying as tenants in that rented property for the past few years. On calling the residents, the eldest brother, Shambhu, came out and bowed at us with deceitful reverence. I asked his name and place of original residence. On being questioned about his occupation, he smiled sheepishly and said, *"Biznish."* "What Business?" I asked. Without uttering a word, he gestured, as if to say, "You already know, Sir." A search was then conducted and we recovered many sacks full of stolen copper wires from the house. Some of the wires were half burnt and some had the insulation intact. Obviously, the brothers had just begun burning the wires to remove the insulation; our unexpected arrival had brought the project to an abrupt halt.

Shambhu could not satisfactorily explain how he and his brothers had obtained such a large quantity of wire or from whom. Being old hands in the trade, they began pressuring me to 'settle' the matter there. Some other men from the neighbourhood also joined in and requested for a settlement. I remembered Surinder's words as I quietly marvelled at the brothers' audacity. Without another word, I began preparing the seizure list. My silence gave Shambhu and his henchmen the impression that the matter would possibly not go to the Police Station and would be settled there itself. I finished all the paperwork, arrested the brothers and started for the police station along with the stolen property. It was probably then that the reality dawned on the brothers and their henchmen.

A stolen copper wire theft case had been solved after a long time. Happy with the success, we returned to the Police Station. Surinder, too, was happy as his challenge had led to the recovery and the arrests. I was very close with some 8-10 junior officers of the Police Station. We shared a very cordial personal relationship apart from our professional relationship. Thus, we had a culture of celebrating each other's success. But that day, the warmth of camaraderie was conspicuous by its absence. Instead of showing any enthusiasm, Paresh babu too raised his eyebrows and quietly returned to his work as soon as he saw the arrested persons. I somehow overlooked the unusual behaviour of my colleagues.

Shambhu and his brothers had not stolen the wires themselves and were only the receivers. So to extract information about the thieves, I began interrogating them. However, the brothers did not open their mouths. Meanwhile, Paresh babu suggested that before producing the arrested persons in the court, a certificate has to be collected confirming that the stolen property belongs to the P&T department. So, I proceeded to procure the required document by meeting the P&T officers and getting the wires examined by experts. It was almost 9 p.m. by the time I returned. I was on night duty that night, and thought that it would be a good idea to catch about an hour's rest. Right at that moment, a senior officer summoned me. I entered the officer's chamber to see the three arrested brothers along with him. The ring leader, Shambu, was standing next to the officer as if he was very close to him. I was miffed to see an ordinary receiver of stolen goods getting such adulation from a senior officer. I felt even worse when the officer asked me for an explanation, "Where's their money? They have alleged that you have misbehaved with them and have misappropriated their money." I was really disgusted at this affront as the officer was seeking an explanation without checking the veracity of the allegations. Still, to allay his suspicion, I asked the two constables who had accompanied me and the Police Station sentry, who had conducted the search before locking up the brothers, to come to the officer's room. It was proven that these people only had some petty cash, a wrist watch and a few rings in their possession when they had been locked up. They were not carrying 'a lot of money' as alleged. Then, I said to the officer in English, "Does it not diminish our respect and authority if we police officers are falsely implicated in front of suspects?" "If someone makes an allegation, I have to make enquiries. Why should you feel so upset about it?" the officer retorted angrily.

As the officer had raised his voice, Shambhu thought that he was admonishing me. In his enthusiasm, he craned his neck and began whispering something in the officer's ear. I could not restrain myself as I saw this audacity and reacted spontaneously. Shambhu was completely shaken as he had never expected me to do something so daring in front of a senior officer. He stepped back meekly, nursing his cheek. Aghast, the officer got up and tried to pacify me, "Wait, wait…remember, you are a probationer. You will not get your confirmation if you get an adverse report." "To hell with your confirmation," I cursed mentally, but gathered myself with great effort and apologised, "Sorry Sir, I had lost my temper because of the false allegations," and walked out of the office. A minute later, the officer stormed out and boarded his car.

That night, I thought hard and long about why the senior officer had behaved the way he did. But I could not reach any conclusion. Of course, I understood very clearly that he was well acquainted with Shambhu. But, when I recollect the incident today, I feel that the officer was probably trying to pressurise me and bail out Shambhu and his brothers.

The next day, after finishing my duty, I was about to leave at about 8 a.m. A man dressed like a politician, wearing kurta-pyjama, who had been loitering around in the Police Station corridor for quite some time, introduced himself as Constable Sipahi Singh and enquired with great humility when I would go for breakfast. In those days, I used to have breakfast at the Ashoka Restaurant near the Police Station. For many reasons, I was not feeling like having breakfast that morning. But Sipahi Singh, who was on suspension for over 18 months, kept imploring me for breakfast, which I refused.

I had assumed that Sipahi Singh was probably overdoing his sycophancy act by trying to take me out for breakfast at the very first meeting. I did not suspect anything or distrust him as he was a policeman and never thought that he could have any malafide intention, even though I had heard a lot about him. That my trust was misplaced became clear when I returned to the Police Station that evening.

After some rest in the afternoon, when I returned to the Police Station for evening duty, I learnt that some Police Station staff including Surinder Singh had manhandled Sipahi Singh. Before I could find out the reason, Inspector Sarmah called me and asked if Sipahi Singh had wanted to take me to the restaurant. When I told him about the incidents of that morning, he said that I had done well by not heeding to Sipahi's requests. "Sipahi Singh was a decoy who had been entrusted to fix you in a fabricated bribery case," he added. So this was a trap to avenge Shambu's arrest, I thought.

Later, I was told that Surinder and a few others were furious when they came to know of Sipahi's nefarious plans, prompting their action against him. That was my first and last meeting with Sipahi Singh. That day, I realised the value of the advice of an experienced hand, especially in the context of the difficult task of policing.

I still had some more surprise in store that day. At night, I went to the Police Club and heard that my transfer was being discussed. Apparently, the DIG had received many complaints about my carelessness and the most important allegation was that I was extremely obstinate and that "it is very difficult to work with him. He needs rectification." Therefore, I was to be sent to Mizoram on deputation. The order was about to be released.

After the recent uprising, Mizoram was still on the boil and a transfer to hilly and inhospitable place was regarded as punishment posting. I became a little depressed on hearing the news, not because I would probably be transferred to Mizoram, but at the reach and audacious clout of the ordinary receivers of stolen property. I now understood why Surinder Singh had warned me that I would be in trouble if I stirred the hornet's nest.

Though the investigation of the case was taken away from me, the earnest desire of those who wanted to see me in languishing in Mizoram was not fulfilled either. Neither did this story come to an end that night. Six years later, Shambhu was arrested again. The invisible power punished him, ostensibly to break his blatant disregard for the law and the law-enforcing agencies, and his erroneous presumption that he could buy his way past anything.

From Guwahati, I was transferred to two other districts before being posted as the Officer In-Charge of a police station in the undivided Cachar district. Soon after taking charge, I went to Silchar, the district headquarters, for a courtesy call. Finishing the meeting with the SP, I headed to meet the Additional SP. There, I also met a few other senior officers of the district. After a formal round of introduction and exchange of greetings, one officer wanted to know about my previous work experience at various Police Stations. In the course of this discussion, I told him that I had been posted at Guwahati during my probationer days. I also learnt that about 40 copper wire theft complaints had been filed in various Police Stations across the Cachar District. A police team was being assembled to go to Guwahati and arrest the accused criminals. I was also told that during investigations, it was found that the copper wires stolen from Cachar as well as other parts of Assam, were sent to Guwahati. And from there, the material was dispatched to various other States with the help of inter-state gangs.

Most of the receivers of the stolen copper wire were residents of Guwahati. And their kingpin was one Shambhunath. The officers further shared that one confessing accused was in the remand of Silchar Police. He knew Shambhu and a few others in the gang, and was ready to identify them and help the police apprehend them. But the problem was that the district's investigating officers involved in the copper wire theft cases did not have a good knowledge of Guwahati. So, they were discussing under whose leadership the team should be sent. I told the officers that I had arrested one Shambhunath in a copper wire case in Guwahati about six years ago. “But I am not sure if this Shambhu is the same fellow whom you are trying to track. The man I had arrested was a small fry but your culprit looks like a big fish.”

During this discussion, two officers slipped out one by one. They returned a few moments later and said, “You too have to accompany the investigating team.” “But what will I do? There is no pending copper wire theft case in my Police Station,” I protested. They said, “That’s okay. It is the SP sahib’s order. Please meet him immediately for a briefing.” I did not feel any enthusiasm then as I did not realise that the small fry Shambhu had grown into a big fish and had become the kingpin of the copper wire theft racket in Guwahati. Mentally, I cursed myself for putting the foot in my mouth.

As asked, I met Shri D. N. Sonowal, who was then the senior-most among all the District Superintendents. The benign gentleman said that since I had prior experience of the terrain, I was being sent along with the investigating team. My job would be to guide the team and liaison with the local police in Guwahati and obtain their cooperation. I was immediately reminded of the suspended Sipahi Singh and how the gang is well entrenched in official circles. Hence, I told the SP that while we will have to take the help of the local police, our efforts will come to naught if our presence and objective is revealed beforehand. The accused persons will immediately go underground as they have moles at all levels of the administration. Sonowal sahib understood my concern and said, "To maintain secrecy, I am giving you a Demi-Official (DO) letter addressed to the Kamrup SP, Shri K.P.S. Gill. You hand it over to him personally."

That night, I along with the investigating officer SI Dulal Dutta, confessing accused Qutub and a few junior officers and constables took a train to Guwahati. Reaching the city the next day, I decided not to take Qutub to the Guwahati Police Station but keep him in the Government Railway Police (GRP) lock-up in Guwahati. Thereafter, I took Sonowal sahib's letter to the Kamrup SP. The SP, in turn, directed me to see the City DySP, Guwahati, with the assurance that he will provide the necessary assistance to our team. So, I met the DySP and requested his help in arresting the accused. He asked me to see him the next day.

In the evening, we visited the narrow lane from which I had arrested Shambhunath. The place had totally changed. Instead of huts, there were some big houses including a few mansions. I learnt that Shambhu and his brothers had moved out of the place a few years ago. A few inquiries further led credence to the suspicion that the small fry Shambhu had now grown big and become the kingpin of the receivers of stolen property. He had also made quite a name for himself after being arrested in a few security acts. My colleague, Dulal remarked, "Vanijye basati Laxmi (the Goddess of wealth, Laxmi, is in business.)" We could not ascertain Shambhu's whereabouts that night, but we had enough leads to give us some hope that his present location would be identified in a day or two.

We met the City DySP the next day. He directed us to contact the Inspector OC, Guwahati.. I was somewhat uncomfortable with the matter going to the Police Station level even before the accused had been identified. Evidently, Sonowal sahib's letter was of no use. However, I met the officer in charge and sought his assistance in arresting the accused and requested him to send an experienced officer with our team.

The OC then asked for the list of the accused persons. I complied but refrained from sharing the name of Shambhu. I also did not disclose about the presence of the confessing accused, Qutub. That day, I and Dulal again went out in plain clothes. We searched and found Shambhu's new house. He now lived in a posh locality of the city in a sprawling mansion. His children studied in a convent school. He had now become a wealthy person and his meteoric rise in a matter of a mere 4-5 years was unbelievable. We were relieved to identify the house of the real culprit and returned to the hotel.

Running over the pages of a local Assamese daily the next morning, I spotted a brief news that blew my mind. The news item mentioned that a team from Cachar Police had arrived in the city to apprehend a gang of interstate copper wire thieves in association with the city police and a 'massive hunt' was on to apprehend the accused. How the journalist may have got whiff of the news was not very difficult to imagine. But we pretended as if nothing had happened and met the Inspector OC. We were hopeful that there could be a strategy in planting the news story. But our hopes were dashed when we received nothing but empty assurances.

Given the uncertainty, we concluded that there was no point in waiting any longer. We had to do something and do it soon. But to conduct a raid, a local officer's presence is necessary. We had to resolve this issue ourselves. So we spent the day preparing for the swoop. Luckily, we also found an officer of the local Police Station, who was enthusiastic. I cannot remember the name of the young officer, but he suggested that next day he would be on night duty. "Come tomorrow night; I will drive you to the spot."

As planned, the next night, we went with the local officer to arrest the accused. We also picked up Qutub from the GRP lock-up, as he would have to identify Shambhunath and also lead us to some of the others involved in the racket. As Shambhu was the main target, we went to his house first. He was called out from outside the house, but there was no response. We then banged the door. Still no response. By then 3-4 minutes had elapsed. Shambhu's house was surrounded by other houses on three sides and only the front, where we were standing, was the only way out. Still, I was worried that he would try to somehow escape if we did not arrest him in the first attempt. It would be very difficult for us to lay our hands on him later. As there was no response, one constable climbed on the shoulders of another and peeped inside from the ventilator. "Sir, one person is trying to climb the rear wall and trying to escape," he said.

I immediately called out loudly, "Shambhu, *bhago mat, bahar aao.* (Shambhu, don't run, come out.)" A trembling voice replied, "Chakraborty sahib na kya? (Is that Chakraborty sahib?)" I replied, "*Haan,* (Yes)," even as I marvelled how the fellow had recognised my voice after so many years. "*Aaa raha hoon, aaa raha hoon* (coming, coming)," he replied. I was sure that he would not escape now because he remembered how he had been dealt with once and would not want a repeat.

Once Shambhu came out, Qutub immediately identified him. The suspicion was then confirmed - it was the same Shambhu whom I had arrested six years ago. After Shambhu's arrest, we raided a few other places but were not successful. Everyone had escaped. In one house, we even found warm tea cups on the table.

After Shambhu's arrest, we had to stay back in Guwahati for a few days to apprehend his accomplices. The moles and agents of the gang, who were keeping a watch on the hotel we were staying in, now became very active. A man who looked like the yesteryear Bollywood film villain, Hira Lal, and was the owner of a common gaming house (gambling in a gaming house was legal back then), approached me directly and wanted to know if Shambhu could be released on bail. On being refused, he indicated that while this might be a difficult task, but if it was done then there would be no miserliness on his part in adequately compensating the effort. When even this did not work, he started pestering Dulal. I had forewarned Dulal about this possibility and so he was on his guard. Failing to get his way with Dulal, he again began pestering me. These people have a false notion that with money power they can bend any law. Hence, when they saw that we were not relenting, they thought that the money offered was probably less. So, in private, he offered me a blank cheque and said, "Please fill in the amount yourself." I had read about 'blank cheques' in novels and dramas but had never imagined that I would ever set eyes on one.

But I had a different equation to resolve with Shambhunath. I wanted to teach him that the law and the police were not toys that could be played around with impunity. And not everyone was up for sale. Hence, in spite of having a large amount of black money, he had to spend a long time behind the bars. Many years later, I heard that his ego had been so badly bruised by the jail term that he had left Assam for good.

CHAPTER

7 A Day in A Policeman's Life

Now, let me return to my probationary period. After spending two-and-a-half years at Guwahati Police Station and its outposts, I was transferred to the Borjhar Airport as the Outpost In-charge. Though this was a police outpost, the In-charge's work had been recently limited to inspecting papers and permits of foreign nationals. Notably, at that point of time, the movement of foreigners in Assam was restricted and they were required to have an inner line permit to enter Assam. Earlier, Borjhar Police used to investigate crime in its jurisdiction, like all other outposts. However, things had changed and the Borjhar Outpost In-charge was supposed to look after the foreigners' movement only. In other words, the In-charge's jurisdiction was restricted merely to the airport. The law & order and criminal investigation activities were taken care of by the parent police station at Palashbari.

My colleagues and friends lamented when they learnt that I had received such an unglamorous posting. I, however, was very pleased and looked forward to some peace after all the physically taxing activities and the seemingly unending graveyard shifts, oblivious of what awaited me at Borjhar.

On the first day, I was quite exasperated to see the dilapidated condition of what was supposed to be the outpost office, which was situated adjacent to the airport. A long, bamboo walled, mud plastered hall like kuchha thatched roof structure had been partitioned into three and had been rented out. The central part was served as the Borjhar Police Outpost; on the right was a south Indian snack shop selling idlis and dosas and on the left was the Office of the Inspector of the Assam Excise Department. The spartan outpost had two chairs, a table, a General Diary and a Foreigners' Register and nothing else. I thought, "What a shame! What would the foreigners think of us, seeing the condition of this outpost?" One of the four constables was able to read my mind and told me with an air of assurance, "Sir, do not think about the foreigners. All our work is actually carried out inside the Airport building. So, no one comes here or sees anything."

The Borjhar airport received about 5-7 flights and only about a dozen foreigners on average in a day. There was no extensive security check or baggage check unlike present times. Dignitaries such as the Governor, the Chief Minister or other leaders or senior officials would arrive only once in a blue moon. Otherwise, there was very little work. Expectedly, boredom set in within a few days. But, as I got acquainted with the staff members at the Airport and grew friendly with them, gossip and games in the evenings kept me busy. I used to thank my stars for such a hassle-free posting. But in a few months, I realised that good luck does not last for ever.

Some days in one's life become unforgettable because of the unexpected or unusual nature of experience they bring in. In my life, one such day was January 24, 1968. Assam was simmering as the bifurcation of Assam and the creation of the new State of Meghalaya had caused widespread discontent. Agitated students spearheaded the protests. That day, the powerful students' union, All Assam Students' Union (AASU), had called for a 12-hours state-wide bandh (shut down), but the airports were kept out of the purview of the lock down. So, there was no additional security. The district administration or the local Police Station also did not bother to send out any alerts. At the time, the tarmac's protection was being handled by a dozen armed police jawans. There was no additional security for the main building or other installations. The Outpost In-charge and the four lathi-wielding constables were considered good enough for taking care of the security issues. No major law & order issue was expected and no one gave it another thought.

On January 24, the day of the agitation, I arrived for the day at the airport as usual, without any apprehensions. It was expected to be a lean day as there would be only few a passengers. I learnt that the passengers who had arrived from Delhi and Calcutta (now Kolkata) in the morning, were stranded at the airport as the agitators were not allowing any vehicular movement. During the afternoon, the flights were scheduled only after 12:30 p.m. So, at about 11:30, I headed for some food. I had just sat down for a meal when a porter informed me that a few students from the Guwahati University located in nearby Jhalukbari had visited the airport area for a stroll. On their way back, they found a small tea shop open on the day of agitation and had an altercation, which later escalated into a fight, with a porter named Dara Singh. Some of the students were hurt in the incident and one of them was critically injured. I knew Dara Singh, a burly, well-built man. The incident was entirely believable because thrashing two-four ordinary people would have been no big deal for him. But I was filled with consternation at the report as I knew that a retaliation by a larger group of students was imminent. In that case, the porter would be attacked severely. So, I immediately rushed to the airport to find out the whereabouts of Dara Singh. I was relieved to learn from his supervisors that they had sent him to the adjacent Indian Air Force cantonment area.

As I had anticipated, within an hour a large group of students arrived and encircled the airport, demanding that Dara Singh be handed over to them. Soon the demand turned into a threat.

Amid the mayhem, a plainclothes Indian Air Force police official posted at the airport, who looked 'big and burly,' was mistaken by a group of students as Dara Singh and was manhandled. The man had a big moustache while Dara Singh had none. However, with the help of the student leaders, I was able to rescue the man. I heaved a sigh of relief as he was sent off to his camp. Unfortunately that relief was short lived. The students were adamant that they wanted the real Dara Singh. They began searching all over the place and raised a demand that no flight would be allowed to fly out of the airport that day. The aerodrome officer and others officials pleaded with the students to keep the airport out of the purview of the bandh. I had an inkling that the agitating students would not leave the airport that day.

By then, some local anti-social elements joined the students and began creating a nuisance. Seeing the deteriorating situation, I became apprehensive. I had only three lathi wielding constables with me and one was guarding the outpost. It would be difficult to control the situation with so few men. So, helplessly, I tried to contact the SP at Guwahati and the Additional SP for some support, but in vain. I also learnt that about 100 trucks had been torched on the Guwahati-Shillong Road. There was trouble in many other parts of the city. Timber godowns in Palashbari and Bijoy Nagar, which were just 8 miles away from the airport, had been set on fire. The SP and other senior officers were engaged in trying to restore normalcy, so no one was available. At last, I climbed the three stories of the airport building to reach the Airport Control Room and tried to call the Guwahati Police Control Room on telephone. I was able to connect after a long wait. I explained the dire situation to the DySP who was in charge of the control room and requested for some reinforcements, but received a negative response. No additional force was available. The officer, who had just finished his training and joined the force, wanted to know what the chief demand of the students was. As soon as I apprised him, he nonchalantly responded, "So what's the big deal? Dara Singh can be handed over to the students." I first thought that the officer was joking. But soon I realised that he meant what he said. I fathomed that there was no point in prolonging the discussion any further. Dejected, I slammed the receiver, vowing that I would not call again. I had not anticipated the scenes that would unfold over the next few hours and therefore did not realise how many more times I would have to climb those stairs and speak on the telephone.

At about 1 p.m. two more aircraft landed. The passengers were stranded in the midst of the hundreds of agitators and waited for sunset as prior to that no movement of vehicles was possible. In such a situation, another unexpected and unsavoury incident took place. Agitated with the manhandling of the Indian Air Force policeman, a Squadron Leader, along with a posse of armed Air Force police personnel, arrived on the scene and disregarding the sensitivity of the situation, began yelling at the students. That day's student agitation was not an ordinary agitation. It was based on a very sensitive matter and the agitators had the goodwill and support of the people of Assam. That's why they did not give any regard to the Squadron Leader or his armed personnel. All the yelling and shouting went in vain. Heavily humiliated, the team turned back. However, this emboldened the agitators. Now they placed a fresh demand: They would not allow any aircraft to fly in or out of the airport that day.

I had no manpower and that is why I had to heavily rely on some of the student leaders, who had been helping me in maintaining order from the very beginning. But by then, many anti-social elements had joined the students. Slowly, the situation began slipping out of control of the student leaders. As the large groups of agitators loitered aimlessly inside the airport complex, the shops and restaurants hurriedly downed their shutters and tension gripped the area. Adding to the woe, a transit flight from Mohanbari destined for New Delhi landed at the airport. A Union Minster was flying in that aircraft. The Minister was unaware that the airport had been almost taken over by the agitators. He got out of the aircraft and wanted to go to the VIP lounge to take some rest. Seeing the crowd on the way, he expressed his displeasure and had an altercation with the students, who heckled him. I got to know of this situation when an aerodrome officer rushed to inform me. I was aghast as we had no prior information about the minister's visit. Wasting no time, I along with a few student leaders and the constables, I rushed to the spot, rescued the Minister and put him back on the aircraft, which immediately took off for Delhi.

Soon after the flight took off, the agitators became adamant that no other aircraft would be allowed to fly out during the duration of the agitation. The hapless Aerodrome Officer and the Indian Airlines officials had to unwillingly accept the demand of the students. With this, the airport too came within the agitation's purview.

As all the demands of the students had been met, some time elapsed peacefully, without any incident. I prayed that the remaining part of the agitation period may also pass uneventfully. But I had never imagined that this passing phase was merely a lull before the storm. The drama had just begun and the climax was yet to play out.

After some time, a flight arrived from Calcutta. The airhostess of this aircraft was Miss Chitra. Unaware of the situation, Chitra, the pilot and some other crew members came to the lounge and were disturbed with the chaos. So, the pilot asked

Chitra return to the aircraft and rest there, instead of the lounge. As the airhostess proceeded to cross the gate separating the main building of the aircraft and the tarmac, some of the agitators accosted her and questioned her, "Why are you going back to the aircraft? Will it fly out?" Chitra, curtly replied, "What nonsense? Am I a pilot?" The agitators picked up the word "nonsense" and gave it an undesirable spin. "She has insulted us by calling us 'nonsense.'" Some of them rushed towards her threateningly. With the agitators on her heels, Chitra somehow managed to run to the aircraft standing on the tarmac and shut its door. The agitators, followed her. The tarmac, which was prohibited for the general public, was flooded with the agitators. Only two jawans responsible for the security of the tarmac were no match for the hundreds of the agitating students and stood aside. Just then, another aircraft landed and its passengers too had to face great harassment.

Not being able to lay their hands on Chitra, the students demanded that she has to apologise for insulting them. Hearing this demand, I was worried because there was a possibility that the anti-social elements would assault her physically if they could lay their hands on her. I shared my fears with the Aerodrome Officer and the Indian Airlines officials, and requested them not to accept the demand. I ran to the control room on the third floor to report the deteriorating situation. I did this many times and requested for support. While I was reporting the deteriorating situation to the Guwahati Control Room for the third time, I saw that the Aerodrome Officer, pilot and other officials heading towards the aeroplane in which Chitra had taken refuge. I immediately sensed that the officials must have agreed to the illogical demands of the agitators and a chaos was imminent. So, I rushed down at great speed and headed towards the gate opening to the tarmac and saw that Miss Chitra had opened the door of the aircraft. With folded hands, she stepped on the ladder. Within a fraction of a second, some miscreants pulled the ladder away. The poor airhostess could not keep maintain her balance and fell from the aircraft – some 15-20 feet below – immediately losing her sense.

Witnessing this situation, I could not resist myself. I forgot that this was a student agitation and that I had no manpower or support. I immediately rushed out and grabbed the sten gun from the armed police havildar and rushed towards the spot where Chitra was lying. The constable was taken aback and began running behind me. He was followed by the other armed guard and my three constables. Seeing us rushing and brandishing guns, the agitators fled the spot, emptying the tarmac. They must have realised that the attack on the airhostess was an audacious and outrageous act. Since they had faulted, the police now had a strong reason to take action against them.

In the meanwhile, the pilot, to everyone's amazement somehow managed to pull Chitra into the aircraft and took off for Calcutta without any announcement or even without the aerodrome control's permission. The passengers of that flight were stranded at Borjhar. Due to the unnatural action of the pilot, it was later rumoured that the pilot was in a romantic liaison with the airhostess. I too felt that I was witnessing a drama.

Meanwhile, seeing the agitators flee from the tarmac, the others too disappeared from the scene. Only a few student leaders remained. As I chased some of the agitators out of the main building of the aerodrome, I cursed myself for not being able to avert the accident. If only I had some manpower, maybe this could have been averted. I also randomly thought if Chitra was alive and what my next course of action should be.

As I was thinking thus, a city Additional SP, along with Circle Inspector Bairagi, and a few jawans arrived. I remember that I had exasperatedly said, "Why have you come now, Sir?" Because I had thought that the day long drama had ended. The two officers consoled and patiently heard my account of the day's ordeals. Listening to me, in their minds, Chitra's situation was uppermost, so they asked me about that several times. But let alone me, no one who was present at the spot, could give any accurate information about her condition. Everyone awaited information from Dum Dum Airport. But before any information could come through, the scene here warmed up.

The officials of the airport began discussions with the Additional SP on the next course of action. Chitra's condition continued to be a major question and everyone was apprehensive of what was to be done. Meanwhile, some of the airport officials accused that the student leaders, who were still present there, were responsible for the incident. Based on the allegation, the Additional SP took the student leaders to the VIP lounge for interrogation. I could not interrupt the interrogation but I expressed that these student leaders had helped us right from the beginning and are not the real culprits. The senior officers of the airport were aware of this fact but they did not say anything. Perhaps, they wanted some action against the students. But this action invited greater danger.

Within no time, rumours spread like wildfire that the student leaders had been arrested. Hundreds of students and some anti-socials arrived in droves and surrounded the airport. They demanded the unconditional release of the student leaders. Within minutes the mob turned violent and they went on a rampage and stone pelting spree. The stranded passengers, especially the women, were caught unawares. I mounted a quick rescue along with my team of constables and herded them to a safer part of the building. During this commotion, I came to know that Indian Airlines Junior Engineer, Shri Hiren Sen, had become a target of some of the local anti-socials. They had spread the rumour that the student leaders had been arrested at the behest of

Sen. Sen's nickname was Sunny Liston, because he looked like the famous Negro boxer. The very jovial man usually wore a sombre look, which dissuaded many. Due to his personality, the local 'dadas' did not mess around with him even though they bore a misplaced grudge against him. But today, they had got a great opportunity to pin him down and hence the rumour was spread against him.

Anticipating the evil designs, I started searching for Sen in the crowd to forewarn him. Before I could reach the VIP lounge, I saw that the student leaders had been released. The students were exhilarated with this and began proceeding towards the main exit gate. With the release of the student leaders, some miscreants, who were waiting for an opportunity, went berserk. They began breaking whatever came their way and pelted stones. Suddenly, I noticed that someone was being thrashed in a room. With the three constables in tow, I rushed to the room and saw that Hiren Sen was being attacked. With the four of us and the Circle Inspector reaching there, Sen got a respite but made a tactical mistake. To save himself, he ran out of the room and into an open space. The attackers surrounded him and began thrashing him at will. A bleeding Sen fell on the ground. Within a second, I saw an attacker pick up a long wooden stool and rain it on Sen. "He's finished," I thought as I almost instinctively raised my left hand to thwart the attack. And then began the invisible power's play. The stool struck six inches above the wrist of my left arm.

Though the strike was powerful, only the skin of my arm had peeled off but I wasn't hurt much. But when the attacker realised that he had hit a police officer, he let go of the stool from a height of about 6 feet. The furniture fell on the floor with a loud clamour, stunning everybody to silence. The pandemonium stopped for a brief moment.

I took advantage of the weakness of the attackers and with a loud moan, I fell on the blood soaked Sen so that he was not directly attacked any more. I had fathomed that the attackers would not directly hit the police.

But seeing me fall, my three constables thought that I was badly hurt. And this drove them to a rage that was beyond my imagination. Nipen Kalita, a youngster from Palashbari, and Ram Singh, who hailed from Patna, Bihar, both of whom were well built, yelled loudly in their respective mother tongues. They lost all composure and charged with their lathis. The elderly constable, Deka, broke down to tears and admonished the attackers, "Tohoti Saarok marili, aaji huda ne-eru dei!" (You guys have hurt our Sir! I will not let you off today!), saying this he banged the ground with his lathi to express his anger. The constables' sudden and explosive display of emotion worked like magic for us. The agitators were taken aback and retreated swiftly. Just then, the Additional SP too arrived with reinforcements. He rushed to my side, kneeled down and began checking on my condition.

Seeing that the agitations had dissipated, a plan flashed in my mind. I whispered in the Additional SP's ears that I was okay. "But please keep this to yourself and tell the agitators that the police officer has been badly hurt and if they did not disperse immediately, then you'll order the police to open fire." The Additional SP was not ready to accept that my injury was not grave. So, with a disbelieving tone, he asked, "Are you sure?" To assure him, I grasped his hand with my left arm and pressed it firmly. "See? I am fine." Thus assured, the Additional SP did as was planned and sternly warned the agitators. The medicine worked and the agitators began to disperse slowly. The student leaders, before leaving met me and apologised. I told them to forget whatever has happened, "Let us not think about it. I have taken it sportingly," I said.

In Durgasaptashati (Sri Sri Chandi) we find, *"ahankarang mano buddhing rakshen me Dharmadharinini".* Today, I feel that it was the invisible power that had given the idea to do some acting and inspired the constables to get fired up. Had it not been for that moment, it is difficult to fathom how that day's drama would have ended.

After the agitators and anti-social elements vacated the airport, the passengers left the airport under the supervision of the Additional SP. By then it was almost 9 p.m. But some of the officers and employees of the airport refused to go home without police protection. They approached me and asked me to arrange for police escort.

Dear Ma, I hope you can understand the situation. These people were witness to the ordeal we had been through throughout the day and knew very well that there were no additional personnel, yet they now wanted us to escort them to their homes. From their demeanour, it was obvious that they just wanted someone in khakhi uniform to accompany them, not necessarily the real police. The episode proved the value of a policeman's uniform during a crisis.

I knew that I would have to give an explanation for the mayhem and the damage and above all the heckling of the Union Minister, because in the eyes of the law, the district superintendent's order asking the In-charge to take care of only foreigners' affairs would not stand. I would be questioned, "After all, you were present there on duty in uniform. Then what the hell were you doing there?" So, I told the airport officials, "Do not fear, we will escort you. But give me a short while, not to rest but to make a general diary entry."

I came to the outpost to pen down the details of the day's events. Many men and women followed me. My outpost must have received so many visitors for the first time in its life and felt really elated. These people were tense but waited quietly. Today, this poor policeman's dilapidated office was not a butt of jokes. To many of these fear-stricken people, this outpost must have appeared like a fortress. Under the glare of many pairs of curious eyes, I penned a 12-14 page entry with all minute details. Thereafter, we escorted everyone to their homes. After I returned to my quarter and gulped down a jug full of water, breaking my 12 hour long nirambu (without water) fast.

The next day, on January 25, I woke up to the loud banging on the door. I woke up with a startle and opened the door, only to find my anxious friends from Guwahati. They had arrived to see me after learning about my 'hand fracture.' But they were surprised to see me unhurt. "But then what about the rumour in town about you being grievously hurt?" they demanded. I lifted the veil from the mystery. My friends had a hearty laugh and jokingly advised me to try my hand at becoming an actor.

After bidding goodbye to my friends, I got ready and reached the airport on time, where I received a hero's greeting. A Delhi-based elderly woman passenger was eagerly awaiting to meet the 'gallant officer' who had fought the anti-socials. She must have imagined a big, burly man. She was surprised to see a man weighing merely 63 kgs and exclaimed, "Oh, he's just a young man!" The other passengers commented, "Yes, he's a young man and has not yet been married, that's why he jumped into the fray. Would he have done so otherwise?" Now, who will explain to these people that those who jump in, do so at all ages?

During the afternoon, the SP and DC came to the airport to inspect and assess the damage. Both of them were tired after fighting the fire that had spread across the entire district. They expressed satisfaction after listening to the praises heaped on our small team by the airport officials. But they also warned me that the next day was January 26 (Republic Day), and there was every possibility of strong protests taking place. They wanted to know if I was prepared to handle the situation. I confidently said, "Yes, I can, but I'll need additional support." They assured me of reinforcements.

On January 26, I was mentally prepared for another day of strife. It was almost 8 a.m. but the promised reinforcement had not yet arrived. However, in a short while, I saw that the airport was flooded with army men in olive green uniform. They were led by an elderly Colonel and at least a dozen commissioned officers. The Colonel, saw me and said, "Don't worry my child, we are here to protect the airport." He then gave a list of wars he had fought and the bravery he had shown on the warfront. Mentally, I thought that this was akin to bringing in a cannon to kill a fly as at that point, I was unaware of the fact that the assault on the Air Force police officer, the attacks on Chitra and Hiren Sen and above all the heckling of the Union Minister had gone a long way. The State Government was busy giving explanations and affixing responsibility.

To prove that the government was already in action, the SP and DC were immediately transferred. A departmental enquiry was initiated against the Additional SP who had come to Borjhar airport. And a DIG was entrusted to probe 14 instances of alleged negligence against me. If any one of the 14 alleged lapses was found to true, then a departmental proceeding was to be instituted, aiming at my dismissal from service. During that time, in the entire state of undivided Assam had only 7-8 DIGs. So, the importance of the inquiry can be imagined.

Dear Ma, after doing so much, when you have to undergo such harassment, then what is the state of your mind? However, I was not the only victim of the system. There are many such instances. But how many people know about the situations policemen have to go through? If they knew, then maybe they would not turn police bashing into a fashion.

Be that as it may, as I had mentioned earlier, due to the grace of some invisible power, I always managed to evade any bruises. In this case too, something similar happened. A senior officer had arrived from the Police Headquarter in Shillong for a spot enquiry. While enquiry was going on, the Comptroller of Aerodrome flew down to Borjhar from Delhi just at that moment. He shook hands with me and said, "We are all grateful to you for whatever you have done. I have come all the way only to congratulate you." Then he addressed the enquiry officer and said, "We want to see him promoted soon." I laughed at the suggestion mentally. Finally, my long 12-14 page general diary entry, the endorsement of the airport officials and the Comptroller of Aerodrome's arrival at that opportune moment had probably saved me from an immediate suspension or an insulting transfer. But the enquiry into the allegations continued for a long while.

Episode of Ramu and Lakshmi

Often in life, trouble does not come alone. During my tenure at Borjhar, I faced a similar double whammy. The enquiry probing the alleged 14 lapses for the fiasco on January 24 did not find anything against me. But the enquiry report had not been submitted. Meanwhile, we were supposed to receive our confirmation in a few days. I had little hope of receiving confirmation as the enquiry was still to officially exonerate me. Worn out mentally and physically, I was one day sitting in a despondent mood in the veranda of my quarter, thinking about my uncle's piercing words: Policing is a notorious job. At that moment, the wife of Shri Hiren Sen, whom I respectfully addressed as *boudi* (sister-in-law) arrived with a complaint. Ramu, an anti-social, and his wife, an equally notorious woman, were up to activities that were becoming unbearable for her and her three daughters. With each passing day, Ramu's anti-social activities were on the rise. Earlier, he used to trade in illicit liquor, but now he was running a brothel. "The activity goes on till late in the night. Please do something," she pleaded.

I had met Ramu in the market soon after having joined Borjhar. He saluted me reverentially as soon as he saw me. He had a deep scar on the left side of his forehead and the deeply injured eyes made his face difficult to forget. His demeanour made me feel suspicious. Who was he? A few days later, I saw him along with his wife. Ramu saluted me and urged his wife to do the same. His wife's name was Lakshmi. On seeing the middle-aged woman, I felt that I had seen her earlier. Later, I remembered that about two-and-a-half years ago, soon after joining, I had seen her and her sister a few times in the Guwahati Police Station. The two dark complexioned but sharp featured South Indian women would sit in the police station for hours together. I used to wonder then whether they were the complainants or the accused. After about a month or two, an officer from the Paltan Bazar outpost caught the two women and brought them to the Police Station. I then came to know that these two were sisters, who were apparently in great demand. With their youth gone, they had now become penniless. Without any customers, they had taken to addiction and were often involved in petty thefts or fisticuffs. They were first rate trouble makers.

On the other hand, I came to know that Ramu was once a notorious wagon-breaker. Maligaon and Pandu (near Guwahati) were his areas of operation. A few years ago, he was grievously injured during a gang war, which led to the disfigurement of his face. He had now shifted base from Maligaon and lived in a village near the airport. Seeing the couple, I understood that the notorious Ramu from Bihar and the once famed Lakshmi from South India, had now joined hands to survive in the harsh world. But little did I realise that I would have to go through much trouble at their behest.

Though Hiren Sen was elder to me, I had become very friendly with him. I used to occasionally visit his residence, which was located at a corner area of the airport. That is when I came to know that Ramu and his wife lived in a hut near Sen's residence.

Boudi had once complained about the drinking at Ramu's place, leading to altercations and how the family was affected. As Ramu lived outside the airport area, (and so, they were out of my jurisdiction) therefore I had informed the local Assam Excise Department Inspector about the ongoings and requested him to take action against the illicit liquor trade. But, when Boudi complained again, I concluded that the Excise Inspector had not taken any action, emboldening the accused and giving them the licence to further expand their illegal activities, with scant regard to the fact that a gentleman's family was living in the proximity.

I was already very irritated. Hiren Sen had not recovered fully. Hence, listening to Boudi's complaints I decided to take some action against Ramu. Also, explaining jurisdictional issues to Boudi would have been difficult and it would have been equally improper to ask her to go and lodge a complaint at the Palashbari police station. So, along with three constables, I raided Ramu's residence that evening.

A few customers had just started arriving at Ramu's den and the evening of merrymaking was poised to commence. But, seeing us, some of the customers quietly slithered away. As there was information that Ramu had brought a woman from outside, I ordered him to call out those who were inside the hut. It was dark and from a distance we had noticed a lone kerosene lamp burned inside. As soon as we reached the entrance, the lamp was blown off. Ramu began touching the feet of the constables, pleading and crying loudly, seeking forgiveness. On the other hand, Ramu's customers who were in the darkness, and his companions tried to scare us by making ferocious moves. In this chaos, I sensed an arm slipping into the hut's door past my right foot. Lakshmi had brought out a long sickle and was about to hit me. But before she could do any damage, I instinctively stamped her wrist with my foot. In great pain, she let go of the weapon and began crying loudly. Hearing Lakshmi's cries, Ramu became aggressive. The alert constables overpowered him swiftly. As soon as his companions realised that Ramu had been overpowered, they stepped back. After the chaos ceased, a non-local young girl came out of the hut. She had just begun putting on rouge make-up. Questioned about her identity, Lakshmi insisted that she was her sister and had come to visit her. "What's your name," I asked her firmly. "Bano," she replied, exposing Lakshmi's lie.

Criminals are known to employ many tactics when they face an imminent threat. To escape being taken to the Police Station, Ramu laid down with his back pinned to the ground and refused to budge. With no other option, we had to drag him up to my police outpost.

On interrogation, Bano admitted that she had been in the trade for the last two years but did not operate independently. I inferred that she had taken this recourse only to survive. Finally, Ramu also admitted that he had to get the girl to keep a few noveau rich and some contractors happy.

The next day, I challaned Ramu and Lakshmi under section 109 CrPC for bad livelihood. Bano was sent to the Guwahati Court with a 'safe custody' request. Later, after listening about that evening's raid, an experienced officer had opined that I should not have gone to Ramu's den without adequate preparation and should not have allowed my emotions to overpower my reason. These anti-socials are notorious and can go to any extent. This apart, it is necessary to have adequate manpower, prepare adequately and take precautions before raiding any women, liquor or gambling dens. Even though I was aware of all these things, I had reacted due to the circumstances and taken emotion-driven decisions. The results could have been both good and bad. In this case, the result was not very good.

After about a week of Court Challan of Lakshmi and Ramu, I had to go to Guwahati for some work. There, I heard that a court case had been filed against me for outraging the modesty of Bano. Summons had also been issued against me to appear in the court. I had no inkling that something like this could happen. What a shame! I felt that this allegation was more insulting than the allegation of the 14 points of negligence. I felt fuzzy and could not think about what I should do. I had only one thought: whatever I had done was done in good faith and since I had not done anything wrong, nothing wrong could happen to me. Since the summons had already been issued, I would have to fight it out in the court. And since these matters cannot be discussed with everyone, I was in a fix about whom to consult. Then I remembered the experienced Manoranjan Choudhury, who had been with Guwahati Police for a long time. Though he was senior, he was quite a sport and had good relations with juniors like us. I sought his counsel and shared all the details with him. After listening to everything, he asked, "What is the girl's name?" As soon as he heard, "Bano," he said, "Oh, seems she is a member of Baccha Khan's gang." I did not know who Baccha Khan was. So I asked, "What should I do now?" Manoranjan Da said, "You don't have to do anything. I will do whatever needs to be done. Just ensure that you remain present at the court on the appointed day, without fail."

With Manoranjan Da's assurance, I returned to Borjhar, but my mind was in turmoil. Earlier, I never used to think of bad time, bad planetary influences or astrology. But during that period I felt that I was going through a very bad patch. Else, why would I have to face an enquiry after the unprecedented events of January 24 and now a court case for trying to help someone?

After about a fortnight, I presented myself at the Guwahati court and for the first and last time in my life, I stood in the dock of the court. The magistrate was again, Srimati Sucheta Raychowdhury. On seeing her, I felt embarrassed. But I also felt hopeful as I thought that I would get justice. The magistrate asked, "Don't you have an advocate?" "No," I replied.

By this time, Ramu's lawyer requested the court that his clients want to withdraw the case. The magistrate now became adamant and said that she would not let them withdraw the case. "Either prove the allegation or face penal action," she said firmly. Ramu's advocate was roundly chastised and told, "If false allegations are levelled against the police, how will they work?" Without dismissing the case, she gave a date and instructed me to be present in the court on that day at all cost.

With the magistrate's uncompromising stand, Ramu and Lakshmi fell in a trap. On one hand the court was unhappy. On the other hand, Bano had refused to present herself in the court. So they were in danger, as they could be imprisoned for levelling a false allegation against an officer. Seeing no other way out, they fell at my feet. "We did not want to file a case against you, Huzoor. The case was filed at the behest of the Excise Inspector. It was he who arranged a lawyer for us. Do you not believe us, Sir? Please see this case filing; the handwriting is that of the Excise Officer." I read the paper and saw that it was the draft of the case against me. I kept the paper with me.

Later, the constables from the Excise Officer's office confirmed that the writing was of their boss's. I could not believe it that a fellow government officer would make such a damaging conspiracy to malign another officer and instigate anti-social elements to do the job. Ramu did not have the gumption to file a case. Then why did the old inspector push him to file the false case? Possibly, the Excise Officer was angry because of the police raid on Ramu's den. The officer must have thought that police was trying to usurp his fertile land. Such a corrupt man would never have thought that a police officer could take action without any personal interest. These officers believe from the bottom of their heart that one joins government service only for the proceeds of corruption. Taking bribes is a matter of their birth right and this is what gives them satisfaction. Carrying on loot under the garb of government service is their dharma. Notably, the Excise Officer had probably figured out that the cover on his dirty game had been blown. That is why, he never visited his office during the rest of my tenure at Borjhar.

That is how three months flew by after the fateful day of January 24. The agitation had let to immense losses for the trading and business community. The Chief Minister of Rajasthan flew in to express his solidarity with the local traders. An enquiry commission was set up to determine the extent of damages, identify lapses on the part of the administration and the police, and affix responsibility.

On the other hand, the enquiry against the 14 alleged instances of negligence on my part continued for a long time. Under such circumstances, one night, a closed cover letter from the office of the Guwahati SP was delivered to me. I received the letter but did not open it, as I thought that it was perhaps my suspension letter. I decided to have my dinner at peace and then open the letter. After dinner, the letter remained unopened. Then, I remembered that a few days ago, the DySP from the DIG's office, Faziruddin sahib, had confided that during the departmental enquiry, nothing adverse had been found against me in any of the 14 allegations. In fact, a favourable report with high praise for me had been submitted. A resident of Sivasagar, this jovial officer was not someone who would have said things lightly. Finally, I opened the envelope out of curiosity. In it were two letters. The first one instructed me to meet the Deputy SP (Law) Phani Roy, who was helping the indicted officers facing the enquiry commission, and take instructions from him. After hesitating to open the second letter for a while, I pulled up enough courage to read it. It said "...SI is highly commended for his sincere and successful attempt on 24.01.1968 to save Shri H. Sen, IAF employee, from the attack of some rowdy students." Reading the order, I felt that I was on seventh heaven. But, a reward after such a long time? What could be the matter? The next morning's newspapers provided an answer to that question.

The day before was the first day of the commission's hearing. The barrister representing the business community spent the whole day explaining how the administration and the police had been a complete failure. To prove his statement, he called the first witness, who was none other than Shri Hiren Sen. After Sen concluded his long statement, the counsel for the State questioned him: "You were a victim of the agitation. But who saved you that day?" Sen gave a short reply, "Chaku." ('Chaku' was the shortened form of my surname and I was popular by that name among friends at Borjhar). The counsel immediately asked:

"Who is this Chaku?"

"My friend."

"So, what does your friend do?"

"He's a police officer."

"Where?"

"At Borjhar Airport police outpost."

"So, you just said that police was inactive that day. But now you are saying that you were saved by a police officer."

"Chaku saved me because he was my friend."

"What you are saying is that even though he is a policeman, he saved you only because he is your friend. Is that logical?"

Hiren Sen buckled under scrutiny and then admitted that it was in fact the police that had saved him that day. This admission effectively demolished the allegation that police and administration were inactive, on the first day of the hearing itself. As a result, a reward was handed over to me by the end of the day. I also understood that I had been instructed to see the DySP (Law) to prepare as a witness in favour of the State. I thought, this is what is called *"Din bhaley aahise"* (Good days are here!). Things unfolded just as I had predicted. Within a few days, I received the Confirmation Order. I was thus baptised by the fire during my probationary period.

On the eve of my departure from Borjhar, I had tea with colleagues in the evening and exchanged goodbyes. As I stepped out of the outpost, I saw the constables of the adjoining Excise Office standing in attention. They saluted me warmly. There was a tinge of sadness on their faces. The eldest among them hugged me and said, "Our Inspector was inimical towards you but you never bore a grudge against us. We were fearful for many days. But aapuni belek, Sir (you are different). You are like God!"

I smiled at this. It is so easy to become a God in this land!

CHAPTER

8 The Strange Doctor

After receiving confirmation, my journey through the next one-and-half years was a complete potpourri that gave me all-rounded experience. I am penning down these pages as a witness to those experiences. I was transferred from Borjhar to the then undivided Sivasagar District and posted at Borholla outpost (now a Police Station) as its In-charge. The village outpost was located at the southern end of Borholla, abutting the Nagaland border. The population comprised people from Ahom, Kochari, Thengal, Miri and several other tribes, apart from the plains people. The fertile soil of the place earned it the epithet, 'Granary of Assam.' Though not everyone was equally well off, I felt that the simple villagers were much happier than the city dwellers. I was impressed with the fact that the common people considered policemen as valued members of the society. They were happy with the success of police and were never shy of expressing their support for the police. A few incidents left a deep and indelible impression on me.

One day, a man walked into the outpost with his 14-year-old son. On being asked why he had come, he said, "Hakim," (the police in-charge was locally addressed as Hakim in those days) "my son has gone astray. He steals the utensils of neighbours and sells those off. The neighbours do not want to file a police report. But I know that my son is a thief and he should be punished. So, I have brought him here. Please punish him. I will not take him home till he is punished." After hearing him patiently, I realised that the simple man was hurt because of his son's waywardness. A round of scolding followed by some counselling of the worried parent would be enough, I assumed. But, even after a lot of persuasion, not much could be gained. The father was adamant. He strongly believed that a thief would never reform if he goes unpunished. Without finding any other means to convince the man, I tried to explain that the child was very young and had committed a petty crime. But the man continued to stick to his guns. So, I had to 'punish' the boy. The man, after much persuasion, agreed to take the boy back after three days.

This incident reminded me of another father, a city-dweller. A 15-year-old boy, Ratan, had earned tremendous notoriety as a pick-pocket in the city of Guwahati. He was a great hand and had become a headache for the police. No amount of chastisement through courts could reform him. On the morning of the shashti (sixth) day of Durga Puja, some people dragged him to the police station on suspicion of pick-pocketing. Since there was no specific evidence against him, he was let off the next day after a strong reprimand. Within a few hours of the commencement of Durga Puja festivities, Ratan was caught red-handed. The public thrashed him roundly and the bruised kid was dragged to the police station again. After a while, the boy's father arrived at the police station to bail him out. I spoke to the man at that time and noticed that the father was annoyed with Ratan, not because of his criminal acts, but because of something else. He alleged, in the course of the conversation, that his son had amassed a lot of money, but did not share a penny with him. What a difference in the thought process! One father is hurt because his son has committed a petty theft. Another one is unhappy because his son does not share the loot. Strange world, indeed!

I came across another instance of simplicity and implicit trust of these village people. Borholla had two large weekly markets. One was at Rajbari and the other at Nagabaat. Rajbari was earlier a tea estate, which had by then been abandoned. This market was located just at the Nagaland border and hence was frequented by people from the neighbouring State, including the Toolong (members of a former Myanmarese tribe) and the Cha tribesmen. Hence, at every weekly market, police had to make adequate arrangements to maintain law and order. On my first day of bazaar duty, the bazaar supervisors became a little worried about where I should sit. At last, they decided that I should sit at the Doctor's house. They therefore requested me, "Sir, please come along to the Doctor's house." I was surprised to know that the village had a doctor. Mentally, I thanked the doctor for his service. I also felt that I should meet the noble person who had such great regard for the poor village people. But when I learnt that Doctor *sahib* was not around as he had gone to Nagaland on a call, I did not proceed to his house. The next time I went to the Rajbari market, people again insisted that I should go to the Doctor's house and hence I decided to pay a visit. But as luck would have it, the Doctor had again gone on a call to Nagaland. My respect for the Doctor grew further after I saw his simple dwelling place. I felt that he was making a huge personal sacrifice while trying to serve the poor people. That day, I inspected his small pharmacy. Large glass jars had pink, green and white mixtures. I remembered having seen such mixtures in the tea estate hospital in the 1950s. Those mixtures were usually prepared by the compounders at the hospital. I had a sneaky suspicion that the doctor could possibly be a compounder. An experienced compounder in such a remote location was no less, I thought. I had been to the Rajbari area on quite a few occasions after that but never met the doctor. Every time, I would hear the same refrain – he's gone to neighbouring Nagaland on a visit.

After a few months, I heard something that startled me. An informer said, this doctor was actually a former guard at a tea estate hospital. That is where he had learnt the art of making mixtures. With that knowledge, he was masquerading as a 'doctor'. The village people, on the other hand, swore by his medicines and had no trust on anything else. And did he prescribe only medicines? Nope. The patients on the other side apparently insisted on the doctor's bezi (injection). The frequent visits to the other side was mainly because of the great demand for 'bezi', I was told. Alas! I thought, a quack doling out injections? Catastrophe can strike at any moment. My informer allayed the fears and said, "No Sir, nothing to worry about." The fellow is very smart. The injection vials contain nothing but distilled water."

Not every story had a happy ending, though. Nagabaat, which was situated at the State border, had a history of bloody clashes. Before the State of Nagaland was carved out, the people of the adjoining villages had conflict over the right to land and forest resources. The villagers on the other side apparently had the support of extremists. A few years ago, the conflict took the shape of a veritable war between the two clashing groups. The Nagabaat residents had organised themselves, resisted the onslaught bravely and protected their rights successfully.

Due to the unresolved border dispute, the grouse simmered underneath. Possibly, the conflict affected the people psychologically, making some of them suspicious and intolerant, especially of unknown people. I recollect an incident with a heavy heart. It was the bazaar day of the week. A labourer who used to do white-wash jobs and was a resident of another State, headed towards the bazaar to find some work. He carried a sack on his shoulder that contained a few clothes and a few brushes. Unfortunately, the sack had a red paint mark. Some of the vagabonds and miscreants observed the red spot and began following him. They spread a rumour that this fellow is a 'lora dhora' (child lifter). Soon a large gathering began hounding the poor youth. The young man felt insecure and began running in a bid to escape. Unfortunately, this made the villagers even more suspicious. Some people caught him and began questioning him. But since he did not know the local language, he could not convince the agitated people that the red mark was merely paint and not human blood. Meanwhile, some people forcibly opened his sack, in which they found a trouser and a T-shirt that had some red paint smeared on it. Someone cried out, "Hey, this is nothing but human blood." Within no time, the mob began lynching the youth.

The news reached us and we rushed to the spot. We found the youth lying on the ground, bleeding profusely and gasping for breath. His eyes had bulged out of the sockets, possibly due to a severe impact on the rear of his head. He was senseless but was making a grunting noise. I thought that he might survive if he receives treatment. So with the help of a constable, I tried to make the youth sit up. But what was this? I was unable to grip him properly as the blood smeared body had become very slippery.

After much effort, the injured youth was put into a vehicle and we rushed towards the hospital. It was a 20-25 minute drive. All this while, as I held the youth firmly and I could feel his agony. His painful grunt continued and I concentrated to hear if I could understand anything. At times, I felt that the youth was pleading, "Do not beat me." Then again it appeared that he was crying deeply. But at the end, he seemed to be asking, "What was my fault?" Before he got a reply, he went over to the other side where there was no pain, narrowness or suffering.

I have come across many cases of gruesome murders and ghastly deaths in my life, but the 20 minutes that I spent with this unknown youth remain indescribable. I can still feel the unnecessary haplessness, pain and suffering this fellow human being went through and my heart becomes heavy whenever I remember this incident.

I bore witness to another death wherein the play of fate was evident. The incident took place during my posting at Borholla. A young jawan with the armed police battalion posted at the Kakodonga Reserve Forest died due to a gunshot fired from another jawan's gun. During spot visit and inquiry, I inferred that the death was accidental and an act of providence. The victim was on 'daak' duty that fateful day. He had collected the sack of daak and was walking out of the barrack when he stopped momentarily to tie his wristwatch. At that very moment, another jawan was cleaning his rifle in another barrack about 20 yards away. After cleaning the weapon, he negligently pressed the trigger without realising that a bullet was stuck in the chamber. The bullet pierced through the bamboo walls of the barrack and fatally wounded the jawan, causing his death. Destiny had come calling for him. Had the victim been a feet farther away or had he not stopped to tie his watch, he would perhaps have escaped death. The death was very unfortunate as he was supposed to soon proceed on leave to see his ailing father. But fate had other plans for him.

It was decided that after the post-mortem, the body would be sent to his home immediately. The next evening, as the police team reached the slain jawan's home, they witnessed another pathetic scene. A funeral procession was leaving the house; the jawan's father had died a few hours earlier. As the friends, family and mourners saw an ambulance stop outside their house, they were anxious. The scene that followed was heartrending. Later, the father and son were cremated together. The deaths appeared pre-ordained, and both of them had to leave this mortal world at the predestined time. But what would have been the situation if the father had died a few hours later?

During my tenure, Borholla was not totally crime free, but there were no organised crime or large groups of dacoits. Among the important cases was one wherein a new gang had murdered a plains tribesman and took away his licenced weapon. The murder's only eye witness was the deceased's 13-year-old son, Mayna Chutia, who hid himself to save his life. He gave a vivid description of the assailants. Based on his statement, the gang was captured along with the stolen weapon. The gang was eventually punished with a jail term.

A new dacoit nicknamed Bormurhia (the big headed one) had been spreading terror for quite some time. The big, burly man was evading capture and posed a challenge for the police. One day, he was caught quite unexpectedly.

Winter was not over yet. That morning, I was standing on the veranda of the Police Station and enjoying the warm sunshine. Suddenly, my attention was drawn to the squeaking of a bicycle on the gravel road in front of the Police Station. I saw a big, burly man wearing a leather jacket pedalling hard. Right behind him were two of my constables. Obviously, this was a chase and the man was trying to escape the police. Instantaneously, I was reminded of an incident that that took place during my college days, six years ago.

A civic organisation of our town had organised a cycle race competition. I had asked my friend Nantu to pay the entry fee for my participation. The next morning, I reached for the spot at appointed time. Just before the competition was to begin, one of the organisers informed me that I would not be allowed to participate in the competition as my name had not been given on time. I felt depressed and unhappy that I was not being allowed to participate. I pleaded with them but they refused.

The race was flagged off in front of my eyes. I stood at the starting point like a fool and watched the participants race ahead. They must have raced some 200 yards ahead when I thought, "I have to return home through the same route, so why not try and see if I can catch up with the competitors?" I began pedalling and soon I caught up with some of the laggards. Then I thought, "Why not see if I can still catch up with those ahead?" By the time I had reached the finishing line, the nearest competitor was at least 20 yards behind!

As I soaked in the sunshine, the thought energised me and gave me the confidence. Immediately, I saddled on a cycle and began racing. After chasing the fellow for about two miles, I was about to catch him when he turned into the empty paddy fields on the left side of the road in a bid to escape. But unable to keep his balance, he fell on the ground. I pounced on him and pinned him down even as he tried to escape with all his remaining strength. While the youth was struggling, I was wondering what crime he must have committed and why he was trying to escape. The constables arrived in a short while and I learnt from them that this man was none other than the dreaded Bormurhia.

Some of the other major investigations involved kidnapping cases. These kidnappings were affected deep inside the Kakodonga Reserve Forest. As mentioned earlier, the border forest area was disputed. After a successful campaign against encroachers, the Assam Government had decided to establish a few new forest villages in the area. And then began a series of peculiar kidnappings. Miscreants from across the border would often abduct the contractors, managers or labourers engaged in clearing the forest or building roads and other infrastructure. The intent was to terrorise these people and scuttle the efforts of the Assam Government. Hence, such kidnapping cases were treated as Serious Report (SR) cases.

To investigate such cases, we would often have to go deep into the forest. Notably, during that time, only Village Number 10 had some human settlement in that area. The village was situated at one end of the border. During the course of such investigations, I got acquainted with a middle aged man, Makram. The man, who appeared to work as a labourer, would often arrive from nowhere, whenever we went for investigations. He would not only tell us about the many paths and short cuts in the forest but also shared vital inputs. I used to be astounded with his deep knowledge of the area and often admired him mentally. How could a simple villager have so much information? In course of time, a close relationship grew with him. I even went to his house, where his wife and two young sons lived a simple life. Makram's house was located just at the border of the two states. One day I noticed an Assam Police Battalion picket close to Makram's house. Since the deployment of armed police battalion forces was not discussed with the local police, I had no fore knowledge of the development. The reason became apparent later.

CHAPTER

9 Makram and The Magic Lantern

It was the first week of June, 1969. At about 10:30 one night, I was tossing around on a *khatiya* (cot) under the open sky inside the Police Station precincts. Though it was monsoon time, not a drop of rain had fallen for almost a month, making the weather very hot and humid. The Police Station did not have any electricity, making it all the more unbearable.

Suddenly, the Police Station sentry announced loudly that he could spot mashal (torches) at a distance. The villagers were probably coming to inform the police about a murder or dacoity. In a short while, a group of villagers arrived on bicycles and informed that armed Naga miscreants had attacked Village Number 10 that evening and ransacked the place. Makram's house bore most of brunt and they had heard a lot of commotion and lamenting from his house. But the villagers could not give an accurate description of what had happened or the exact number of casualties as they had all fled as soon as they got a whiff of the attack.

My first reaction was that we should reach the spot as quickly as possible, as the victims may need immediate assistance. The very next moment, I was assailed by the practical difficulties – there were no guns at my outpost and I had only a few hands. With a handful of lathi-wielding policemen, how wise would it be to enter the dense jungle? I began mulling over what we should do. My head said it would not help to go there right now and the move could actually be counterproductive; we should wait till dawn. My heart, however, insisted that if a helping hand is not extended at the time of distress, what is the use of police? If we go now, we may be able to save a few people. My mind conjured up the faces of Makram's two children. For Makram's sons, we were the khaki-wearing chachas (uncles). Their glee was apparent whenever we visited Makram's house with candies and biscuits for them. What were two kids doing now? Eventually, my heart won the tussle and I firmly resolved to go to the spot immediately. On hearing my decision, the villagers who had come to inform us, said that they would accompany us only to the point where they could travel on bicycles but would not enter the jungle. By this time, a large gathering had arrived at the Police Station as the news of the Naga attack spread. Some of these people had licensed arms, but no one agreed to accompany us during the night.

My colleagues, too, were reluctant to join me for the nocturnal venture. Perhaps, they thought, "What kind of a mad man is he? He wants to go to a place at night where people do not dare to venture even during daytime." Excuses poured in one after another. Someone reported sick. Someone's children were unwell. I realised that no one would accompany me voluntarily. So, I announced resolutely that I would go alone even if no one accompanied me. I had thought that at least some people would join me following the announcement, but no one ventured out. It was humiliating.

An eerie silence descended. Suddenly, two constables – both of entirely opposite nature – came out to join me. Constable Kon Moina was the first to totter out of his room in a dishevelled uniform. He was followed by the pious and steady Constable Tulsi Dutta. This was both surprising and unexpected.

About five months ago, a senior officer had told me that an obstinate constable, Kon Moina, was being posted at my outpost, with the hope that I would be able to rein him in. He had been suspended and even dismissed due to wilful negligence, incompetence, unauthorised leaves and indiscipline. However, he was reinstated after the court's intervention. Emboldened, he had no fear of departmental proceedings or suspension. His latest exploit was a fisticuff with the officer in-charge. I had heard the officer patiently and somehow convinced myself to take up the challenge. "Please send him, I will handle him," I had said confidently. Then began a test of my patience. I had to spend a lot of time, energy and money to keep him sane. I used both carrots and stick as I had a firm conviction that if this fellow was managed properly, it would be possible to extract a lot from this drunkard. But I had never imagined that this character would be the first to come out to accompany me that night. Actually, as usual, Kon Moina had gone off to sleep after drinking. He had woken up at the commotion and learnt that I was preparing to head towards Kakodonga alone. He somehow pulled himself out, put on the uniform, picked up his cap and cane, barged out of the barrack and announced, "Bolok Saar, moi hazu. (Let's go Sir, I am ready.)"

On the other hand, Majuli's Tulsi Dutta, an aged constable, was a very decent and God fearing person. He would regularly conduct ritualistic worship in the Police Station, waving a lamp and incense every morning and evening. He would never chastise even the lowliest of criminals. "Krishna, Krishna!" was the only refrain that escaped his lips whenever he came across anything untoward. Tulsi, I felt, was like Prahlad, who was born in the family of demons. I would always wonder what he was doing in the police force. But that night, under the difficult circumstances, I realised that he was perhaps both brave and committed. Kon Moina and Tulsi Dutta's extension of a hand of assistance that night was an extraordinary experience. I learnt that it is incorrect to judge one by one's appearance or outward nature. The real test of a human being is during adverse situations.

After Kon Moina and Tulsi Dutta, ASI Makhan Bora too joined us, albeit after finding no excuse. Thereafter, the four of us began our journey to the affected village on bicycles. The torch-bearing villagers accompanied us. I remembered that there was an armed police picket just next to Makram's house. Then how could the miscreants attack the village unopposed? To allay my suspicion and to see if I could get a few armed policemen, I headed towards the Armed Police Battalion post nearby. There, I learnt that the men from the picket near Makram's house along with men from quite a few other posts had been withdrawn to help out with the flood situation caused by the River Brahmaputra.

The inspector in charge of that post expressed inability to provide any armed guards to accompany us for want of sufficient manpower, and especially without the permission of the seniors. Taking the failure in stride, I headed towards Kakodonga forest. The villagers accompanying us bade us goodbye at the outskirts of the forest after giving us directions to Makram's village through the dense forest. We left our cycles under a large tree, prayed to the Almighty and set off towards the village on foot.

Soon, the sky was overcast with monsoon clouds, making it quite dark and difficult to proceed. Somehow, we managed to reach the outskirts of the village and saw a few huts, which were empty. The occupants had probably fled. After trekking another half an hour, we spotted a flickering light at a considerable distance. We proceeded in the direction of the light. Covering a considerable distance, we came across a newly laid mud road, about 8 feet wide. It indicated the possibility of a settlement somewhere close by. Even though we had hit a road, we had to walk carefully as there were deep drains on either side. Traversing further, we could now see the flickering light quite clearly but the source of that light could not be identified. Nevertheless, that flickering light was like the Pole Star for us that night. We kept moving forward towards it and realised that it was perhaps a lantern. Before we could reach the lantern, we noticed a sack-like object lying on the road. As we reached closer, we found that it was man. The body was smeared with dust and the face was not clearly visible. The man's skin appeared moist and slippery, and there was no way of gripping him. We tried to call him but initially there was no response. It was difficult to make out whether he was alive or dead. We thought, maybe he is not responding out of fear. So, we again called out and said we are police. At this, the curled up man tried to speak faintly, without lifting his head. I recognised that this was Makram. The miscreants had injured him seriously with cleavers (Naga Dao). Moments later, he fainted out. We were now sure that we had arrived at the affected village. Close by was Makram's house. We went there and saw that the house had been vandalised. The bamboo structure had been cut at various places and the thin partitions of the hut had been slashed. The floor had blood marks and rice and lentils were strewn all over. Makram's wife or children were nowhere around. There were two-three huts around 100 yards of Makram's house were all empty. Everybody must have fled and the assailants too must have retreated after committing the atrocities.

Makram was still alive but needed immediate medical assistance. But how could we carry an injured and singed man to the nearest hospital, at a distance of at least 9-10 kms? In those parts, the only mode of transport was the bullock cart. I asked the accompanying constables to search around and see if they can find a bullock cart.

Within a few minutes of the constables' departure, a torrential rain commenced. It is difficult to describe the fury of the monsoon clouds. During our tense journey through the forest, we had not noticed that clouds had welled up and a storm was on its way. I also had no experience of how dreadful the rains can be in the hilly hinterlands. Within 15-20 minutes, the water was up to our knees and soon it was up to our waist. On the other hand, the rain made blisters on Makram's body swell like balloons. One who hasn't seen it can never imagine how such large blisters can form on a human body. Meanwhile, the water level kept rising. We somehow moved Makram to a higher place and tied him to a small tree. Makram made no sound or movement and was oblivious of the torrential downpour.

By the time the water had risen to our chest, Bora babu said, “Sir, this fellow is dead. Is there any point in killing ourselves? Let us go and take shelter elsewhere.” His suggestion was not illogical. But I was in two minds. I replied, “He may not be dead yet. And in that case it would not be proper for us to leave him in such a condition.” I still believed that Makram would live if he received treatment. Dear Ma, please think of the situation we were in at that point. The dense forest, the torrential rain, the pitch darkness all around, chest high water and the possibility of snakes or other wild animals attacking us – everything seemed to be against us. But a surprisingly, the lantern was still flickering near a tree in Makram’s house. The chimney had darkened with soot completely, but the lantern continued to flicker. Bora babu said ominously, “Looks like Makram’s life force is in that lantern. Till the lantern continues to flicker, Makram will continue to live.” Perhaps Bora babu was right.

The rain stopped after about an hour and a half. The water began receding after some more time. The two constables, meanwhile, were nowhere to be seen. They must have been stuck somewhere due to the rain. When the water receded below our waist, I and Bora babu set off to look for a bullock cart. We left Makram under the care of the magical lantern. I had never driven a bullock cart, but Bora babu assured me that he had done so. We doubled our efforts and reached the village to look a cart. Soon, we spotted a house and entered it. As luck would have it, both the constables were in the same house. They informed that the house had both, bullocks and a cart. But we had to wait for the water to recede further.

After about another half an hour, we somehow managed to put Makram in the cart and started our journey towards Borholla. By that time, the sky began clearing up and daybreak was close by. As we crossing a drain, my thoughts turned to Makram, "Was he still alive?" To find out, we began calling out his name, one by one. But there was no response. There was no way to physically check as his entire body was covered with big and small balloon-like blisters, except the sole of his feet. We scratched the sole, but to no avail. Then I felt a little remorseful that perhaps we were taking a dead body with us.

By the time we reached Borholla, it appeared that the entire village was awake all night. Hundreds of people including the doctor and nurse were awaiting news from the forest. The doctor at the dispensary pushed two injections and told us that Makram could live if he was taken to the Civil Hospital. Borholla outpost had no police vehicle and it was difficult to take Makram in a bus. So, we cajoled a businessman, took his van and sped towards the Civil Hospital in Jorhat. There, we admitted Makram. I then headed to the SP's office and reported the entire matter. By then it was 10:30 a.m.

After returning to Borholla from Jorhat, I grabbed a small lunch before dashing towards Makram's village again to find the whereabouts of his wife and children and gather some more details about the attack. On reaching Village Number 10, I was relieved to find that most of the villagers had returned home and that Makram's family members were alive. They had taken shelter at a relative's house. After perusing the statements of the villagers and other circumstances I surmised that the target of the attack was Makram and not the entire village. To prevent Makram's neighbours from coming to his help, a group of the miscreants terrorised and attacked two or three houses. None of the villagers could say who had kept the lantern outside. "Perhaps Makram's wife had hung the lantern on the tree before fleeing the village," I reckoned as I marvelled at the lantern's role in helping us reach the village in the darkness. This is why I was curious about the lantern.

I came to know that Makram used to live on the other side of the border in Nagaland about four or five years ago. He was threatened by the miscreants and was branded a spy. He had then shifted to Village Number 10. I also learnt that the separatist elements had resolved to kill Makram. That was possibly why an armed police picket was posted near his hut. The miscreants attacked as soon as the picket was removed. Makram had never told me that he used to live in Nagaland. But now I understood how he had gathered so much information.

I met Makram's wife and told him that he had been admitted to the hospital in Jorhat. She told me that Makram had gone to the court at Jorhat as a witness on the day of the attack. A group of miscreants from the other side of the border attacked their house after he had returned in the evening. She was cooking when the assailants launched the attack. Because of Makram's valiant opposition, the miscreants could not enter the house from the main door. They cut through the rear bamboo walls of the hut and attacked him with cleavers. Makram fathomed that these miscreants had come to attack him and he also launched a counter attack, injuring quite a few of his assailants. But as the attackers were very large in numbers, they cornered him and injured him grievously. Makram lost consciousness as he fell on the floor. The miscreants mistook him for dead and gleefully poured the boiling rice and dal on his body, singeing him. This explained the blisters.

She further added that while Makram kept the attackers busy, she hid herself and the children under a cot. She covered their mouths so that they would not make a sound. After injuring Makram, the miscreants began looking for his wife and children. One of the miscreants flashed a torch under the cot and said, "There is no one." Another miscreant pushed him aside angrily and said, "Give me the torch...let me see." He too flashed the light under the cot but could not see anyone. The attackers spoke amongst themselves, "They must have fled," and left.

Makram's wife broke down as she recollected the incidents. "Believe me Sir, the beam of torch light fell right on us and I thought that this was the end. But it is the Almgity's meherbani (grace) that the attackers did not see us, as if they had been blinded at that moment. She further said, "When the miscreants left Makram for dead, I sneaked out of the house with the children and took refuge in the house of our relative." She, however, had no knowledge of how Makram had gone out of the house or who had hung the lantern on the tree.

After three or four days of the deadly attack on Makram, I was transferred from Borholla. It was not a demotion, but a promotion of sorts, Ma. From an outpost, I was given the charge of an important full-fledged Police Station, whose officer-in-charge and second officer were both under suspension. Police-public relation was at its nadir and there were many other problems.

On being transferred suddenly, I could not ascertain more about the magical lantern or the condition of Makram. Police life is like that – as soon as one is transferred from one place to another, the connection with the previous post, posting or people fades out.

CHAPTER

10 Madhuram's Feat

I was having a fairly good time at my first mofussil posting at Borholla. My *karma*, however, drew me out and placed me under very challenging circumstances with the very next posting. The Police Station of which I had taken charge had been in a state of neglect for a long time. Over a period, the situation had gone from bad to worse. The local people were annoyed with the Police Station's way of working and the local press minced no words in publishing reports elaborating instances of police incompetence and ineptitude. The situation had reached a point when the drivers and conductors of public transport vehicles refused to allow policemen to board their vehicles. As a result, the Police Station's connect with the district police headquarters and the court was almost severed. If they could, the public would not have hesitated to lynch the policemen.

Under such circumstances and as per the instructions of the SP, I made a General Diary entry and took charge of the Police Station. I realised how hopeless the situation was after I applied myself to set the house in order. As both the senior officers were suspended, the Police Station had only an elderly ASI and no other officer. Of the 12 constables, half were novices. The Police Station's documentation and records were completely off the track. No one knew the number of cases registered at the Police Station, even in the last three months. Evidently, no one had touched the Khatian register in a long time. After searching high and low, a few original FIRs were found. These had not been sent to the court. Along with the original FIRs, some bail bonds were also found, but there were no corresponding case diary records. In simple words, a case had been registered, the culprit had been arrested and had been granted bail, but there was no record of why the culprit had been arrested or granted bail. I asked around to understand why the Police Station was in such a pathetic condition and was amazed by the tales the various sources had to relate.

Apparently, the suspended officer in-charge and his deputy had a wayward work life. By the time they woke up, got ready and reached the Police Station, it would be late in the evening. The ASI babu and the constables would hold the fort the entire day, in their absence. The two officers would then deal with the entire day's work – complaints, counter complaints etc – in about an hour in a manner mentioned in Diwan Jarmani Dass's account of Raja Bhupinder Singh. The Raja, fearing loss of leisure time, had adopted a novel way to dispense justice: All the cases were presented to the Raja in two random stacks. He would kick one pile and announce 'acquitted,' then kick the other one and announce 'convicted.' Our two officer also believed in the quick disposal of cases in a similar fashion. By then, all the friends, middle men and anti-social elements would arrive at the Police Station. Then there would be much merry making and entertainment. Finally, everyone would leave for 'investigation.' Often, the officers would indulge in mischievous activities and to hide their identities, they would make the accompanying criminals wear their uniforms. They would then return to their quarters in the wee hours. On days when the irritated wives of these officers refused to open the door, they would enter their houses through the windows. On some days, they were found with their legs and boots hanging out of the windows. These accounts amply explained why the people were unhappy, dissatisfied and angry with the police.

The suspended officer in charge was senior to me by about five years. Though he was temperamental, he was once upon a time well regarded as an efficient officer. He had fallen in the company of a few middlemen and criminals, who were able to manipulate him as per their wishes. Unfortunately, in the later years, he could not extricate himself from the clutches of these criminals and was eventually caught, convicted and jailed in a murder case. He died during his incarceration. The officer's case was a live example highlighting a negative aspect of police life.

Thus, on one hand, there was a mountainous pile of pending cases and on the other, the Police Station records were in a state of complete disarray. The matter was compounded by the lack of cooperation and faith of the general public. I was torn between which problem I should tackle first. After due consideration, I decided to concentrate on improving police-public relationship first. After about 15 days of successfully pursuing this objective, the town was rocked by a spate of crimes, especially, house breaking at night. Not one or two, but at least a dozen such cases were reported every night. I had a hunch that the aim was not to commit burglaries but to bump up the crime rate. The main objective, it appeared, was to prove the new officer's incompetence. But at whose behest? Who would benefit the most? Before I could get to the bottom, my senior officers understood what the problem was and my SP did me a great favour. The suspended officers, who were occupying the official residential quarters, were hounded out. With this, the burglary cases abated somewhat but did not stop completely.

As mentioned, there was a huge pile of pending cases and the new cases of burglary only added to the workload. I was under pressure to take some action. But the problem was who would help? The elderly ASI Khadim-ul Hussain was mostly engaged in record keeping and had little idea of crime or criminals. The old hands and the adept constables had been transferred. So the Police Station's VCNB (Village

Crime Note Book) was my only source of information. I pored over the records day and night, identified the criminals and suspects of every area, and drew up a list of the village headmen and other respectable people. A list was handed over to each of the constables and they were instructed to meet these persons regularly. They were also tasked with finding out more details about the new criminals and the old ones. Simultaneously, Village Defence Party (VDP) meetings were held regularly and the members were activated. These initiatives led to a considerable drop in fresh crimes. But I was restless as the old cases were still pending. So, laborious day and night patrolling continued without a break. The entire team patrolled the 300-odd villages under the Police Station. Gradually, the people noticed that police personnel were visiting their villages regularly but no one was being unnecessarily disturbed. As a result, the negative sentiments about the police began to soften. Slowly, information began trickling in. A few criminals were arrested, but the big fish were still out of the net. I continued the efforts with renewed determination. Perhaps, the invisible power was pleased with the penance and gave me a small clue.

One night, we were patrolling a village about 4-5 kms away from a village on our bicycles. Suddenly, I noticed a shadowy figure slip away quickly besides a large bush on the left side of the road, about 15-20 yards ahead of us. I was not sure if it was a human or an animal. To allay my suspicion, I dismounted from cycle and walked down to the bush. I tried to see all around but could spot nothing in the darkness. The accompanying constables looked around but they too did not find anyone or anything. I was about to return when I suddenly noticed something lying under the bush. It was a cheap blanket. Instinctively, I felt the blanket – it was still warm. So, someone was lying there and had made good his escape. The objective obviously was to evade the police patrol. But who was here? Surely, he lives somewhere close by. Without telling anything to anyone, I asked the accompanying constables to wake up the owners of the three nearby dwellings and check if everything was okay. Two of the house owners came out and reported that everything was okay. But third house was locked. On inquiry, I came to know that the locked house belonged to one Madhuram. Madhuram's neighbours informed that he lived alone in the house and would often disappear. Constable Jatin, an old hand, spoke to some other villagers to find out the house owner's whereabouts. "Sir, this Madhuram is the same fellow who supplies vegetables to us," Jatin reported. Madhuarm was a very amiable person and quite old. "He cannot be a thief," I thought. There was no reason to suspect him, so we continued with the patrolling and returned late at night, as usual. But the warm blanket continued to haunt my imagination. Then, I noticed that Madhu had stopped coming to sell vegetables for a couple of days. This raised my suspicion and I resolved to question him even though I had no reason to do so.

I told Jatin about Madhu's absence and asked him to call on him and convey that I wanted him to see me. "Maybe he is unwell," Jatin proffered. "Still, ask him to see me," I told him.

I don't know what Jatin said to Madhu, but after about two days, Madhu arrived at my residential quarter early in the morning. I had thought that I would not reveal that I suspected Madhu but would pin him down by asking him questions about who was sleeping on the blanket outside his house and where he was that night. But Madhu never gave me a chance to ask any question. Dropping the basket of vegetables outside the room, he sought my permission to enter the room. But, without waiting for my reply, he plunged and fell straight at my feet. I had not expected this at all and was completely taken by surprise. I thought, "He might now plead that he is not guilty." But Madhu said nothing of that sort. "Sir, I will explain everything," he began with a trembling voice, fear writ large in his eyes. "But whatever you do, please do not thrash me. After all, I have a prestige as a Guru." What! Madhu was no ordinary vegetable vendor but the coach of thieves and burglars? This was absolutely surreal. I was reminded about Kalita, the boy in Guwahati, who had confessed a major burglary after mere scolding. I figured out that Madhu was scared of the police cane and played it up. "I will spare you, but you have to reveal everything or else..."

After listening to Madhu, I realised that I had stumbled upon a gold mine while searching for coal. "I have been involved in crime (burglary, theft) for about three decades now," said Madhu. "But over the last 8-10 years, I have stopped doing the 'work' myself. I have 'disciples' all around and they respect me a lot because I had never been caught. When I was active in the Moriani Police Station area, I found out that the police is suspecting me. I moved base to this area, which now falls under your Police Station jurisdiction. Even if I do not go to the field any more, I have information about everyone." He further revealed, "The sudden spurt in theft cases after your taking over was at the behest of the previous officers. An 'A Class Bad Character,' Manik Das and his gang members have committed the crime at the direction of the officers. If you give me an opportunity, I will help you catch all of them one by one, I promise. But please take care of my izzat (honour), Sir." To ascertain if he was speaking the truth, I probed him with many questions. He gave satisfactory replies to all my queries. I then assured Madhu, "Ok, I will not tarnish your reputation by arresting you on the condition that you will help me arrest all the criminals." Madhu promised that he would not renege on his words.

Normally, it is unwise to rely on the words of people who have a criminal antecedent. After considering the matter deeply, I decided to take a risk and let Madhu off quietly but not before letting him know in no uncertain terms that he would have to repent severely if he did not keep his word.

Madhu, mercifully, did keep his word. Within a month, many criminals were caught and a good deal of stolen goods were recovered. This created a strife in the world of crime, bringing the industry to a grinding halt. Due to the drop in crime and the posting of two additional officers, most of the pending cases were disposed of quickly. After a few other smart detections and action, the local press, which earlier left no opportunity to criticise the police, gloated over the success of the police. The happy police chief wrote, "...the officer in-charge has achieved a Herculean task by clearing the 'Augeas' stable' of the police station."

One day, a senior officer dropped in and said in mock seriousness, "Your Police Station will no longer be required." As we had not committed any negligence, I asked humbly, "Why are you saying so?" The officer smiled and said, "If there is no crime, why would the Government maintain a Police Station?" I smiled back at the joke and mentally thanked Madhuram, who deserved the real credit. To this day, I remain eternally grateful to the invisible power, who gave me keen sight to watch the shadowy figure slip by quietly in spite of the darkness, and the wisdom to feel the blanket rather than use the cane or kick it that night.

CHAPTER

11 Inexplicable

The crime graph declined rapidly, thanks to the availability of two new officers, a few smart detections and some strong police action. Local newspapers were heaping praises on me and police higher ups were overjoyed at the turnaround.

I, too, felt relaxed just as a student does, after passing a difficult test. The situation, however, did not last long. An apparently ordinary crime brought me to the brink of calamity, because the complainants in this case were no ordinary people. They belonged to a particularly powerful family of the State. And they expected everyone to work according to their wishes. However, what they desired, in this case, was illegal and this resulted in a chaos that eventually shook up the entire district administration. The incident began in a very ordinary way.

That year, during the rains, about 300 fishing families were rendered homeless due to the erosion of the Brahmaputra riverbank, where they lived. The poor people took shelter in a vacant fallow land adjoining a tea estate, which was located in my

Police Station's jurisdiction. It was learnt that the Satradihkar of Auniati in Majuli (now a district) was the Spiritual Mentor (Guru) of these fisherfolk. The land they had taken refuge was half of the Guru's property, and they had his permission to occupy the land. The Guru had leased out the other half of the land to the tea estate's owner, who was politically well connected. The government had provided the refugees with some tin sheets and other relief material, with which they had erected bamboo huts. The tea estate's owner, however, was unhappy with this. This led to a conflict, which acquired a serious hue in no time.

One day, the tea estate's owner came to the Police Station and complained that the fisherfolk were trespassing his property. Accordingly, a case of criminal trespass under section 447 CrPC was registered against the fishermen. As soon as the case was registered, the complainants (owner of the tea estate and his accomplices) started pressing for the arrest and forcible eviction of the poor fishermen. As the case was a civil dispute and also a bailable one, there was no legal provision under which the police could have evicted the people, without court orders. "Even if we arrest them, they can easily get bail and then they cannot be arrested again for the same offence as per law. Besides the State administration is trying to arrange for an alternative place to relocate the displaced fisheremen," I tried to reason, adding, "It would be prudent to wait." But the plea fell on deaf ears and the complainants were adamant. A few days later, they started attacking the fishermen and destroying their huts and shelters, and even forcibly taking away their tin sheets and other household materials in a bid to scare them.

In spite of harassment, the fishermen did not yield and stood their ground. By this time, a Left-leaning group grabbed the opportunity and began giving the incident a political colour. Even if the incident was minor, it got politicised. This made the complainants shaky and they thought that the land may go out of their hand. So, to vacate the land, they continued to pressure the police and the administration for immediate eviction. They even threatened to launch an agitation to cripple the administration by swamping the city with thousands of activists. But both the senior officials of the district (DC and SP) being self-respecting and upright officers, did not bow down to the threats. As the district headquarters turned into the theatre for the power play, I felt that I had no further role in the drama. I was wrong.

One fine morning, information was received about the suspicious movement of a large number of unidentified people. "I hope the tea estate manager is not up to some misadventure," I thought, as he was the brain behind all the attacks and harassment of the fishermen. Immediately, some officers and constables were deputed to identify the actual purpose behind this unusual movement of people. I also informed the SP and Circle Inspector about the developments.

After some time, the Police Station staff came back and informed that under the leadership of manager, about 300 tribal people from a distant area and many tea garden labourers armed with sticks, cleavers and other weapons are marching towards the disputed land, in all probability to evict the fishermen.

I mulled over what my next plan of action should be. The Police Station had only 8-10 people and it was impossible to combat the large number of people. In the meanwhile, the Circle Inspector, a middle-aged person, arrived at the police station and said, "I am proceeding. You get reinforcements from the police reserve at district headequarters."

On hearing the CI's words, I said "There is no point accosting the 300-strong group with a handful of men. If police is inactive or if it retreats, the attackers will be encouraged. So, it is important to keep the arsonists engaged till reinforcements arrive." But that was easier said than done. Since the CI was much older to me and a father of many children, I persuaded him not to go and offered to go instead. "Meanwhile, you arrange the reinforcements. Let me see how I can hold them till then." I asked the oldest grey haired constable, Fazir, to accompany me. The reason was to make it amply clear to the attackers that the police's intent was not to use force.

On reaching the spot, I saw that the situation was quite complex. Huts in a large area of about 20-25 bigha had been set ablaze and the scared fishermen along with women and children stood at a distance, watching the horror. They found some courage at the sight of two policemen and became combative. I stopped them because the attackers were overwhelmingly large in number and a direct confrontation would have led to significant bloodshed and loss of life. As I dissuaded the fisherfolk, I kept thinking what should be my next step. Should I be a mute spectator? That would have been meaningless. So I kept advancing and asked Fazir to stay back, instructing him to inform the Police Station if I was attacked.

I don't remember the multitude of thoughts that flashed through my mind as I faced the attackers alone. But I remembered only one thing – I had to march ahead with confidence. I proceeded further towards the attackers and before saying anything, I tried to ascertain who the other people were apart from the garden labourers. Unperturbed by the presence of a single uniformed police person, the attackers nonchalantly continued with their arson. As I went further, I could clearly see the faces of the non-locals who belonged to a certain tribal community. Killing a human being was no big deal for these ferocious people. They usually stayed within their territory and cared two hoots about the law, courts or police. All the crimes within the community were resolved according to their own traditional laws. I knew that even thought they were illiterate, they were simple people and understood straightforward talk. So, I stood on a high spot about 40-50 feet away from them and addressed them loudly, "See, what you are doing is not good. And the fellow who is provoking you to do all this is not your well-wisher. The manager is trying to use for you for the dirty work, so that you go to jail. Look, I am standing alone in front of you. You can kill me if you want. But remember, I am a government officer. If you kill a government officer, the government will not spare you."

After my first burst, I noticed that the attackers were quietly listening to me and trying to understand what the policeman was trying to say. Those in the front sat down on the ground and those standing in the rear could now see me. I saw the manager, wearing in half pants, in their midst, instigating the people to attack me. But the attackers did not respond. I concluded that my words had hit the bull's eye. So, I raised my voice further and said, "Try to understand, the government will not spare you if you mess with a government officer. Your women, children will be in a very bad shape and you will be in jail. And this manager will not be able to save you." And so on...

Oh Ma, I have no clue how I managed my extempore speech. It was as if Goddess Saraswati sat on my tongue that day. I was surprised at my own elocution. My brain was racing at break-neck speed under the duress and in the face of imminent, life-threating danger. Ma, my situation was then like that of a tiger rider. As long as I was on the tiger's back, I would be alive. In other words, as long I could speak, I would live. Stopping for a moment would have meant the end. So I continued speaking, for at least about an hour till the reinforcements reached. You might be thinking that I was speaking about the law, or philosophical concepts such as paap-punya (sins or virtuous acts) etc. No, Ma! The people I was speaking to were least bothered about these things. So, I continued to hit them with my words.

By this time, the manager had become impatient and tried again to persuade my audience to attack me. But the attackers were then all ears, listening to my gospel with rapt attention. Some of them gave him hard and disapproving looks. The manager turned his face away no alternative. The poor manager's dreams of securing a promotion or material gains were further dashed by the arrival of a large posse of armed police force. As the manager saw the armed policemen jump out of the truck, he bolted along with his handful of accomplices. However, they were soon caught. And with this came the abrupt conclusion of my extempore neta-like speech.

As mentioned earlier, that some of these incidents of my life were not only dramatic but bordered on the surreal. The events of that day were similar. I don't know what drove me to accost the 300-odd attackers, with only one accomplice with me. To this day, I find no logical explanation of how I managed to speak for an hour or why the arsonists listened to me motionlessly. I can only attribute this to the invisible power.

CHAPTER

12 Meeting Makram Again

Things moved swiftly thereafter. The manager, 'Babu' and the labourers of the tea estate were arrested on the same night for their role in the arson, intimidation and torching of the fishermen's dwellings, and were eventually brought to justice. No one had ever imagined that the faithful loyalists of the most powerful family in the State could meet such a fate. However, they did get a chance to rejoice during their stay at behind the bars, when they learnt that I had been transferred.

A few days after the arson, an urgent message from the Police Headquarters was delivered to me. I was asked to hand over charge within 24 hours as I had been transferred to the Special Branch, Shillong. The message did not come as a surprise at all as I was expecting some kind of retaliation. Without wasting any time, I handed over charge to the second officer and proceeded to meet the SP to bid him goodbye before heading towards Shillong. When he heard that I had already handed over charge, he said, "Why did you not wait for my orders? Since your actions were aimed at helping the administration and maintaining law and order, we are trying to get the transfer order cancelled. The DIG (Range) is personally going to Shillong to sort out the matter. Please return and resume charge." I returned to the Police Station, but with a heavy heart. The SP, DC and Circle Inspector had also been transferred, although they were not required to relinquish office within 24 hours, like me. However, the thought that the powerful considered me as a threat to their hegemony filled me up with some legitimate pride. "Not a bad show, huh," I thought with a wry smile.

A few days later, the SP reluctantly shared that my transfer order could not be cancelled. After receiving the DIG's request, the IG proffered that since the transfer had been 'requested' by the Chief, it cannot be cancelled. He advised that the transfer order be executed but assured that some appropriate compensatory action would be taken later on.

Two days later, I handed over charge to the new OC in the evening and reached Jorhat town. I decided to check into a hotel for the night as the next bus to Shillong would be available only next morning. That night, the tea estate owner sought me out at the hotel. He behaved as if he had just learnt about my transfer and expressed mocking disbelief. "Heard that you have been posted elsewhere?" he said, condescendingly. "You were doing such good work...but why this transfer? This is not good and we are not at all happy." I could easily fathom the real purpose behind the sudden change of heart and did not react to the insinuations. I quietly bade him a quick goodbye after exchanging a few perfunctory pleasantries.

Even though I had taken this transfer lightly thus far, this audacious meeting, whose obvious purpose was to add insult to injury, made me revolt from within. I mulled over the Catch-22 situation all police personnel have to face. Going by the law and going against it, both may bring undesirable results. In spite of education and decent family background, would I have to now dance to the powerful people's music? No, this is not a gentleman's job. Kaka was right, policing is a notorious job. Even if one sacrifices one's life while performing one's duty, there is no value.

Winter had descended. Early next morning, I braved the chill and fog as I walked to the bus stand and awaited the bus to Shillong. My mind was still very agitated. I kept reminding myself (the lesson from the Bhagavad Gita) that we only have the right to perform karma, not the results those actions bear. But my mind would not calm down. I remembered the dire circumstances under which I was given charge of this Police Station. In spite of being the youngest officer, my DIG and SP had entrusted me with the task. I remembered the struggle and the sleepless nights that went into putting the house in order and winning the trust of the people. But now I felt that there was no practical value of all these things. If not, why be transferred in 24 hours? And for what fault? There was no record. Of course, it was as clear as daylight that my plight was a result of standing against the most politically powerful family of the State. But then, I was only doing what the law had sanctioned me to do. In spite of knowing everything, the administration had failed to stop the insulting transfer order. A depressing sense of haplessness was building up in my mind and I strongly considered resigning.

Suddenly, I noticed a limping figure struggling through the dense fog. Soon, I noticed that he was approaching me. As the fellow came closer, I saw that he had humped back and deep injury marks on his face and head. The face was completely burnt. He was holding something to his chest with both his hands. "A beggar," I thought. But instead of asking for alms, he greeted me, "Aadab". As I responded with a gesture, I felt that the fellow knew me. But I could not recollect him. He too understood that I had not recognised him and said, "Sir, have you forgotten me? I am Makram." The name rang a bell, but I still could not fully recollect. Then, in a flash, I remembered. "Makram from Kakodonga!" I could not contain my surprise even as I realised that the blistering hot rice and lentils poured on him on that fateful night had caused his skin of chest and back to shrink, making him hump backed. I was both overjoyed and sadden at meeting him. "So he's alive…this is a miracle!" I thought in disbelief. Who could return from the doors of death otherwise? I thanked the Almighty and stepped closer to hug him. But before I could do so, he shoved the 'thing' he was holding close to his chest in my hands. It was a fowl. Makram said gratefully, "Sir, I am alive today because of you. I don't have anything to gift you, hence I brought this." I knew that refusing the 'gift' outright would hurt him. So I cajoled him, "Please take this back. I am going to a new city and I have no place to stay. You are alive, and that itself is a big gift for me."

Overwhelmed with emotions, Makram said, "Sir, after being discharged from the hospital, I returned to the village, only to learn that you been transferred. I have been wanting to meet you ever since. But as I am nearly crippled, I could not travel to see you. But yesterday, during a visit to the marketplace, I learnt that you have been transferred again to a faraway destination. My mind was disturbed at this thought. After I returned home, I thought that if you leave, I may not be able to meet you again in this lifetime. So, I thought let me bear a little discomfort and meet you once. I prayed to the Almighty and went all the way to the Police Station, only to learn that you had just left for the district headquarters and would be boarding the bus to Shillong the next morning. Though I was disappointed, I was determined to meet you. I thought, let me give one more try. Unfortunately however, it was already late in the evening and busses to the district headquarters had stopped plying. Seeing my eagerness, the officers at the Police Station asked a truck driver to accommodate me and drop me here. I reached here late in the night and waited all night to meet you. I am fortunate that I have been able to meet you and express my gratitude. I am relieved now."

I briefly chatted with him about his family, children, the developments in the village and his present occupation. The bus was ready to leave by then. Before I bid a final adieu, I curiously asked him how he had ventured out in spite of the grievous injuries that night. Makram recounted, "When I regained my senses that night, I found that my wife and children were nowhere around. The father in me was more concerned about my children than about the unbearable pain and blisters the burn had caused all over my body. I somehow grabbed a lantern and stumbled out of the house in search of the children. But I could not maintain my balance while descending the muddy slope outside the balcony and the lantern slipped off my hands. I fell down and lost consciousness again. I had woken up briefly after hearing your shouts." After a brief silence, he resumed, "Sir, let me tell you something. I had a firm conviction that you would rush to my aid whenever the news reaches you, no matter what time of the night it was. I am indebted to you for vindicating my faith…I owe my life to you." Tears of guileless gratitude welled up in his eyes. The bus was about to depart. I hurriedly shoved some money in his reluctant hands. "Buy the children some sweets,"

I managed to say as I boarded the bus. Makram mumbled something in return as the vehicle began moving. I peeped out of the window and gazed at him for as long as I could. Makram stood still, staring at the bus till it disappeared.

As the bus hurtled towards its destination, I could not take my mind off Makram. I wondered in amazement how this nearly crippled person had mustered strength to travel all the way from the Kakodonga forests to Jorhat and braved the chilly winter night only to meet a police officer who had been transferred, a person with whom he shared no relationship whatsoever. Makram hadn't come only to express his gratitude. He was drawn by a humane sense of bonding with someone he recognised as his own. As the town faded away at a distance, I realised with some satisfaction that the trust, love and affection of people like Kon Moina and Makram that I had earned over the last one-and-a-half years were my real achievements.

Some people understand the value of police work and unflinchingly give the respect it deserves. This realisation was an inspiration for me throughout my career, which stood in stark contrast to the ridicule and the ridiculous demands of those in power. I never forgot Makram or people like him, as they were the true inspiration behind my work.

CHAPTER

13 Moon to The Rescue

It is quite natural for one to be confused at the crossroads on an unfamiliar path. I am sure readers would have confronted such a bewildering situation in their lives. But only a foolish person can take a wrong turn on a familiar path. One night, I too had committed such a blunder – ostensibly at the behest of the invisible power – only to realise that the 'mistake' not only prevented a dacoity and abduction of a young woman, but also a possible riot in the communally sensitive township.

I had completed about six years of service by then and had taken charge of a mofussil Police Station only about a month ago. The Police Station, housed in a British-era building, was located at one end of the township. Electricity had not yet reached this place and hence, darkness would descend soon after sunset. One night, an officer brought a youth to me and said, "This young man wants to have a word with you in private. As you do not know him, he asked me to introduce him to you." With this brief introduction, the officer left us alone.

The youth appeared distraught. On questioning, I learnt that his name was Rafiq, a resident of village Koina, located about 10 kms from the police station. He worked as a primary school teacher. After composing himself, he confided that a Hindu girl, who was married off recently, has returned to her parent's house for the first time after the wedding. Rafiq's neighbour, Nooruddin, was planning to abduct her that night. To help him execute his nefarious designs, Nooruddin had contacted a few large and small gangs of dacoits. As part of the deal, the dacoits would help Nooru abduct the woman and he would in return help them commit a dacoity at the house of the local zamindar. Nooru would have no share in the looted booty. Rafiq further revealed that Nooru had an eye on the girl for a long time. As the girl got married off suddenly, the forlorn Nooru had gone mad with his one-sided affair.

"So, how will Nooru help the dacoits commit the dacoity?"

"He will ask the zamidar to open the door."

"Why will the zamindar listen to Nooru?"

"Because Nooru is the panda (leader) of the Village Defence Party (VDP). Everyone in the zamindar household knows this, hence no one will suspect Nooru.

"How did you learn about Nooru's plans of abduction and dacoity?

"Sir, Nooru is a friend of mine. I know everything about him. That madcap's only intention right now is to capture that recently married girl by any means."

"How are you so sure that Nooru will execute his plans tonight?"

"Sir, the girl's elder brother is a friend of mine. I know all the family members very well and I often visit their house. That is why Nooru is pressurising me to help him."

"How?"

"Sir, Nooru has asked me to visit the household and keep the members awake by engaging them in banter and entertainment till about 11:00-11:30 p.m. so that they can break into the house easily, without much effort."

"But, why are you betraying Nooru and sharing his plans with the police?"

"Sir, I do not approve of such criminal activities. But this Nooru is a dangerous fellow. He will not shy away from committing a murder if someone disobeys him. That is why I could not refuse him outright. But, if I help Nooru, will you spare me? Finding no way out of this Catch-22 situation, I decided to approach you."

"Do you know how big the gang of dacoits is?"

"Yes Sir, about 25-30 people."

"And how many people are there in the zamindar household?"

"Sir, the zamindari is on a decline. So apart from two or three household helps, there aren't many people to offer any resistance."

After probing him for some more time, I was convinced that he is speaking the truth. So I instructed two trustworthy constables to collect the location details from Rafiq. I then spoke to the officer who had brought Rafiq. "I wonder why this fellow has willingly come to inform the police about the impending crime."

"It appears that the school master had initially agreed to the plan. However, he must have chickened out at the last moment. The reason is probably your bad reputation of ruthlessly administering strong medicine," he said with a chuckle. "But that is a half-truth," I protested. "I have a right to hiss if the situation so demands."

By then, the constables had collected all the required information. We did not have much time left at our disposal. I told Rafiq, "Do as Nooru has instructed you to do. Rest assured, you will not be harmed." Like a good school boy, Rafiq agreed meekly. Before returning to his village, Rafiq warned us not to take the main road to the village as Nooru may have appointed his henchmen to inform him about any police movement.

Rafiq had mentioned that the gang of dacoits could be about 30 members strong. I did not have enough manpower to take on such a large gang. I excluded the very senior havildars and constituted a team of about 19-20 men, including three officers, a few constables and other ranks. The only firearms available at the police station were the World War I vintage .202 rifles. Reluctantly, I asked the boys to pick up a few of those, even though I was unsure if they would be of any use if the need arose. As the Police Station did not have any vehicle of its own, bicycles were the only option. But even these were of no use for the present expedition as Rafiq had forbidden us to use the main road. Unfortunately, there was no other road to Koina village. The only way was to trudge through the paddy fields. On learning this, I was somewhat dejected as the fields then had neck-high standing crops and some places had knee-deep muddy water stagnating in the snake infested fields. I was petrified at the thought of encountering snakes. Since there was no other option, I directed a fervent mental plea towards Goddess Manasa and set off for the site of the probable abduction. After an exhausting trek, we reached the spot at about 11 p.m.

The doors and windows of the house were bolted and no light could be seen. That struck me as an oddity. Didn't Rafiq mention that he would be in the house and keep everyone awake? But it seems that everyone is fast asleep, which means Rafiq is not here. Since there was little time left, the team encircled the house from three sides and laid in wait for Nooru and the gang. Soon it was mid-night. Then, another hour elapsed. There was still no sign of the dacoits. I began growing anxious with each passing minute. When nothing happened till 1:30 in the night, my anxiousness gave way to worry.

Did Rafiq mislead us? His cock-and-bull story was perhaps aimed at luring us away from the Police Station and executing a dacoity there. A cold sweat broke on my brows at this thought. I rued myself for not having questioned Rafiq more intensely before trusting him. But I did not share my predicament with anyone. So, what should we do now? It was already 2 a.m. As the chances of any dacoity at the zamindar's house seemed remote, I decided to return. If we were lucky enough, maybe we would have a run-in with the dacoits.

We had arrived in the village through the paddy fields to keep our movement a secret. Since there was no need for any secrecy now, I decided to take the main road, which was about 400 yards to the east. From there, we had to march south to reach the town and the Police Station. I called off the campaign and with a heavy mind, began walking towards the main road. And that is when the invisible power began its play.

Walking by my side, the most experienced constable of the team, Ravi, said, "Sir, did you not want to see the route to Bangladesh that the thief Adil and the cattle smugglers take? That route is not very far from here. A little distance to the north is the Koina marketplace. From there, it is a 20-minute walk." I had heard a lot about this notorious trail ever since I had taken charge of the Police Station, and had wanted to visit the place. But I had failed to make time for the visit. Ravi's invitation sounded tempting as we were close to the spot. I also thought that the miscreants would have done their deed by now and making an effort to rush back would be futile. It would be wiser to recce the trail.

As we hit the main road, I told the team of my intention to visit the smugglers' hidden trail. So, instead of going south, we turned northward. The team members gathered that the plan to accost the dacoits had been abandoned and immediately went into relax mode. The second officer and a few others laid down on the road itself to rest their strained backs. A handful walked with me while the rest followed us slackly. Those habituated to smoking deliberately fell a bit farther behind. After a short walk we reached the Koina market. A few shops and shanties became dimly visible in the moonlight that shone brightly from the northwest.

Silence reigned as we trudged along. Suddenly, I saw something that was spine chilling. On the black-topped road surface to my right were several elongated ghost-like shadows, marching one after another like soldiers. From the shadows, it appeared that they were innumerable in number. The identity of the group, of course, was abundantly clear to me. I turned around and was dismayed to see that I had only five or six others with me. Immediately, it dawned on me that if the dacoits come to know that we are only a handful, they will overpower us in no time. Without losing another moment, I rushed at them so that they would be taken by surprise. "Charge… charge," I commanded as I whipped out my whistle and blew hard. By then, a few of the dacoits had come very close. The rest, taken aback by the police presence, ran helter-skelter. Both the dacoits, who were at the front of the group, were armed with guns. One of them stuck the gun barrel on Constable Anil's chest and was about to shoot point blank when another constable landed a bone-cracking baton blow on the dacoit's arm, instantly disarming him. The two constables then overpowered the dacoit. The other dacoit was also armed, but his gun too proved powerless against the humble police cane. By then, the other members of the police team reached the spot and chased the fleeing dacoits. A few dacoits tried to save themselves by taking shelter in the shanties, but could not evade the policemen's eyes. The police team surrounded them and eventually, three dacoits were apprehended from the shanties. A gun, several other weapons and a new black burkha was recovered from them. The fellow carrying the burkha in a bag was identified as Nooru.

Four others accompanying Nooru were apprehended without much trouble. Though Nooru was too surprised to offer any resistance initially, he acted like a man possessed the moment he realised that his plan had come to naught. It was our turn now to be surprised at the strength of this middle statured person and it took five or six of us to subdue him. Though the entire encounter had caused quite a commotion, only the zamindar and two other villagers turned up at the spot, ostensibly either out of fear or to evade 'problems' at a later stage. A loaded gun, weapons and the burkha were seized and the three witnesses signed the seizure list. On learning that his house was the target of the dacoits, the zamindar thanked us profusely and invited me to tea at his place. I assured him of a visit whenever I could find some time and returned to the Police Station along with the arrested dacoits and the seized goods.

On interrogation, the dacoits revealed that they were 23 in all. Of these five-seven were debutants, who were on their first soiree, evidently at the behest and instigation of Nooru. Though most of them had reached the planned get-together spot by 11 p.m., one group was delayed because their supplier could not deliver the promised arms on time. They had arranged for weapons from another source and were thus delayed by several hours. All the dacoits sang to the cane's rhythm except for Nooru, who did not open his mouth in spite of all efforts. A chargesheet was finally submitted against Nooru and four other dacoits for attempt to commit dacoity and under various sections of the Arms Act.

Fortunately, the case came up for hearing in the Sessions Court in about a year. There were no civilian witnesses of the capture of the dacoits. As mentioned earlier, the zamindar and two others were witness to the seizure of the fire arms, weapons and the burkha. However, as is common in our country in many criminal cases, all the three seizure witnesses turned hostile in the court and gave a statement to the effect that the police did not seize any guns, weapons or burkha from Koina bazar that night. They also said that they did not know how their signatures appeared on the seizure list, adding that the police had called them to the Police Station and asked them to sign on a blank paper. Probably, that blank paper was later turned into the seizure list, they alleged. On the other hand, Constable Anil, on whose chest a dacoit had pointed a gun, failed to identify the dacoit in the court. These made the police case weak.

Whilst the three seizure witnesses had probably turned hostile either out of fear of the dacoits or due to some other allurement, Anil's case was a bit different. Anil was actually a Literate Constable (LC), whose job was to maintain documents of the Police Station. Due to a shortage of manpower, he had accompanied the team on the night of the incident. As he had never previously stood witness in a court proceeding or faced a lawyer's questioning, he may have been unnerved. Moreover, Bashir, the dacoit, had grown long hair and a beard, which made it further difficult for Anil to identify him. Due to the absence of any witnesses, the culprits were about to be acquitted. Unfortunately, a police statement does not have the same evidential value as that of a common citizen in the eyes of law and police statements are often treated with some amount of doubt and suspicion.

The defence lawyer's argument was that the police was falsely claiming to have arrested his clients from the Koina bazar. The police had acted out of prejudice against his clients and had arrested them from their homes, embroiling them in a false, fabricated case. He further alleged that the statements of the zamindar and the other two witnesses corroborated the fact that no seizure of fire arms, weapons or other objects were made by the police. The case, therefore, was malafide.

The case, which was on a downward free fall, took a miraculous turn when the defence lawyer attempted to corner and question me in the court. My response to the allegations was that as I had joined the police station only about a month before the incident and did not know the accuseds, the question of being prejudiced against them did not arise. I stood my ground and reiterated that the accused persons had been arrested from Koina bazar, and no other place, as claimed. I also explained in detail how I had apprehended the dacoits after spotting their shadows.

The defence lawyer rejected my statement as false and challenged me. He sarcastically asked which 'instrument' the police had used to spot the accused in the darkness of the night. I replied that even though it was dark, the moon was shining. And it was the moonlight, not an instrument, that cast a long shadow of the approaching dacoits revealing their presence. As we had prior information of their possible movement, we could apprehend them. The defence lawyer immediately countered that if the police could see accused, the accused could have also seen the police and escaped easily. He made a fervent appeal to reject the police argument. My counter-argument was that we could see the shadows of the approaching dacoits but they could not see our shadows. This was because of the peculiar position of the moon at the time of the incident. At that point, we were travelling from north to south and the dacoits were headed in the opposite way. The moon, which was at a steep inclination in the north-western sky, shone its light on the rear-right of the southward moving column, casting a long shadow of the miscreants on the south east, which fell to their left and our right. As our shadows fell beyond their sight, the dacoits were unable to realise our presence. I further explained that had the moon been in the south east or south west, then they would have seen us and we would not have seen them.

Even though the defence lawyer rejected my clear and precise statement again, calling it completely fabricated, the honourable judge called for a panjika (panchang – Hindu calendar) to clear his doubts. After perusing the calendar and considering the positions of heavenly bodies, the honourable judge concluded that the moon, on the night and time of the incident, was indeed positioned on the north-western sky. The position of the moon on that night turned out to be the clinching evidence of the case. The defence lawyer could not challenge this fact with any argument. The judge accepted the police statement as true and admissible. Though there were no other witness in this case, all the accused were convicted and punished with rigorous imprisonment.

Decades later, as I reminisce about the incident, I cannot be but overwhelmed by the handiwork of the invisible power. I can only thank providence for guiding me that fateful night. Had I not been foolish in proceeding towards the hidden trail and headed towards the Police Station instead, the outcomes would have been very different. But then, who can challenge destiny?

And oh moon – the subject of innumerable romantic plays and poems – did you have to end up as the nemesis of love-lorn Nooru? Or, were you merely play a dispassionate role by taking up a particular position that night to save the modesty of a newly married girl, and save the police from a disgraceful aftermath had the accused succeeded in their plans?

CHAPTER

14 Whodunit – The Case of A Minor's Murder

There is a popular Bengali saying, "Morar opor kharar gha," which essentially means 'double whammy.' I have had to face such a situation on many occasions throughout my career. Before one fire was doused, a bigger blaze awaited me gleefully. I was caught in a similar situation when I took up the investigation of a clueless, gruesome and sensational murder.

I had to complete about three Serious Report (SR) case diaries before preparing for a Crime Conference barely four days later. Returning that morning to the Police Station after night patrolling, I instructed Purakaysthya babu, the Second Officer, "I will not be in the police station today and shall concentrate on wrapping up the pending documentation work at my residence. Please ensure that I am not disturbed, unless it is critical." Back at my quarters, I applied myself to finish the task at hand after a brief rest. At about 1 p.m. in the afternoon, I heard a knock on the door. "These fellows don't understand exigencies and depend on others for minor things," I rued in annoyance, as I answered the knock without getting up. "What's the matter?" Debananda, the Police Station sentry, replied, "It's a murder case, Sir."

"So what?" I shot back. "Ask the Second Officer to file an FIR and commence investigations."

"But Sir, the case is koolooless and quite kiti-kul," said Constable Debananda, who was fond of showing off his English vocabulary whenever he had an opportunity. His voice, however, conveyed the gravity of the situation. Reluctantly, I headed towards the Police Station.

A middle-aged school teacher, whose surname was Bora, along with a few residents of Korengaghat village, was waiting for me. The school teacher reported, "This morning, at about 8 a.m., I was grazing my cattle at a pasture at the edge of the village, when I suddenly heard a cry. I ran towards the direction of the cry, but found no one. The grass, however, had some blood stains." The scared school master had then turned back and informed a few villagers. On searching the area, the villagers spotted a blood smeared dead body in a nullah adjoining a sugarcane field. The body was lying prone and upside down on the bank of the nullah. The villagers identified the victim as a 12-13 year old boy, Robin, who was from the same village. They suspected that the child's throat had been slit with a sharp-edged weapon. However, they were unable to shed any light on who could have committed the crime and pleaded with the police to arrest the suspect and ensure the strongest punishment to the culprit.

On the basis of the complaint, a case of murder under Section 302 of the Indian Penal Code was registered and I took up the investigation myself. Bora and the accompanying villagers further said that Robin's family, including his father and uncles, was in a state of shock and therefore did not accompany them to the police station. In fact, they had not even visited the crime spot to see the dead body. On probing the enmity angle, the villagers said, "Robin's father is a very gentle person and does not have any enmity with anyone. And Robin? Who could have any grouse against a mere child?"

As the preliminary queries did not yield anything worthwhile, I headed for the crime spot along with the ASI and a few constables. The concerns regarding the forthcoming Crime Conference and completion of the Serious Report case diary were completely forgotten as I fully concentrated on the new challenge at hand.

At about 3.30 p.m., we reached the crime spot at Korengaghat. The accompanying villagers showed us the spot where the dead body lay. I spotted Robin's body in the nullah by the sugarcane field, which was about four feet deep. The face was not clearly visible and it was unclear if the head had been completely severed from the body. Opposite the cane field was a jungle full of bamboo clusters, trees and shrubs. In between was a clearing of about 30-40 feet. In the middle of this clearing, about 5-7 feet away from the body were large patches of clotted blood. Possibly, Robin had been attacked with a sharp edged weapon at that spot and his lifeless body was later dumped in the nullah so that it is not easily visible to passers-by. The crime spot was a deserted place at the southern end of the village. There was no dwelling within 200-250 yards of the area. About 40 yards further south from the spot where Robin's body lay was a narrow road, running east – west. Robin lived in a house about two miles to the west on that road.

Robin had left home at around 7-8 a.m. on a bicycle with two rupees, to buy betel leaves from a shop located to the east of the crime spot. He never returned home.

The crime possibly took place at about 8 a.m. As the news spread, hundreds of curious onlookers thronged the spot to see the dead body, drastically diminishing the possibility of getting any clue about the criminal or criminals. Still, we conducted a preliminary search but found nothing suspicious. Mercifully, no one had touched Robin's body.

As there were no apparent clues and the area was surrounded by jungle, it was obvious that we would need more hands to conduct a thorough search and investigate further. I sent a message to the Second Officer to send a few more constables.

Thereafter, we combed the entire area of the crime scene, primarily to locate the murder weapon. Over an hour of painstaking search yielded nothing. However, Robin's bicycle was found abandoned about 250 yards to the north of where Robin's body lay. We left the bicycle untouched. Evidently, the murder or murderers must have fled this way. Darkness was fast approaching, so I called off the search for the day.

I then rushed to Robin's house and met his father, elder brother and other relatives, who were all stunned, stoned and shaken by the sudden untoward event. In spite of a lot of effort to elicit any actionable information, they could only share that they did not suspect anyone. They had no serious dispute or transaction with anyone in the village, which could have led to Robin's murder. The villagers present at the spot agreed with Robin's family.

The village consisted of about 80-90 dwellings. Though the people were not very rich, they were all well to do and had enough to eat. Certainly, no one would have killed a child for mere two rupees or a second-hand bicycle.

I then returned to the crime spot. By then, four more constables had arrived from the Police Station. One of them was Bapukon. No sooner had I spotted Constable Bapukon, I mentally criticized the Second Officer's judgement. "Did he not find anyone else?" I thought, "Why did he have to send this foolish fellow for assisting with a serious case?" Among all the constables, Bapukon was the worst when it came to policing acumen. His face, demeanour and even his moustache invariably reminded one of the famous comedian, Charlie Chaplin. His professional abilities were just as lackadaisical. Hence, he was never entrusted with any significant task. I asked the rest of the team to fan out in the village and discreetly collect pertinent information while making Bapukon stay back with me at the crime spot.

As mentioned before, the crime spot was at one desolate end of the village. The clearing was surrounded by jungles on one side and a sugarcane filed on the other. A small rivulet passed through the low land and no one lived anywhere near the vicinity. Evidently, the possibility of an outsider committing the crime was remote and I strongly suspected that it was the handiwork of a village resident. A strong resolved grew within to spare no efforts in solving the dastardly murder and bring the perpetrators to justice.

According to police procedure, after a preliminary inquest, police is supposed to hold a 'surat-e-haal' or inquest and send the body for post-mortem at a Government Hospital. However, as the body was still untouched, I thought this was a fit case to use the services of a Police Dog. At the very least, the dog could possibly be a great help in recovering the weapon of offence, I surmised. With this plan of action in mind, I decided that the body would not be moved till the dog operation ended. However, back then in 1969, conducting a sniffer dog operation was a troublesome and time consuming affair. A Dog Squad had recently been established with only two trained dogs for the entire undivided state of Assam. The Squad was then stationed at the Capital City of Shillong. If the SP agreed to my request, I would have to wait for another 24 hours for the dogs to arrive. Mentally, I prepared for the long haul as my resolve to take the investigation to its logical conclusion grew stronger. I then addressed a report to the SP, sharing all the available case details and explaining the urgent need for a dog operation. Since the chances of success was high, I requested him to requisition the services of the Dog Squad at the earliest.

I could spare no one else, so reluctantly decided to send Bapukon to hand over the report to the SP at Jorhat. I had little faith on him, and hence I repeatedly reminded him about his task. "So, where will you deliver this envelop?" "At the SP's office, Sir," he replied with an air of pride and confidence. I then explained to him that it would be quite late in the night by the time he reaches Jorhat. The SP would probably be at his residence at that hour. I instructed him to first visit the SP's bunglow. Bapukon was beside himself at being selected for this all-important task. Taking his seat on the motor vehicle, he commanded the driver, "Jaldi chalo" (drive fast).

It was the Hindu month of Kartik (October-November) and the Raas festival was being celebrated in most of the villages in the area.

As the dusk turned into night, the dead body was covered with a cloth. "We'll have to guard the body through the night," I told the accompanying ASI. "Please make arrangements for everyone to rest." The crowd of onlookers had thinned substantially by then. An old, inebriated man tottered towards me.

"Sir, I was told that you were looking for me."

"Who are you?"

"I am the owner of the sugarcane field."

"Yes, I did want to have a chat with you."

I was completely at sea with the case in hand and clutched at every single straw that came my way. I reckoned that if I was lucky, the old man could possibly share something useful. "Let's go to your house and talk," I said.

The old man lived in a house quite far from the sugarcane field. The house was spacious but ill maintained. "The family must have been well off at some point in time," I mused. The house had a large courtyard, surrounded by rooms on three sides. A pond was located close by. A smart girl, in her early twenties, brought a couple of garden chairs for us to sit in the courtyard. She then served us water in sparkling glasses and then, after a while, she returned with some tea and biscuits. Her confidence and extrovert character was in stark contrast to the nature of most village girls. The old man introduced her as Runi, his sister's daughter, who lived with the family since her childhood. There was no one else in the house then, as his wife and son had gone to the Raas fair.

Of his own volition, the old man said that he had visited a Raas fair the night before at an adjoining village, about four-five miles away. He had returned very late in the night and went off to sleep. He was awakened by the commotion, the next morning. He had run to his sugarcane field and found Robin's body there. Though the body was found close to his fields, he had no role in the ghastly crime, he pleaded. He could offer no information about the criminal – or criminals – nor share any possible motive.

I probed him further to ascertain more details about the village, the murder and the possible bad characters who could have committed the offence. But the old man had nothing to share. He also said that he did not know if Robin's family had any dispute and certainly there was no dispute regarding property. Disappointed, I took leave of the old man and returned to the crime spot. On my way back, I kept thinking about the possible motive behind the heinous crime.

The facts known till now clearly ruled out a dispute of any kind, including property dispute, as a possible motive. So, was it a murder for gain? Even that looked improbable as the murderer had left the bicycle behind. Sexual exploitation could be a reason, but that could only be ascertained after a post-mortem or at least an inquest. Also, it was possible that Robin saw or knew something about the assassin, which could have been damaging if it were made public and hence Robin was silenced once and for all. But no pointers towards such a possibility had emerged till now. "Now what?" I thought, as disappointment clouded my mind. "But then, the murderer is certainly from this village and not someone from outside," I thought the very next moment. "Then, why won't we succeed if we put in our best efforts?"

Another suspicion that began brewing simultaneously was a possible link of the murder with the ongoing Raas festivities. Even though it was a religious festival with deeply devotional underpinnings, the fair had, of late, acquired notoriety as an opportunity for some unscrupulous elements to indulge in drinking, gambling, cheating and making a fast buck. Many villagers fell in the trap and lost everything in gambling, including their minds. Was Robin was a victim of such a perverted mind?

I reached the crime spot, lost in these thoughts, only to find the DySP (HQ) waiting for me. I saluted him and he greeted me in return, saying "SP sahib asked me to come over to review the case." Evidently, my letter had reached the SP and he had taken it seriously. I shared the details of the investigation so far with the DySP and outlined the possibilities even though the motive behind the murder was still unclear. I also expressed my conviction that the offender was a village resident and not an outsider. The senior officer agreed with my assessment and left after wishing me good luck with the investigation.

After the DySP left, I thought that since there was nothing to do at night, I should return to my quarters and rest for the night so that I could start with renewed vigour and energy the next morning. "No," I thought the very next moment, "there are wild animals in the jungles and any damage to the dead body will scuttle the investigations." The ASI and other Police Station staff assured me that they would take care of the situation and requested me to return. Though I did not distrust them, I decided to bear the inconvenience and stay back at the spot.

By then, Constable Bapukon had returned from Jorhat. A bonfire was lit a short distance away from the body with dry twigs from the jungle. The staff members arranged dinner for everyone. A few blankets were arranged but the mosquitoes would not allow anyone to sleep. I wrapped myself completely in a blanket as I stretched on a thin cushion of straw on the ground and tried to catch a wink.

The time was past 11 p.m. Two jawans stood guard near the body. The rest battled the mosquitoes. To lighten the mood, someone shouted out, "Hey, Bapukon…tell us about your visit to the sahib's bunglow at Jorhat." The comedian in Bapukon seized the opportunity. He cleared his throat and began relating his journey in minute detail in his own funny way. I was in no mood for humour but as I had no choice, I listened to his tale half-heartedly.

"Our Sir wrote a letter and handed it over to the ASI, who in turn handed it over to me. He asked me to deliver the letter to SP sahib. I took the letter, folded it carefully and put it like this in my pocket," Bapukon said in all seriousness. "I then picked up my lathi and marched to the vehicle. I sat on the front seat, much like the officers, and instructed the driver to drive me to Jorhat."

"As the vehicle hit the tri-junction at the end of the village, a young man frantically waved at our vehicle and urged us to stop," Bapukon continued. "As we screeched to a halt, the youth approached me and introduced himself as Robin's cousin. He enquired where we were headed. On learning that we were going to Jorhat, he asked for a lift as he had some important work there. I felt sympathetic towards the young man, who had lost his dear younger brother, and asked him to hop in. I didn't let him sit in the front though," said Bapukon authoritatively. "Sitting in the rear, the youth kept murmuring to himself throughout the journey. On questioning, he said that he was disturbed due to his brother's death and did not know who could have committed the crime. After a while, he said, 'Let's see what the Police does. I shall see to it thereafter'."

I sat up. "Did the youth go to the SP's bunglow?" I asked Bapukon. "No Sir, he sat in the vehicle parked on the road outside." "Then why did he go to Jorhat?" I thought and promptly asked Bapukon, "Did he return with you?"

"No Sir."

"What's his name?"

"Alas, Sir…I forgot to ask that!"

"How old is he? How does he look?"

"He appeared around 25-26 years old. Fair complexioned, medium built. I can recognise him promptly if I see him, Sir," Bapukon offered apologetically.

The driver too assured that he would be able to recognise the youth.

Silence prevailed as everyone sensed that I was seriously mulling over Bapukon's description of the youth and his activities. Even though I tried to lay back and relax, the new turn of events perturbed me. Maybe the youth was Robin's elder brother, but why did he say "I shall see to it thereafter."? Does he suspect someone? "Something's fishy here," I thought, as I made a mental note to question the youth first thing in the morning. Tired to the bone, I drifted off into sleep. The day broke a short while later. Everyone freshened up and got ready for another day's battle.

Suddenly, I remembered the school master, who had not shown up. We needed to know exactly where he was grazing his cattle, where he heard the cries and the route he took to the spot where he saw the blood patches. As I splashed water on my face, I asked the ASI to send someone and have him summoned.

A short while later, the gentleman arrived. Before he took me to show the various spots, I instructed the team to comb the entire area properly to see if they could find anything suspicious. The team split into two and commenced a search. The ASI, the driver and Constable Bapukon set off to catch the youth who claimed to be Robin's elder brother.

Teacher Bora took me to the pasture where he was grazing his cattle and showed me around with cooperative enthusiasm. He recounted how he heard the cries and showed the meandering trail he had taken to eventually see some blood patches. I recorded his statement in accordance with the statutory procedure. After a while, Bora apologised and said that he could not stay back any longer as he had some urgent work. I asked him to see me again after his school duties.

After his departure, I tried to reconstruct his activities on the day of the crime, based on the description recorded in his statement. This compounded my worries. The pasture was at a fair distance from the actual crime spot and there were many large trees and thick vegetation in between. The possibility of hearing a cry from that spot appeared remote. Correctly ascertaining the direction from where the cry came was an even bigger improbability. Further, the path from the pasture to the crime spot was not a straight one due to the intervening vegetation; one would have to take a U-turn to reach the spot.

Finally, Bora's statement that he had seen blood marks but had not seen Robin's body appeared untenable as the body lay barely 5-7 feet away. The boy's feet were propped a few inches above the nullah, which would have been very apparent to anyone.

Clearly, the school master was not being truthful. But why? What could be his compulsion? What is he hiding? I continued to mull over these questions as I tried to fathom why Bora was putting up a smokescreen to hide the truth behind the ruthless and gruesome murder. Perhaps he feared for his life. Or, was he merely trying to evade the harassment of a brush with the law? Or worse, did he have a role to play in the crime? Whilst this could be a possibility, my mind was not ready to accept it. Had he been directly involved, he could have simply stayed mum and not call the other villagers to the crime spot. Nor would he have visited the police station to file a complaint. However, irrespective of my logic and analysis, I mentally placed Bora at the top of the list of suspects, as he was being untruthful.

Meanwhile, the ASI, who was out to find Robin's 'dada' (elder brother), learnt that no one from Robin's immediate family had gone to Jorhat the day before. None of the relatives fitted the description of the physical features of the youth who had claimed to be Robin's cousin, the family said. Stumped, the officer made painstaking enquires only to learn that the youth was none other than the only son of the old owner of the sugarcane field. His name was Droneshwar, but was better known as Drona. Even though the youth was identified, I avoided accosting him directly and asked the team to discreetly collect more information about this character. A few other bad characters of the village were identified but as there was no evidence against any of them, I decided to avoid any direct questioning. All of them were put under surveillance.

At about 5 in the evening, the elderly Additional SP arrived to enquire about the progress of the investigation and the motive behind the murder. I shared all the details and explained the multiple possibilities that could have led to the crime. The ASP was in agreement with my assessment and asked me to continue my efforts. Before he left, he told me that the sniffer dogs were already on their way from Shillong and would arrive by midnight. Since the search party had not been able to find anything suspicious till then, I felt a bit relived with the news.

Hopefully, the trained dogs would be of some use in leading us to the culprits. At the very least, the dogs could be helpful in finding the weapon of offence. I was almost certain that the criminals would have disposed of the weapon in the jungles close to the crime site.

My attention now returned to the school master and I decided to call his bluff by pinning every lie he had woven in his cock-and-bull story. But where was he? I had asked him to see me in the evening but he did not turn up. His wife too could not shed any light on his whereabouts. "How far will you flee, buddy?" I thought.

By 9 p.m., a good deal of details about this Drona character had been amassed. Mischievous by nature since childhood, the youth had managed to join the Home Guard (a voluntary organisation tasked as an auxiliary to the police) for some time. He was suspended about two years ago for some reason and since then, he stayed at home. The father and the son were both habitual drinkers and gamblers. Both had been to the Raas and stayed there till late on the night before the murder. Most people kept a safe distance from Drona because of his noxious and temperamental nature.

By then Purakayastha babu, the Second Officer, had arrived to help out with the investigation. Since most of the information known so far was collected under his supervision, I asked him and his team to keep an eye on Drona and hunt for the school master. I also forbade them to arrest or directly accost either of them.

The day had seen a few spells of rain and there was a possibility of a few more showers during the night. The dog operation would begin the next morning. I thought of taking some rest before the action began. The next moment, I shrugged off the idea. "A matter of one more night," I thought. "Who knows, I might just manage to get a lead." I asked Purakayastha and his boys to return and instructed them to come back at 7 a.m. sharp in plain clothes and earnestly commence working on their allotted tasks.

The next day, November 27, was the third day of the investigation. The sniffer dogs had arrived in a special vehicle at about 2.30 a.m. At 7.30, Robin's body was carefully pulled out of the nullah and placed on the grass. I noticed that the head had not been severed completely and was still attached to the body by a thin slice of the skin on the left side of the neck. Clearly, the assailant had used a sharp and heavy weapon with significant force, as the child appeared healthy. He was also handsome, for a boy of his age.

Havildar Gogoi from Shillong accompanied the two dogs, Jiya and Jyoti. After a brief consultation with Gogoi, one of the dogs was brought to body and made to sniff the neck. The dog immediately bolted towards the south and then ran towards the road on the west. For a brief while, the dog stood near the gate of a house, and then began running again, Havildar Gogoi in tow. I ran behind the duo, and behind me ran a large mob of extremely excited, unruly and uncontrollably curious onlookers. After running for about two miles, the dog ran straight into a house on the right side of the road, entered a room, hopped on an empty bed and sat puffing on it triumphantly. It was Robin's bed.

Red faced, both at the anti-climax and the two-mile run, I asked Gogoi what the reason for the faux pas could be. Gogoi explained that the dog had perhaps picked up the smell of Robin and not that of the assailant. Though the first attempt had ended in naught, I was amazed at the natural endowment of the animal and marvelled at its ability to pick up a particular odour from a three-day old dead body, pursue it for nearly two miles on a road that is traversed by thousands of people every day and precisely reach the boy's home. This, in spite of the fact that there were several spells of rain in the interim.

We again returned to the spot with the dog. At around 9 a.m., the other dog was made to sniff the handle of Robin's bicycle that lay in the jungle. The dog picked up a smell, bolted for about two miles and stopped at the tri-junction of a black-topped road. The residents of Korengaghat normally boarded buses to Borholla or Jorhat at this point. Again, we returned to the crime spot empty handed. We had jogged a lot since morning but no one thought of taking any rest and our primary aim was to achieve a breakthrough in the case.

On our return, we found the SP and the Circle Inspector waiting for us at the spot. I appraised them about whatever little progress had been made with the investigation thus far and debriefed them about the dog operation. Without naming anyone, I also indicated the possible suspects.

Meanwhile, sitting arrangements were made for the officers at a shady clearing in the lawn of a large house nearby, overlooking its kitchen.

I felt somewhat reassured at the presence of Circle Inspector Brikodor Deka. He was a committed, accomplished and brave officer. I had learnt a lot from him and revered him as my Guru. “Sir, I have been waiting for you every moment for the past three days,” I confided. He soothingly shared that he had to travel to distant Karimganj to appear as a witness in a case and had returned that very morning. While strolling on the veranda outside his quarters in the early hours, he had noticed a large number of people, mostly on bicycles, heading towards Cheenamara. On enquiring, he had learnt that a boy had been ‘sacrificed’ at Korengaghat. Without wasting another minute, he had started for the place of occurrence. The CI patted me and said, “Don’t worry. The case will be solved.” He also shared that he had already identified the probable culprit. I was startled and wanted to know whom he suspected. “I will not reveal anything now. You continue with the investigations,” he said.

I did not have much time left with me. The body would have to be sent for post mortem after conducting the inquest proceedings. Another attempt would have to be made before the Dog Squad left, as it would be very difficult to solve the case otherwise.

I collected all the information gathered by Second Officer Manamath babu and his boys. Their inputs strengthened my suspicion. Most people in the village despised Drona. However, there was no direct allegation against him. Manamath further stated that Drona had been keeping a close watch on the police activities, especially after the arrival of the SP and the CI. He was oblivious of the fact that the police had an eye on him as his movement was completely unhindered. I, too, concluded that Drona had been emboldened as he did not know that he was under surveillance. Instead of making any attempt to escape, he was brazenly moving around near the police.

The Second Officer further added that the CI had questioned the school master and that he was at his residence. The other bad characters were also being shadowed even though nothing suspicious had emerged against any of them.

I began to wait for some more evidence to confirm my suspicion. The main suspect was Drona. Then we would arrest and interrogate him. With this plan of action in my mind, I returned to the place where the SP was hosted. The village womenfolk had prepared some tea and refreshments for the officers. Among them was Runi, the smart looking girl. I noticed that every now and then, she would come to the kitchen window overlooking the lawn where the SP and other officers were sitting. She was trying to eavesdrop, ostensibly on behalf of her cousin.

We continued our conversations casually. At an opportune moment, I whisperingly requested the CI to reveal whom he suspected. "The school master," he said, keeping his voice low. I replied, "Sir, though there are many discrepancies in the school master's statement, I don't think he would have committed the crime." When the SP wanted to know my opinion, I said, "Drona is a bigger suspect than the school master," and substantiated the reasons for my suspicion with the details available. "Time now to call the bluff," the SP said after he heard me patiently and asked me to move quickly as time was short.

Though there was no incriminating evidence against Drona, my suspicion was growing stronger. But I wanted to be doubly sure. At that moment, I recalled another case that took place about two and a half years ago at the Guwahati Police Station. The case was solved on the basis of the suspect's behaviour and a study of his mental condition. The case pertained to the frequent theft of self-starters (an engine component) from trucks parked near a dhaba (road-side eatery). Two suspects, residents of a state in western India, were picked up after the investigation. The two began accusing each other after they were made to accost each other. The accusations led to verbal abuse, which soon escalated into a fisticuff. During the fight, the behaviour of the two opponents was starkly different. One was fighting aggressively in a fit of rage whereas the other was merely trying to defend himself, even though he was the stronger of the two. On the basis of this observation, I pursued the second suspect, who eventually broke down and confessed to his crime. On the basis of his confession, a large number of stolen self-starters were recovered from a burial ground located about 150 miles away from the city of Guwahati.

As I recollected this incident, I thought it would have been good if I could observe Drona closely. But the fellow had been keeping a safe distance and was keeping an eye on us instead. After a brief consultation with and permission of the SP and the CI, a new plan was put to work to bring Drona to close proximity. A job announcement targeting the local youth was made, asking the able bodied to come forward for a preliminary examination. The ploy worked like tonic. Immediately, about 15 young men queued up, our friend Drona included. They were asked to take off their shirts and present themselves one by one in front of the SP, for a screening.

I strongly believed that if Drona could be brought near the SP, his reaction and demeanour would give away a lot about him. A close observation could be a big help in arriving at something more definitive.

Drona's turn came after the interview of a few youngsters. He walked in like a trained jawan (soldier) and stood in front of the SP. However, he could not contain the anxiety residing deep in his heart, in spite of his conscious efforts. His facial expressions and a peculiar observable thumping of the left side of his chest gave away that he was hiding something. As we witnessed this, my eyes met the CI's. The SP, too, noticed everything and nodded in silent agreement. Though my suspicion was confirmed, I did not arrest him or the school master immediately, as the dog operation had not yet concluded.

The Dog Squad was scheduled to leave in about an hour and a half. A dog test of Drona, the school master and the other suspects would have to be concluded prior to that. "Now what?" I thought in a moment of bewilderment. And that is when the invisible power began guiding me in an astonishing way. I instructed all village residents aged between 15 years to 75 years to queue up on the road and asked all the police personnel to ensure that the order was invariably complied with. Finding the school master, I took him aside, gave him a final warning privately and asked him to speak the truth. The master, however, stuck to his guns.

Meanwhile, about 200 men, including Drona, the school master and the other suspects, had queued up on the road, as instructed. Drona stood right at the middle of the queue. The Dog Squad van stood about 200 yards away. As I had suspected that Robin had been sexually assaulted before being murdered, the sniffer Jyoti was brought to Robin's dead body and was made to sniff the boy's posterior. The canine picked up a smell, bolted towards the queued up men and began the operation from one end. On reaching Drona, the dog stopped briefly for a moment, sniffed hard from toe to naval and climbed to his face, as we waited with baited breath. Then it climbed down and while it was still sniffing, the dog swiftly held Drona's right wrist between its jaws, without causing any physical injury. Havildar Gogoi signalled to confirm the import of Jyoti's action. Some of the villagers began applauding and one group wanted to punish Drona immediately. All of them were sternly warned to stay calm.

Meanwhile, Jiya, the other sniffer, who was kept in seclusion so that it would not be able to witness Jyoti's activities, was now brought and made to sniff the body. The dog commenced its operation after the men in the queue had been shuffled. However, just as Jyoti did, Jiya too pointed at Drona. The crowd began applauding again and now many, including Robin's family members, began baying for Drona's blood. Oblivious of the law and its procedures, the simple villagers believed that Drona's guilt had been proven beyond doubt. In a court of law, dog evidence is not considered conclusive proof unless it is accompanied by other substantial evidence, witnesses or recoveries. Though the dog operation had given us enough ground to arrest Drona, I knew very well that this was hardly enough to even file a chargesheet, let alone earn a conviction.

We still had a lot of work left. An inquest proceeding had to be conducted apart from conducting a search at suspect Drona's house. Another attempt had to be made to recover the murder weapon. However, it was clear that unless Drona was safely removed from the emotionally charged village, nothing would be accomplished. Accordingly, Drona was formally arrested and arrangements were made to send him to the Police Station safely.

I needed a few able hands to finish the work at hand, so I could spare no one but Bapukon to take Drona to the Police Station. Havildar Gogoi would have to go to the Police Station for a General Diary entry before he left for Shillong and I thought it prudent to send Bapukon and Drona along with them. Accordingly, I instructed Bapukon to take Drona to the Police Station in the Dog Squad van and put him in the lock-up. Bapukon was elated. He must have thought that the all-important assignment had been given to him because of his substantial contribution, leading to the arrest. "Don't worry, Sir. This criminal will not be able to escape from my watchful eyes," Bapukon said with a crisp salute. I thought, "Yes, with Gogoi and the two trained dogs in the vehicle, I am pretty reassured."

The SP and CI asked me to carry on with the search and other procedural formalities. "Meanwhile, we will begin questioning Drona and the school master," they said as they left for the Police Station with the school master, who was also arrested.

Before I left to conduct a search at Drona's house, I instructed the second officer and the ASI to conduct an inquest procedure and send the body for post-mortem. I especially reminded them to seize Robin's trousers.

During the search at Drona's place, a pair of recently washed but unpressed trousers was found. The knee area appeared to have been scrubbed forcefully, perhaps to wash away blood or some other suspicious stains. The apparel was seized for a forensic examination. No weapon or other suspicious material was found. Notably, Runi was very cooperative during the entire operation. Though she must have been disturbed at Drona's arrest, she did not express anything. She however requested me to see to it that Drona is not physically harmed. Even though it was daytime, Drona's father was inebriated and kept cursing the police. In the midst of all this melodrama, the proceedings, including the recording of a few witness statements, were completed and I returned to the Police Station, after a good three days.

At the Police Station, I learnt that Drona had promised the SP and the CI that he would show them where the murder weapon was concealed. He had taken the two officers on a wild goose chase to quite a few places and fishing nets were cast at a couple of ponds at his behest. Predictably, nothing was recovered. The SP had returned to Jorhat soon after returning from the expedition. The CI was still around and together, we began questioning Drona and the school master again.

Drona had obviously realised that the murder weapon was crucial for the investigation and that it would be difficult to prove his guilt without it. He now flatly refuted any role in the murder and maintained that the dogs had obviously made a mistake. "This fellow will be a hard nut to crack," I surmised.

It was then the school master's turn. He too continued to stick to his statement and adamantly stated that he knew nothing other than what he had already disclosed. With no further progress, the CI bade adieu at about 11 p.m. The Crime Conference was scheduled to begin the next day.

Readers can easily gauge my precarious physical and mental condition at that moment. After struggling continuously for over the preceding 50-60 hours, all we had was two suspects. Even the reason or the motive behind the murder was unclear. There was no more time at hand. The suspects would have to be produced before a court before 10 a.m. the next morning. The possibility of getting a police remand was uncertain. If something had to be done, I would have to stay awake the whole night. But my body refused to listen. Purakayastha babu suggested that I should go and have a bath. "You'll feel fresh," he proffered. Though I heard him, I could not decide what I should do and slumped on the wooden chair, shutting my eyes in a bid to relax a bit.

Not only the boys in the investigating team, but the entire staff of the Police Station had become completely involved in the case. No one thought of going to sleep. The constables rested in the barrack adjoining the Police Station and a pall of gloomy suspense enveloped the police station. To brighten up the mood, someone poked Bapukon. "Hey, Bapukon! You're quite a hero, man! Why don't you tell us how you brought that dreaded murderer from Korengahat and locked him up?" As expected, Bapukon pounced on the opportunity. Like a seasoned thespian waiting in the wings of a stage, Bapukon stepped into the imaginary limelight with the practised ease. He began relating his tale with indescribable enthusiasm, minutely detailing how he had escorted Drona from the clutches of a ravaging crowd to the

Dog Squad vehicle stationed about 200 yards away. Bapukon continued dishing out his delicious tale to the relishing satisfaction of his audience. I, however, found it quite insipid. At one moment, I thought of asking them to stop. But I had no strength left to speak.

Bapukon continued, "Though many people in the crowd perhaps wanted to assault Drona, no one dared to touch him. How could they? After all, I had a big cane in my hand. As Drona was getting into the vehicle, a youth yelled, 'Take him to the Police Station and thrash him heartily. Bloody devil!'" I woke up with a start as soon as I heard this. I asked Bapukon if he knew the youth. "I haven't made any mistakes this time, Sir. I have taken down his name as well as residence. His name is Debo and he stays close to the place where the van was stationed."

A ray of hope dawned in my mind. Why did the youth call Drona a devil? Why does he want Drona to be thrashed? Perhaps the youth nursed a grouse against Drona and hated him. But why? Without wasting a moment, I took Bapukon along and headed straight to Korengaghat.

We reached Debo's house and called out his name. An extremely handsome, muscular youth resembling the Greek Gods, answered the door. He appeared some 20-22 years old. Bapukon immediately identified him as Debo. As time was running out, I asked him to accompany us to the Police Station. Debo readily agreed, as if he was waiting eagerly for us to arrive. Perhaps he wanted to share something important with us. "Good," I thought. My hopes, however, were dashed after the preliminary questioning. When asked as to why he wanted Drona to be punished and why he had called him a devil, Debo said, "No special reason, Sir. Since he has murdered Robin, I wanted him to be punished. And isn't a murderer a devil? What's wrong if I called him one?"

"But how do you know that Drona had committed the murder?"

"Why, didn't the police dogs identify him?"

Even after probing him with various questions, the fellow would not share anything else. I surmised that this was another tough one. I decided not to push any further, especially since I could keep him in custody for another day. I instructed the staff to take him to the constables' barrack in order to keep him separated from the others.

Meanwhile, the lock-up sentry informed me that Drona and the school master were visibly anxious and uncomfortable as soon as they saw Debo being brought to the police station. I immediately summoned the school master. "Listen, why are you asking for trouble? After all, you are innocent. Debo has already revealed everything," I took a shot in the dark. Instantly, the school master turned pale. The next moment, he fell at my feet. "Sir, I lied as I feared for my life. This butcher would not have spared me alive had I uttered a word. I will tell you everything. But please save me," he pleaded. Then, he began relating the sequence of events.

"That morning, I was grazing cattle near the sugarcane field. I saw Drona tottering in an inebriated state. Debo was walking with him. Drona had a large Naga dao (a single edged, long blade cleaver), with which he chopped some standing sugarcane stems. The two then began munching on those, sitting by the nullah. Short tempered by nature, Drona was doubly dangerous when he was drunk. So, I took extra precautions to hide myself from his line of sight. A few minutes later, I saw Robin on a bicycle, pedalling towards the east. Drona spotted him and forcibly pulled him to the sugarcane field, bicycle in tow. I saw Drona intimidating Robin. Petrified, Robin caught his own ears and pleaded for mercy. But Drona was adamant and kept shouting, 'I won't spare you today'."

"Debo tried to reason with Drona but he was livid and not ready to listen," the school master continued. "Then, Drona sodomised Robin in front of Debo. But, even after the torture, Drona's anger had not subsided. He kept yelling that he would kill Robin. Crippled by fear Robin did not even dare to stand up. Drona then ordered Debo to pin Robin to the ground and Debo complied. Drona then slit Robin's throat with the dao just as animals are slaughtered during halal. I froze as I witnessed the horror unfold before my eyes and wetted my trousers in fear."

"After committing the murder, Drona and Debo dragged Robin's body and threw it near the nullah, picked up his bicycle and walked towards the jungles. Stunned, I returned to the village and told the villagers that I had heard some cries and saw the blood patches, and that something untoward had taken place. Sir, trust me. I am not involved with this crime in any other way. I feared for my life and that's why I did not say anything even though I am an eye-witness to the crime. I lied to you as well...please save me," he pleaded.

"Ah, so here comes out the truth," I thought. "If only this fellow had spoken earlier, it would have spared us much trouble." But, I was not very enthused. We would require more solid evidence against Drona to submit a chargesheet. If only we could find the weapon of offence. Lost in these thoughts, I didn't realise when my eye lids had shut themselves.

The invisible power, however, had other plans. He had already set the board for the next move. We, the pawns, merely played out the invisible directives of the divine. Suddenly, I awoke with a start. Manmath babu was sitting upright and wide awake. I asked him where the school master was.

"He has been kept in seclusion."

"And Debo?"

"Why, he is in the barrack. All is well."

According to the school master's statement, Debo was not only a witness to the crime but had also helped Drona commit it. "So, he's lying. He needs to be taught a lesson now." I used all my strength to get off the chair and told the Second Officer, "Come on, let's interrogate him properly now."

I was aghast the moment I stepped into the barrack. The youth had been hung upside down and he was happily hanging that way. My heart skipped a beat as I did not know for how long he had been kept in that position. If an untrained person is kept upside down for a long time, blood accumulates in the head and may cause serious brain damage. "Who has done this?" I demanded as the constables hurriedly brought Debo down. The moment he was made to stand up, the young and healthy lad began yelling, "Sir, I can't see a thing, there's complete darkness before my eyes," and fell nearly unconscious. Sure that he was not pretending, I held him close to my chest. As I comforted him, I mentally shot an urgent prayer to the Almighty – the only saviour who could come to my rescue at that moment.

After about 5-7 agonizing minutes, Debo began returning to normalcy. I fathomed that to help him regain his composure, it was important to take the fear of police out of his mind. I therefore did not keep any stone unturned to humour him. My foremost concern was to ensure that he remained stable. I asked all the Police Station staff to leave us alone as I began befriending him. He soon warmed up and we spoke about friends, family, sports and many other matters, but not a word about the murder. About an hour later, the youth had become completely normal. Though Debo was about 20-22 and I was about 28 years old then, he began treating me like a bosom friend and spoke freely. He must have thought that this young cop was a "good fella; if I can keep him in good humour for a while, he might even let me off the hook." He spoke unhesitatingly about his affair and an illicit affair with another woman. By then, the time was 'brahma-muhurta.' I mentally cursed myself as I continued to listen to his unending banter in mock amusement. "People meditate and offer prayers at this hour. And look at what am I doing?" I also realised how demanding the policing profession is and how much thankless effort goes into solving each case.

As Debo showed signs of complete normalcy, I was tempted to begin questioning him about the murder. But, I resisted the urge. If he sensed trouble, he could have gotten into a shell. I preferred to wait it out for an opportune moment. And then magic happened. As if prompted by the divine, Debo broached the subject on his own and said, "Sir, will you let me go? I haven't committed the crime. It's is Drona's misdeed."

And then he began singing. "I and Drona have been friends for a very long time. He confides many things to me. Over the past year or so, Drona had developed a physical relationship with his cousin, Runi. On one careless day, Robin had seen them in the act. From then on, Drona and Runi feared that Robin would exposed them in front of the villagers. Runi even contemplated suicide. Drona used to intimidate Robin on one hand and heap allurements on the other, in a bid to stop him from exposing his incestuous affair. About a fortnight ago, Drona confided that Robin had been threatening to expose him. I was sure that Robin would not have done anything like that and he was merely blackmailing harmlessly and having some fun at Drona's expense, and I told him so. But he was adamant and decided to kill Robin."

"Drona had been to the Raas fair on the night before the incident. He had spent almost the entire night there and returned home early in the morning, completely intoxicated, only to have an altercation with Runi. This infuriated him further and he stepped out in a fit of rage, without having a morsel. I met him on the way. He was very hungry as he hadn't eaten anything in hours, and ate a few sugarcanes. The sweet cane juice perhaps further aggravated his intoxication. As fate would have it, Robin happened to pass by in a bicycle at that moment. Drona flew into a rage as soon as he spotted Robin and seized him forcibly. He angrily asked him why he had been blackmailing him. Taken aback, poor Robin pulled his own ears and pleaded that he never meant it and would never say a word to anyone. But Drona would not listen. He frightened Robin into submission and sodomised him. But even after the torture, Drona continued to boil. Possessed by the devil, Drona slaughtered Robin with his cleaver. When I tried to obstruct him, he attacked me as well. I pacified him with much effort. He then threw Robin's body in the nullah and picked up Robin's bicycle as we walked away from that place and headed toward the jungles in the north. After walking some distance, Drona threw the bicycle on the ground and suggested that we should go to a river about a mile away. We bathed in the river and returned to our homes separately." Debo concluded by saying, "Sir, do you realise now why I called him a devil?"

He then persistently pleaded for his release. I patiently told him that even if I accept his statement to be true, I would still need more evidence to establish Drona's guilt. Debo thought for a while and then said, "Sir, there is more proof."

"What else?"

"The weapon which was used to kill Robin."

Though I rejoiced inwardly at this unexpected revelation, I did not express any interest. "That won't be enough. I'll need more. Tell me everything once again in detail. Let me see if I can find something more incriminating."

Debo then recounted the entire incident in minute detail, recalling where he had met, where they had gone and how the murder took place. He added that after the murder, Drona had warned him of dire consequences if he dared to open his mouth. Drona had forced him to go to the river. At the desolate riverside, Drona pointed at a hillock and commanded Debo to dispose of the weapon there.

Debo did as instructed. He further stated that the place is hardly visited by anybody and firmly believed that the weapon would still be there, untouched by anyone else. He was confident that he would be able to retrieve it.

I questioned Debo several times and in various ways to verify the exact location of the weapon and was convinced that he was speaking the truth. An hour later, we were able to retrieve the weapon of offence, as indicated by Debo. After about 65 hours of continuous pursuit, I could finally heave a sigh of relief.

Drona continued to deny any role in the murder even after the recovery of the weapon of offence. The court, in the meanwhile, granted police custody of the three suspects – Drona, Debo and Bora, the school master – for 24 hours. During this period, Drona broke down and confessed to his crime but did not disclose the motive behind the murder. He refused to acknowledge any illicit relationship with Runi. Nor did he share any role of the girl in the murder.

During the investigation, however, it became apparent that on returning home after committing the murder, Drona had first washed his trousers himself and then he made Runi clean up the marks near the knee of the trousers. He then took Runi to Jorhat in a bus. There, he bought a new pair of trousers for himself and a mekhela-chador (traditional womenswear) for Runi. The two then had a meal at a restaurant and returned home before dusk.

During interrogation, Runi accepted that after returning from the river, Drona had confessed to her that he had "finished Robin." She also said that during their journey to Jorhat in a bus, Drona had said that he would kill Debo if the police came after him. She, too, denied having any illicit relationship with her cousin.

Even though both Drona and Runi denied their relationship, it was quite clear that the main motive behind the murder was to keep the affair under wraps. Since Runi had said that Drona had admitted his crime to her and had threatened to kill Debo, an attempt was made to have her statement recorded by a magistrate. She, however, turned hostile at the last minute.

On completion of investigation, a chargesheet was filed against Drona and Debo, implicating them in the murder. The school master was made an approver. The school master's eye witness account, the dog evidence, recovery of the weapon of offence and its identification eventually led to a conviction and resulted in a life sentence for Drona and Debo, in spite of an inconclusive forensic report.

Today, as I reminisce the incident many decades later and mull over the peculiar turn of events leading to the detection in this sensational case, I feel thrilled to note how justice prevails at the end. Why else did Bapukon get drafted to help out with a serious crime? Bapukon, I believe, was the real protagonist of this incredible episode. It is also quite intriguing to note that Debo's sudden brush with death, which was completely unscripted, was the turning point in the case that would have remained unsolved otherwise.

CHAPTER

15 Peculiar Personalities and An Untold Story

Assam is extremely rich and diverse not only in terms of geographic, cultural and natural resources, but also from a demographic perspective, resulting in a significant variation in administrative challenges and crime patterns of the various districts. The crime pattern of a particular region largely depends on its peculiar demography, or what is referred to as *'jono gothoni'* in Assamese. For instance, Central Assam's Nagaon district and most of the districts adjoining the Bangladesh border have a significantly higher number of theft-dacoity cases and crime against property, as compared to the other parts of the state.

During my early service days, the Thanadars (Officers In-charge) of these regions were held in high esteem by the public. The DC or the SP were relatively unknown entities in these parts of the world as they would rarely visit such far-flung places. The Thanadars, on the other hand, were more influential because of their presence on ground. To an external observer, it would appear that these officers were leading a cool life without facing too many pressures or problems. But this was far from the truth, as can be inferred from the following account.

On my arrival to take charge of one such Police Station located near the Bangladesh border, I noticed about a dozen-and-a-half civilians, dressed in their best possible, waiting outside the Officer-in-charge's office room, puffing *beedis* anxiously. I instantaneously knew that these people had not come to share any grievance. But who were they and what were they doing here? Soon, I learnt that they had come for a 'meet-and-greet' session. A little more probing brought out the reality – these were the 'middle-men' who masquerade as the be-all-and-know-all. They roam about freely in the Police Station precincts and create an illusion that the police or the public are completely dependent on them. Though they introduce themselves as social workers and behave as 'helping hands,' in reality, these people do not play any constructive role in reducing crime or apprehending criminals. Their only objective is to make some money by cheating the hapless citizens. Worse, these people create an unnecessary and imaginary barrier between police and the public by instilling fear in the minds of people. "Beware! Do not go to the police station alone or you'll be in trouble," is a narrative they purposely push into gullible minds. Many people fall prey to such elements, not realising the fact that reaching out to the police in case of any crime or injustice is a fundamental right of every citizen. Falling prey to such nefarious designs, many people, especially in rural areas, believe that these middle-men are their only solace. Unfortunately, some police officers do little to bridge the artificial police-public divide as they believe that this ecosystem works to their advantage.

Whenever a case is reported to the police, these middle-men immediately sniff out what the complainant's real intention is. Will he really fight the case and take it to its logical conclusion or make a quick buck mid-way and retract? Is the dispute aimed at punishing the accused or is it merely driven by some personal agenda? After ascertaining all these facts, they then share 'tips' with the officer. "Sir, maybe you needn't register a case and just conduct a superficial inquiry." And then, they commence playing their role of being a relative of both, the groom and the bride. Fortunately though, not all police officers are indulgent towards these middle-men, and I was one of those.

As I made it clear in no uncertain terms that day, a section of my visitors began lamenting, "What kind of officer is this? We will die of hunger if he puts a spanner in our works." The other section, which considered itself superior to the others, had an indignant look on their face. "Let's see how long this officer survives here without our support." A few days later, this group too realised their folly.

Another group, however, puts the Thanadar to test and tries to infer what kind of officer one is. Does he have a strong spine or is he a weakling? Intimidation tactics include showing proximity to political leaders, money power or support of a particular community. And those who have stood in elections or tasted some political success have a different air about themselves. Let me share an incident.

A few days after taking charge of the Police Station, I noticed a timber merchant weeping and pleading in front of the Second Officer for quite some time. I enquired what the matter was after the visitor left and learnt that the man was incurring losses in his business. Moreover, someone had shot at and killed his elephant, which was used to transport the logs. He alleged a conspiracy against him and pleaded for police action against the culprits. A few days later, the harassed merchant turned up again in panic and complained that some tea garden labourers were forcibly looting his logs. He would lose everything if the logs were taken away. I heard him and thought that that the merchant was going through a rough patch. I felt empathetic, so I took up the case myself. On reaching the spot, I saw in disbelief the logs being sawed into planks openly. A couple of large manually operated crosscut saws were being used by a number of people. Others were busy loading the planks on trucks and bullock carts. The men included locals as well as residents of adjoining states. The audacious loot in broad daylight surprised me. The saws, planks and other equipment were seized and the men were arrested and brought to the Police Station.

I had not shifted to the police residential quarters yet and was temporarily putting up at a Dak Bungalow accommodation, close to the Police Station. At about 10 p.m. that night, the chowkidar, Haradhan, informed me that a local 'neta' was waiting to meet me. Stepping out, I found six-seven tea estate managers and the short-statured 'neta' seated in the veranda. On enquiring the reason for their visit, the political leader unceremoniously thrust a chit in my hand without uttering a word. It was a note from the SP, who had scribbled, "I have heard the defendants and this appears to be a case of civil dispute. The arrested persons may be released on bail." I was offended with the attitude of the tea estate managers. Instead of approaching me, they thought it fit to take a politician along and approach the SP, 80 miles away. I thought if I released the arrested persons immediately, the managers of about one-and-a-half dozen tea estates in my jurisdiction and the local politicians would gain an upper hand and try intimidatory tactics in the future as well. I was also annoyed with the neta's impolite behaviour, and said firmly, "The arrested persons cannot be let off on bail tonight. I will think about it tomorrow." Neta ji was visibly agitated. "You are disobeying the SP's orders," he threatened. "I'm not disobeying," I retorted. "I need to mull over various aspects. Evidence is required to prove that the case is actually a civil dispute. Besides, some of the arrested persons are from distant places and it would not be prudent to release them at this late hour. If something untoward happens to them en route, I will be held responsible." "All right then," said the ruffled Neta. "We will obtain the bail from the court." "As you wish," I dug in as I turned back, stormed into my room and purposely slammed the door shut.

I had a sense of déjà vu as I recollected how I had been transferred within 24 hours after a similar brush with the political class, about five years ago. The tea-estate scenario and the involvement of a political leader was all too familiar and fresh in my mind. "Perhaps I won't be able to stick around this place for more than a week. Couldn't have cared more, nonetheless," I thought, as I cast a glance at my still unpacked luggage. I was lost in thoughts when I heard a knock on the door. "Now, what does Haradhan want?" I thought as I opened the door. It was Neta ji. Before I could bat an eyelid, he had entered my room and bolted the door. "Hey, hey" I thought, "What's this fella trying to do? Hand-to-hand combat?" But before I could react, the Neta stepped forward and clasped my hand. "My political career depends entirely on the votes of these tea-estate people," Neta ji got to the point in a soft, polite voice, without wasting a moment. "I hope you understand that people like me who are into politics have to do many things unwillingly. And I had no intention of ignoring you when I approached the SP. Since we had never met earlier, I thought it better to see the senior officer first. Please forgive me." As the reason why the gentleman wanted to have a closed door, one-on-one conversation became amply clear, I relented. I called Haradhan and asked him to tell the officer on duty to conclude the bail formalities and release the arrested labourers in small groups. As I recall this incident, I feel that belling the cat that night turned out to be a blessing in disguise as I did not have to endure any unfair pressure from the tea estates or the political class during my fairly long tenure at this Police Station.

Through the course of my career, I had the opportunity to meet many people. Of these, a few peculiar characters have left an indelible impression on my mind. One such person was Insan Ali. Eversince I took charge of this police station, located close to the international border, I noticed that a short-statured 70-75 year old man, wearing a lungi, fatuwa (traditional half-sleeve cotton shirt) and tarkki (white skull cap worn by Muslims) would often visit the Police Station. He never entered the building premise or spoke with any officer. He would merely wobble in with a walking stick in one hand and an umbrella in the other, walk past the gate, meet the sentry, exchange a few words and walk out slowly a few minutes later. After watching this monotonous activity for a couple of months, I became curious. Especially intriguing was the fact that the man always wore the same dress.

On enquiry, I learnt that this unimpressive looking old man was no ordinary person. He was Insan Ali, one of the richest farmers in the Police Station jurisdiction. He lived in a village some 15-20 miles away. He had inherited vast property and his children were all well settled in the city. Insan, however, preferred not to abdicate the land of his forefathers. "But why does he come to meet the Police Station sentry every week?" I posed the question to the senior-most constable, Chowdhury.

He tried to evade the question initially but on being pressed, he shared reluctantly that Insan comes to contribute Rs. 10 to the Police Station sentry. But why? “For the welfare of the Police Station staff.” I casually asked him if the amount was more and if he was lying. “No Sir,” Chowdhury protested. “Insan’s father used to give Rs. 10 a week. He is continuing with the tradition for the past 30-40 years. He’s such a miser – he’d probably fall dead if he has to pay a penny more.” I quizzed Chowdhury thoroughly and finally concluded that he was speaking the truth. But if Insan was such a miser, surely he wasn’t very rich? However, how rich – and how penny wise – Insan Ali was became amply clear a few days later.

My Police Station was notorious for theft and dacoity cases. Crime was almost like a cottage industry in this region. During the investigation of a bunch of such cases, I realized that Ajeer, a relatively new name in the world of crime, was behind the spate of crime and he was trying to expand his footprint in the area. As it would be dangerous to let this fellow go unchecked for long, I put in strenuous efforts and finally nabbed him from a border village.

Ajeer’s interrogation led to a treasure trove of information regarding the criminal activities of his gang. Incidentally, he mentioned having committed dacoity twice at Insan Ali’s residence. There was a gap of about two years between the two episodes. Ajeer and his gang had decamped with Rs 2 lakhs in cash during the first expedition and about Rs 2.5 lakh during the second. In those days, these were astronomical amounts of money. I was a bit perplexed with this confession. Would anyone keep so much cash at home, especially after being bitten once? To verify Ajeer's claims, I searched the Police Station records and found the document reporting the loot of Rs 2 lakhs from Insan's house. I further learnt that an armed police picket was posted outside Insan's residence for about a month after the sensational dacoity. Curiously however, there was no record of the second dacoity. Even after questioning the Police Station staff and a thorough search of the records, no report of the second case could be found. Ajeer, however, adamantly stuck to his statement.

To verify the truth, Insan Ali was summoned to the police station. On being questioned, Insan acknowledged the first dacoity but made no mention of the second one. Ajeer was then brought face to face and he described in detail how he and his gang had tied up Insan Ali, threatened his wives and grabbed the keys from them before disappearing with the cash. Finding no escape, Insan reluctantly admitted to the second dacoity. This added to my perplexity. Why did he not report the crime then? After a lot of cajoling, Insan finally exploded in frustration, "What would have been the use of reporting the crime? After enduring a loss of Rs 2 lakhs, I had to spend another Rs 200 for a month's chai-pani of the policemen who were posted outside my house. Had I reported again, I would again have to bear the loss of some more money." I was dumbfounded with Insan Ali's logic. However, I definitely became curious to know more about this interesting character.

Among my acquaintances, Noni Babu, the son of a rich man, knew Insan Ali. I learnt from him that Insan was actually one of the wealthiest farmers in that region. However, he was an epitome of tightfistedness and was extremely austere in his habits. Lungi, fatuwa and tarkki were his only apparels. He does not wash any of his clothes and replaces it only when it is torn or worn. Noni babu further shared that he did not know of the second dacoity. But after the first dacoity, his family members had pleaded with him to keep the cash in a bank. A branch of the United Bank of India had recently opened in the region. After much persuasion, Insan Ali decided to visit the bank branch for an inspection. He took a round or two of the bank building and said, "This building is not stronger than my house. No point keeping my money here." He then added another floor to his single floor residence, but did not build a staircase, for 'security reasons.' Every evening, he would have an early dinner before dusk, use a bamboo ladder to climb up to the first floor along with his two wives and then pull up the ladder. He would not climb down till daybreak next day, not even if his son, son-in-law or other close relatives plead with him to do so. I had the opportunity to meet this penny pincher on another occasion.

It was the middle of 1975. Emergency had been declared across the country. On that backdrop, the rural areas saw an uprising of landless farmers. The land owners began losing sleep as the slogan *'langol jaar zomin taar'* (the land belongs to the one who tiles it) began doing the rounds of the villages. The police station received dozens of complaints against the agitating landless farmers. The rich landowners, who had exploited the landless peasants under the garb of barter, now feared land-grabbing by the poor peasants.

Some land owners, instead of approaching the police or courts, attempted to forcibly evict and intimidate the protestors with the help of armed henchmen. Some such complaints were filed in my Police Station also. Insan Ali, too, adopted this route and used force to evict some of the peasants who had grabbed his land. To compound things, the victims of the assault were Hindus. As my Police Station was located in a communally hyper-sensitive zone, the flare-up could have taken an ugly turn any moment. I rushed to the spot and somehow managed to bring the situation under control. However, fear of a communal clash continued to haunt me. Even though Insan Ali was not physically present during the attack, the victims as well as the local public were sure that the attack was done at his behest. To obviate the possibility, I decided to arrest Insan Ali and went to his home. The timid-looking Insan was livid and said, "I have been visiting the Police Station for the past 50 years, but on my own accord. No one has been able to take me to the police station forcibly." I had neither the time nor the inclination to get into a verbal duel. Accordingly, Insan was quickly carried to the vehicle waiting outside and we headed for the Police Station without allowing the matter to escalate any further. On my way back, however, I anticipated that it wouldn't be a peaceful day as some pressure to release him was bound to come from various quarters, and that is what exactly happened.

At about 1 p.m., the SP called up. I assured the senior officer and told him that since the offence was bailable, I would definitely release him, but after a while. If he is released immediately, it will provide an opportunity for the unscrupulous communal elements to foment trouble. It was also necessary to send out a message to the rich landlords and dissuade them from taking the law into their own hands. The SP agreed but advised me to "release him by the same night."

After spending the rest of the day dodging pressures from various quarters to release Insan, it was time for the roll-call parade at night. Just as I was preparing to release him on bail, Insan Ali did something that I could never have imagined.

The roll-call parade procedure had commenced. I was sitting behind a desk in the centre and Insan sat taut on a bench on my left. Behind me were two lock-ups, the male lock-up, which housed the people arrested during the day, and the female lock-up, which was empty. Suddenly, I noticed Insan walking towards me. I assumed that he must be coming to request for an early release. Instead, he walked past me to the female lock-up to my rear and shut the iron grill behind him. As I watched his activities in bewilderment, he addressed me, "I will pay Rs 100 only. If you agree, then it is fine. Else, I will obtain the bail from the court." The churlish behaviour of such an elderly and rich person was beyond my wildest imagination. Making an offer of Rs 100 to secure his own release must have been really tough for him!

Dear Ma, as I travelled down the memory lane, I suddenly recollected my encounter with another strange 'witness.' Though he was not a calculative person like Insan, he had his own calculations behind his insistence to become a witness. This was a time when I had gained some popularity after a string of successes. I was often complimented with words like: "The criminals in the city have fled, fearing your baton."

I had just gone to bed after dinner on a wintery night when the Police Station sentry called me out. "A case witness has arrived, Sir. He wants to spend the night at the police station itself. Should I let him stay overnight?" "Who can this 'sincere' witness be?" I thought, but could not figure out. I could perhaps recollect if I knew his name. So I asked the sentry to find out his name. "He is not sharing his name, Sir. He is repeatedly calling himself a witness and insisting on spending the night at the police station." "Is he mad?" "No Sir, he appears quite healthy and absolutely in his senses." I decided to check out and proceeded to the police station to find an unimpressive looking stout man sitting on the veranda of the Police Station. I could not remember having seen him earlier, so I asked him his name.

"Sir, I am the witness."

"That's fine, but what's your name?"

"Kala Miya."

"So, which case are you a witness for?"

"A dacoity case, Sir."

"Which dacoity?"

"The one that is going to happen tonight."

I gave the man a stern look and thought that he was either deranged or intoxicated. Infuriated, I told him, "So, you want to become a witness even before the crime has been committed. That is not acceptable."

"Still, I am a witness. I am my own witness," he insisted.

"What?"

"I am a witness to the fact that I have no role in the dacoity that is going to take place tonight," he proffered obstinately. "That is why I want to stay in the Police Station tonight."

Clearly, Kala Miya knew a lot about an impending crime and wanted to make sure that he was not implicated. On probing further, Kala Miya finally spilled the beans.

"A gang of dacoits will strike at yonder place at yonder hour. But you won't spare me after that."

"And why would I doubt your involvement?"

"I have just returned home after spending five-and-a-half years in jail. After the dacoity, I will surely be rounded up as a suspect because of my criminal antecedents. And then...I've heard from various quarters that you are a ruthless officer." I could see the fear of the police cane in his eyes as he pleaded again, "Please let me stay here tonight, Sir."

I mentally thanked the man for the timely tip. "Give him a blanket and a cup of tea," I told the sentry before I rushed to apprehend the gang of dacoits. Relieved, the man must have thought, "The Daroga may be a stern one but he has a heart of gold."

A co-incidence too many ...

Dear Ma, you must be thinking that I was having a leisurely time at the remotely located Police Station. In reality, however, I had to face a lot of troubles as all police officers have to face. Though my professional reputation as an "iron-handed officer who never spares criminals" helped ensure peace and tranquillity for the public, it brought me very close to a personal tragedy. Let me reveal, for the first time in my life, how a dastardly conspiracy to harm my family was exposed in an incredibly surprising and unexpected manner.

A daring group of criminals had suddenly become active in the area. The kingpin of this gang was Ghona, who, along with his gang of wagon-breakers, looted material from goods trains at the railway station and the yard, located at some distance from the main city.

As this criminal activity pertained to the Railways, investigating it was juridically the responsibility of the Government Railway Police (GRP). That is why, the gang evaded the local police's notice for a long time. Emboldened by their success, the gang soon became greedy and got into multiple crimes beyond the railway yard. I got whiff of this gang and its nefarious activities during the investigation of one such case. However, in the absence of any solid and reliable evidence, we were unable to take any effective measures against them. This encouraged Ghona and his gang further. Getting a grip on this gang quickly was therefore an imperative and I deputed a team to keep a close watch and collect evidence.

One day, Bhola, the strongest in Ghona's gang, fell in our trap. Burly Bhola belonged to a respectable family, but had fallen in bad company, which eventually led him to the world of crime. In a way, his impressive physique had become the cause of his downfall. He had been freshly recruited by Ghona, who was fond of big and brawny aides. The neophyte, however, had an addiction, which was exploited by constables Dhiren and Nitya, and they were able to apprehend him. The two enthusiastic and smart constables spent the entire night brainwashing the fellow. They soon sensed that Bhola, who would beat his victims to a pulp without batting an eyelid, was actually petrified at the prospect of being at the receiving end. The two constables took advantage of Bhola's phobia and warned him of dire consequences. "You don't know how ruthless our OC is. If he suspects that you are being untruthful, you've had it."

Thanks to the constables' night-long good work, making Bhola sing hardly required any effort. He soon revealed many secrets of his gang and confessed to its involvement in a number of criminal activities. On the basis of Bhola's confession, Ghona's secret hideout was busted and a huge cache of stolen goods as well as other illegal material was recovered from a cremation ground. Ghona, Bhola and several other gangsters were arrested and sent to jail.

After about a month of Ghona and his gang's departure to the jail, two crimes were reported from two villages located adjacent to each other but a considerable distance from the Police Station. Though the crimes were petty in nature, I decided to investigate those myself. I had never been to that part of the countryside earlier and thought this was good opportunity to visit those places while also conducting the investigation. Setting out for the task, I and a small team reached a small railway station where we learnt that the places of occurrence were located to the south of the railway track. There was no motorable road and hence we would have to trek for about 4 miles. I mentally calculated that completing the investigation and the formalities would require another 6-7 hours. I also learnt that we could return in a local passenger train, which was scheduled to arrive in the evening. I had not taken a train ride in a long time and decided that we would take a joyride on the train while returning. So, I instructed the Jeep driver to report back to the Police Station.

After a hard day at work, we returned to the railway station and waited for the train to chug in. Only a few trains passed through this rather small, decrepit station; some stopping for only a brief minute. As the local train arrived at a leisurely pace and screeched to a halt, I saw a door ajar right in front of me. The moment I set foot on the pedestal to board the compartment, I was taken aback to see Mr Bhola staring down at me. He was hurrying to scramble down. Bhola was even more surprised – and visibly scared – at this entirely unexpected encounter. He stepped back hastily and began mumbling and trembling as he folded his hands in salutation. "When did he get bail?" I thought suspiciously. Considering the legal provisions under which they had been booked, Bhola and his gang members should not have got bail before 60 days at the least. "Must have done some hanky-panky to get bail so soon."

The train started chugging almost immediately. As the compartment was full and there was no seat available, Bhola and I stood near the door. Without any coaxing, Bhola confessed that as advised by his lawyer, he had feigned illness and got himself admitted at a hospital. After spending a few days, he managed to get the required medical certificates. He had got bail on 'health' grounds that very day and was on his way back home. "But why were you getting off the train two stations before reaching the city?" I asked. "To evade your eyes, Sir," he responded sheepishly.

Bhola was obviously cursing his fate, fearing arrest and a return to jail in some other case. He kept pleading innocence and tried to cajole me and keep me in good humour through the short journey. Suddenly, he turned serious. "Sir, I cannot keep myself from sharing something important with you. A conspiracy against you is brewing in the jail barracks." I ignored his words as most criminals use such tactics when they are under pressure. Finding my response unenthusiastic, he continued, "Vengeful Ghona is nursing an extreme resentment against you. To avenge his insulting incarceration, he is hatching a conspiracy to commit a heinous crime."

"What's new in that," I thought at Bhola's words. All thieves, dacoits, murderers and criminals dream of taking revenge on police persons for putting them behind the bars. I dismissed Bhola's statement as another ploy to distract. Aghast, Bhola made another attempt. "Sir, you have an infant son, don't you? Ghona has made all arrangements to abduct your son." I remained unperturbed. "Sir, you don't believe me, do you? But trust me, I am not lying," Finding me unmoved, Bhola suddenly questioned, "Sir, doesn't a tribal domestic help carry your son to the river front for a stroll during the evenings? And sometimes, a few jawans play with him by carrying him around in a large bucket?" While these statements were true, these were no secret. Finding me completely disinterested, Bhola resigned indignantly with one last attempt, "Sir, please do not take this lightly. Ghona has tasked a hardened criminal who is about to be released from jail very soon. An advance payment has also been made. The criminal's henchmen had been keeping a watch on the movements of your family. They have collected the information and conveyed it to Ghona and the criminal inside the jail. They have made all plans to abduct the child from the river front. The criminal, on his release, will commit the abduction himself. Please take some precautionary action swiftly, Sir. And please don't blame me if things go wrong." As the train halted at the destination, Bhola bent down to touch my toes in a gesture of seeking blessings and quickly disappeared in the crowd.

On returning to the Police Station that night, I mulled over Bhola's words. His conspiracy theory did hold some water. After all, Ghona's decade-long reputation as a criminal with no police action against him had been dented. Obviously, this must have hurt his ego. He also had access to lots of funds, so making an attempt at avenging his insult was quite possible. I decided to scratch the surface a bit more.

The next day, I received confirmation that the criminal who had been tasked with the abduction was indeed going to be released from jail in about a week. If Bhola's words were true, then the criminal could possibly make an attempt as he would be in need of money. To scuttle the plan, it was necessary to let the conspirators know that their cover had been blown. Further, they needed to know that the person who should have been the last to learn about their nefarious designs, has got whiff of it. Hence, going ahead any further would be a grievous mistake. Accordingly, some people were sent to the jail and were explicitly directed to convey the information to Ghona and his henchmen. However, it is difficult to gauge the mind of a criminal. He could have hatched another conspiracy. So, I kept track of Ghona's release from jail on bail.

Soon after Ghona was released about a month later, I had him summoned to the Police Station and questioned him. Predictably, Ghona began shedding crocodile tears profusely, refuting any role in hatching any conspiracy while in jail. However, the large drops of sweat that lined up on his brows gave away the truth. To make sure that he got the message loud and clear, about a thousand rounds of bullets were brought from the store and laid down neatly in front of him, before he left the Police Station. I am not sure what went on in his mind as he glanced at the ammunition while leaving the Police Station, but I did not face any trouble from him ever again.

The incident, still fresh in my memory, intrigues me to no end even today. Why did I decide to take up the investigation of the two cases with the intention of visiting the unexplored countryside? Why did I plan to take the train instead of the road? The chance meeting with Bhola on the train and the subsequent banter leading to the conspiracy's disclosure – were these all mere coincidences? Or was it something else?

CHAPTER

16 Horror in Hojai

It is always agonising to recollect painful memories and writing about such incidents only amplifies the distress. But not sharing my story about the horrific situation that developed before and after the Assam Assembly elections in 1996 will be injustice to truth and unfair to my attempt at recording significant personal and professional experiences. More importantly, I would be failing to tell the story of how police personnel have to face the consequence of the unwanted interventions and actions of the political class.

It was mid-1999. I was then the Commandant of the 4th Assam Police Task Force (APTF) Battalion and was attending a training programme at the Forensic Sciences Laboratory in Guwahati. Suddenly, I heard a voice, "Hello, Mr Lumding Chakraborty!" Surprised, I turned back to find the Additional Director General of Police, David *sahib,* smiling and waving at me. 'Lumding,' by the way, is the name of a Railway town in Assam's Nagaon district (presently Hojai district). Surrounded by lush green hills and thick forests,

Lumding serves as an important railway junction. During my service career, I had the opportunity to work with David sahib for barely a few days and that too in a state of complete anarchy and chaos. As I shook hands and exchanged greetings with the senior officer, my mind was glutted with memories of those horrific days. My situation then was like that of a marooned soldier, left all alone to fight to the finish. Though most people had forgotten my predicament, David sahib obviously remembered it and as a gesture of his appreciation, addressed me as "Lumding Chakraborty."

Dear Ma, you might be wondering how could policemen become 'marooned soldiers'? Such a situation arises when the administrative machinery fails completely and things come to a grinding halt. Let me relate to you the context in which such a situation arose and how it led an entire city to the brink of disaster.

Ten months after being transferred from Bijni to the Lumding Battalion, I was transferred again as the Additional SP of Hojai, a sub-division of the Nagaon district. Like most sub-divisions, Hojai too had a Sub Divisional Police Officer (SDPO). However, an Additional SP post had been created pre-emptively for this hypersensitive sub-division after the Babri Masjid demolition. The position, unfortunately, did not have any operational or financial power and was merely an ornamental one. This fact dawned on me only after spending a few months in office. Initially,

I overlooked the issue but in about a year's time, I understood that the administration was actually running at the will, whims and fancies of the local politicians. The entire law and order machinery was being manipulated, as the officers in charge of the various police stations had received those plum postings with the blessings of their political godfathers. Willingly or unwillingly therefore, they had to do the bidding of their political masters. The officers were completely occupied with serving the narrow interests of their mentors and had no time for attending to the grievances of the general public. A few officers, in blatant disregard and disrespect to their khaki uniform, wore a cloak of sycophancy while tending to their own personal interests. It was impossible for me to fix the anomalous situation without the support of my two superiors, because I had no powers to punish or transfer even a junior rank. All decision-making powers were vested in the District SP. Unfortunately, the SP thought it fit to look the other way while maintaining status quo in all matters. The DIG, too, went silent after throwing his weight around for a couple of days. This attitude of the senior leadership encouraged the corrupt and truant officers. Question them about their absence from duty, pat would come a reply, "I had gone to meet the DIG sahib." The purpose of the 'meeting' of course, was abundantly clear. A criminal arrested during the day would be released that very night. On questioning, the answer would be something like, "The SP had ordered for it last night."

Ma, I am sure you can now understand how emboldened some of the wayward officers had become. So, when would they work? Clearly, everyone was swimming with the tide. For me however, it was too late to change colours. And that's why I was in a dilemma. I often felt like Washington Irving's Rip Van Winkle and could relate to every bit of his predicament. Just as Rip found everything and everyone unrecognisable upon returning to his own village after a 20-year-slumber, I too found everything unacceptably surreal. For the first and last time in my life, I had tried to obtain a transfer in a bid to escape from the bizarre situation. I reposed my trust on a very senior officer. On hearing my plea, the officer said with a tinge of reprimand and displeasure, "Officers line up at the Chief Minister's residence for a plum district posting like this and you...?"

I, however, was not the only one attempting to secure my transfer. Many thanadars and political leaders, including a few petty ones, were trying to get me out of the way. But alas, destiny had willed it otherwise. Due to unexplainable reasons this god-fatherless officer was doomed to stay put. Had I succeeded in securing a transfer, I would have saved myself from the hurricane that was brewing. But then, has anyone been able to evade one's destiny?

One might legitimately question that when the senior officers were unperturbed with the wrong-doings of the Police Station officials, what was the need for the Additional SP to bother? Well, as the senior-most officer of the sub-division, the Additional SP would have been answerable for any misdeed. Moreover, my career spanning over 30 years had taught me that nothing can be more dangerous than the common man losing his faith on the police administration and taking law into his own hands. That is why my intention was to ensure that the public did not perceive the police merely as an instrument of oppression and that the ordinary citizens got some justice at the very least. But the real power to deliver such justice is actually vested in the Police Station officials, the investigating officers and the field officials. These ranks form the spine of the policing and justice delivery system. Fixing the errors of omission and commission made by these officers can sometimes be beyond the scope and capability of even the superior officers. The ugly and violent incidents that rocked Lumding a few days later clearly vindicated my position.

The situation began worsening as the elections drew closer. The Police Station in-charges of a few prominent police stations began to brazenly flaunt their political allegiance. These officers remained occupied with scheming up ways and means of harassing the opponents of their political masters. The devious tactics deployed could well be the subject of an entire book. The rising incidents of murders and violent assaults gave rise to a strong public opinion against the police, seriously denting its credibility and image. People suspected either police hand or its tacit connivance in most case, including those of political murders, harassment of journalists, disruption of political rallies and even instances of bomb explosions. The police protection and free-hand granted to the anti-social elements, who were in fact on the payroll of the politicians, was another major reason for public disgruntlement. Trouble thus began to brew. Any attempt to rein in the delinquent officers was met with stiff challenges from their political bosses while the superior officers preferred to stay quiet.

As I have mentioned before, extremist elements were active throughout the state of Assam during that period, especially in the sub-divisions of Nagaon and Hojai. An officer in-charge of a police station located in an area known to be the stronghold of a particular group of militants, was proven guilty of harbouring dacoits and other anti-socials. This news irritated the public. Finding no other way out, I pushed for the officer's transfer. As was expected, the recommendation attracted the criticism of the political class. After much effort, the officer was finally transferred. Irked by this 'defeat,' a petty politician, who was a relative of the officer in question, issued a dictat that "the offending Additional SP will not be allowed to set foot in the Police Station jurisdiction till he is transferred." The puffed-up petty politician was extremely arrogant, and would often boast of his journey from one bigha of land to 60 bighas. But destiny had willed it otherwise. Before he could relish my transfer, he fell to the bullets of militants.

At another Police Station, a flawless plan to assault the student leaders who supported an opposition party, was neatly hatched. The plan, of course, was carefully kept away from me. Unfortunately, things went awry the day the plan was executed and the irate mob could not be controlled even after police firing. I dashed to the spot on receiving an SOS from the nervous SDPO and dealt with the situation with an iron hand. This, however, 'insulted' the ruling party members and the local leader (a minister) was furious. Humiliated at his grand plan's failure, the Police Station in-charge too, in an inebriated state that evening, vowed to use all his clout to "have the useless Additional SP transferred." The poor fellow was oblivious of the fact that the political game of dice could change any minute and if that happened, his predicament would be unimaginable. The clamour for my transfer, however, did not stop at that.

One night soon after, while patrolling the Hojai-Morajhar area, I stopped a truck carrying timber illegally. A well-dressed gentleman alighted from the truck and said with an air of arrogance, "The timber in this truck belongs to the Professor." I surmised that no police officer is probably supposed to stop a vehicle belonging to the "Professor." Since I had no knowledge of who this "Professor" character was, I ordered the truck's seizure and sent it off to the Neel Bagan police outpost before proceeding towards Morjhar. On returning to the police outpost late that night, I found a Forest Officer waiting for me. He told me that the District Forest Officer had requested that the offending truck be handed over to the Forest Department. Due to compelling official reasons, I turned down the request. A case was formally registered. This triggered an avalanche. A few days later, I learnt from reliable sources that a prominent religio-political leader had left for the State Capital with a delegation to demand for my ouster. "So, is he the Professor?" I mused.

The elections were close by. At such a point in time, the main opposition leader was murdered in the main bazar area of Lumding. Two election rallies organised by the opposition were also disrupted due to bomb explosions and grenade attacks. Many persons, including women, were injured in these incidents, which heralded a new turn in the political scenario of Lumding. Public dissent was palpable and the needle of their suspicion pointed towards the local leader belonging to the ruling party and the anti-social and criminal elements harboured by him. The local thanadar was accused of partiality and wilful negligence in conducting a fair probe. While sending out a strong message to the investigating officers to conduct an impartial investigation and arrest the accused, I had told them firmly, "Why do you fear? You are not going to arrest the Chief Minister." This statement of mine was cleverly distorted by the thanadar and the other boot-licking investigating officers, and presented to their political godfathers. They alleged that I had ordered the Chief

Minister's arrest. As expected, the political leaders were up in arms and began their efforts to push for my transfer with renewed vigour. But this time too, the all-powerful 'transfer' weapon failed to find its mark.

Meanwhile, a new SP had taken charge of the district as the incumbent officer was injured in a militant ambush and was under treatment. The new officer had vast experience but was perhaps unable to gauge the political undercurrent of the region. On his second visit to Lumding, the SP ordered strict action against the local police and the anti-socials who had the blessings of the local politician. Within a week, he was handed transfer orders. This stunned the media and the public alike, especially because the officer was known to be very close to the Chief Minister. A few days later, the previous SP took charge after some recovery, but only for a brief month or two. But let me come back to that later.

Elections were to be held on April 27. Many leaders of the ruling party knew very well by then that they were staring at a defeat. To distract attention, they repeatedly alleged militant attacks on their cadres. This kept the police busy. A few days before the election, the DIG (who had recently been promoted to the IG rank) visited the area. Almost all the thanadars and officers assured him of the ruling dispensation's victory. I, however, differed and shared my assessment of the situation. The senior officer turned grim as he heard me. Later, finding me alone, a Circle Inspector whispered, "Sir, why are you inviting trouble by speaking the truth? No one is interested in the truth here as the future of many people in this gathering depends on the political fortune of the ruling party. The stakes are very high, Sir." Though I did not fully understand the CI's purport at that time, it became very apparent soon after the elections.

On April 27, the election went off smoothly, barring a couple of sporadic incidents. The ballot boxes were transferred to the designated safe locations from the polling booths. At about 9 p.m., information trickled in indicating that militant groups had seized a few ballot boxes at some polling booths in the Kaki Police Station area. Immediately, I rushed towards Kaki from Sankardev Nagar (Sub-divisional Headquarters). Thankfully, it turned out to be a false alarm. The villagers had mistaken a column of BSF jawans and a Commando unit on polling duty to be militants, ostensibly because of their jet black outfits, bandanas, face masks and automatic weapons. This had caused some panic. Relieved, I headed back to Sankardev Nagar, reaching there by about midnight. The SDO requested me to stay the night as many ballot boxes had not arrived yet. I agreed and relieved the SDPO of his duties, assuming the charge myself.

Early next morning, on April 28, I learnt about some disturbance in Lumding the night before. Since I had not received any information from the local police, I dismissed it as something trivial. The SDO too feigned ignorance about the matter. I tried to contact the officer in charge of Lumding, but in vain. A little later, an election candidate informed that there was massive uprising in Lumding the night before and possibly, the Police Station had been gheraoed (punitive encirclement of the police station by a large group of protestors, causing confinement of the police personnel). The news of gherao was confirmed by a message from the District Headquarters. I asked the SDPO to proceed to Lumding immediately. He however pleaded, "Sir, I am ready to go to anywhere but Lumding." Finding the officer reluctant, I refrained from pressing him any further. In spite of not having a wink all of the night before, I decided to head towards Lumding myself. But where was the force to accompany me? Every man in the area had been engaged in election duty. I finally set off for Lumding after a group of 15-16 Black Panther commandos arrived from Guwahati at about noon. This commando unit had been recently raised to combat ultras.

From Sankardev Nagar, we sped past Lanka to reach Udali, from where an 18-20 km a hilly tract took us to our destination. Deserted streets and tell-tale pyres of burning tyres greeted us as soon as we entered Lumding. However, I barely paid any attention as my mind was focused on my immediate mission – that of freeing the besieged Police Station. After crossing the city's main market and taking a left turn towards the Police Station, we accosted a huge crowd of protestors. It took quite an effort to get past the agitated crowd to reach the Police Station precincts, which had been taken over by the protestors. I entered the Police Station office building only to find about a hundred women protestors inside. The officer in-charge was standing in front of his table. Evidently, the crowd had punished him. I felt both sad and outraged at the condition of the senior police inspector. It didn't take long to realise that to bring things to normalcy, we would have to end the siege and free the Police Station premises of the protestors, and that the process would have to commence by dealing with the womenfolk first. Meanwhile, the women protestors began piling up their allegations noisily on me. Without beating about the bush, I told them firmly, "All your accusations will be heard. But first, you have to leave the police station and free up the streets." By then, some of the Police Station staff, who had fled sensing trouble, returned to the Police Station. After much persuasion through hot and cold means, the women were convinced to leave. As they began vacating, some anti-social vested elements provoked them and egged them to not leave the Police Station premises. I noticed their activity and so did the commando unit that accompanied me. I quickly realised that if action was not taken immediately, these anti-socials could gain an upper hand and hence instructed the commandos to use force. The cane treatment worked wonders, breaking the bones and spirit of the anti-socials rather quickly. Soon, the gathering began dispersing. Within an hour, the Police Station and the adjoining area was freed of the unruly protestors. The credit for this success goes largely to the commandos, whose fierce looking jet black uniform and firm and decisive action instilled the much needed fear of law in the hearts of the unruly protestors.

I heaved a sigh of relief and thanked God, believing that we had managed to control the situation with minimal collateral damage. My sense of relief, however, was short-lived. In the absence of any official communication, I was oblivious of the fact that Lumding had been burning since the night before, fuelled by massive public ire. The irate common man had taken to the streets like a tornado and tore down anything that came in its way. Many houses and buildings had been razed to the ground with bare hands and ordinary implements such as rods and shovels, and movable and immovable properties had been burnt to ashes. As mentioned before, people were infuriated with the reign of terror unleashed by the anti-socials, who had the blessings of the ruling party. The efforts of these elements to disrupt the election process the day before by indulging in booth capturing and crude bomb explosions at several places proved to be the proverbial last straw that broke people's patience. Thousands of men and women took to the streets and soon went on a rampage, destroying the property of these anti-socials and their protectors. The destruction was still continuing, as was the search for the anti-socials. Obviously, there was a possibility of these elements being killed if the mob could lay their hands on them.

I learnt about these developments when a few leaders of the ruling party, including the Speaker of the Assembly, who had been confined to their homes since the night before, arrived at the police station and related their tales of horror. They had gathered courage to venture out after they came to know about my presence in the city. The first to arrive was the most powerful of all the ruling party leaders in the area. He had perhaps never imagined that he would have to see such a day in Lumding. As soon as I extended a courteous greeting as per protocol, he immediately went on the defensive and began explaining that he was 'never displeased' with me. "Listen, I never wanted to transfer you. The one to be blamed is the yonder devil," he said, naming another leader of his own party. Then, with an air of regret, he added, "Ah, but had I known that you are so capable of decimating my political opponents, I would never have relied on this useless officer in-charge." In the course of my career, I had witnessed many occasions when political leaders praise the police when they have their backs pinned to the wall. The neta's words, therefore, did not surprise me at all. However, his mention of 'transfer' confirmed my suspicion that an effort towards securing my transfer had indeed been made by the politicians after I had ordered the investigating officer to arrest the suspected anti-socials. There was, however, no time to mull over these things. Just three days later, I had to witness the use of this 'transfer' weapon, which is wielded against police officers with impunity by those in power.

The entire night of April 28 and the subsequent 24 hours went into dousing the raging inferno across Lumding. I had no force at my disposal to quell the riot-like situation. On top of that, the Police Station officers were completely demoralised and the officer in-charge was practically under house arrest. I had to make strenuous efforts to convince the irate public to return to their homes. Though a semblance of normalcy had returned, it was very apparent that the anti-socials of both sides (those supported by the ruling party as well as those harboured by the opposition) were planning a fight to finish and a blood bath was imminent. And this was my biggest worry.

Meanwhile, even after 24 hours after the commencement of rioting, the SP or DIG, who had been recently promoted as IG (Operations), did not arrive. Instead, on April 29, the Additional Director General, David sahib, and a senior Battalion Commandant arrived to supervise the efforts to maintain law and order. I felt mentally relieved at the arrival of the senior officers. But alas, my relief was only momentary as within the next 48 hours, I was again rendered helplessly alone.

The election results had not yet been declared. Three days after the commencement of riots, the SP paid a visit. Lumding continued to simmer as reports of attempts to murder and sporadic incidents kept trickling in. The goons on both sides were active and we received information that both sides were preparing for a showdown. Illegal arms and ammunition were being procured from various neighbouring places, including Dimapur in Nagaland. The weapons were being secretly stored at several places inside the jungles and in the slum areas. Clearly, a major search-and-seize operation was needed to prevent a large-scale armed conflict. For this we required a team of officers and a large force. There was a probability of the goons using the slum-dwellers as a shield during the operation, and hence police had to be extra vigilant. David sahib, too, was in favour of immediate and large-scale action. Curiously, the SP did not show any enthusiasm and returned to the District Headquarters. Meanwhile, I proceeded along with whatever force was available at my disposal to conduct searches at suspected places, based on David sahib's advice.

I returned at about 8 p.m. only to find the senior Battalion Commandant leaving in his vehicle, with a long face. Before I could understand what the matter was, I spotted David sahib marching towards his vehicle. His otherwise calm face could not conceal his extreme mental agony. Realising that like the commandant, he too was probably leaving Lumding,

I dashed to see him even as his vehicle's engine ignited. "Sir, you had come here to guide us and supervise the law and order restoration efforts. Now, why are you leaving?" I demanded in exasperation. The normally cool and collected David sahib lost his composure and blurted many things cathartically, the sum and substance of which was, "Our chief (DGP) has transferred the commandant on the basis of a thanadar's statement and your SP does not want to do anything. In such a situation, is there any point in my staying here?" I felt helpless and cried out, "Sir, please tell me your next destination. What will I answer if I am questioned?" David sahib replied, "I will tell you that but don't call me back again," as he started off for the District Headquarters of Karbi Anglong.

Stunned with the sudden exit of two senior officers, I tried to find out what had gone wrong. I learnt that after reports of a few fresh incidents of violence, the officer in-charge had deployed the police force in certain areas. The Senior Battalion Commandant was displeased with the deployment and accused the officer in-charge of partiality. The officer, who was a pet of the local leader, immediately informed his political master. The rest of the story can well be imagined. The leader used his clout to influence the State Police Chief, who ordered the Commandant to return and report at his own headquarters in two hours.

In spite of the on-ground presence of an Additional Director rank officer, the Police Chief did not bother to consult him or verify the authenticity of the allegations against the Commandant. Obviously, this was unacceptable for a self-respecting and honest officer like David *sahib.* And that is why he decided to leave Lumding immediately.

Though the elections had ended on April 27, the election results were declared a good 14 days later. The new government was formed a few days after that. Thus there was a hiatus of about17-18 days. During these intervening days, speculation was rife about the outcome of the elections and there was a strong public view that the ruling party would be defeated. Sensing a kill, the opposition leaders and their supporters went berserk, leading to sporadic incidents of violence at various places apart from Lumding, including Hojai, Lanka and a few other places.

One day, I received information indicating the possibility of communal violence at Hojai. I called the SDPO to instruct him to take appropriate precautionary measures, but learnt that he had reported sick. I decided to rush to Hojai myself. But the Lumding Police Station officer in-charge's wife would not let me go. She begged me to stay back as she feared for her husband's life in my absence. Even his own Police Station was no longer safe for him. I had to persuade the lady a lot and assure her that I would return in a day. On my way to Hojai, I thought about the predicament of the family members of police personnel, who have to suffer mental agony for no fault of theirs.

Vanishing of the officers

On the other hand, there was no word from the SP or any other senior officer at the District Headquarters. My SDPO, too, was unfortunately unwell. With David sahib's departure, I was practically all alone and on my own once again. Then began the shameful vanishing of officers who had pinned their hopes on the victory of the ruling party. Now, with only a formal announcement of the election results remaining, these officers thought it fit to go into hiding. The first to do so was the officer in-charge of Lanka Police Station, followed by the OC of the Lumding Police Station. Soon, the thanadars of two other police stations and two second officers were untraceable. I kept wondering where the emerging situation would lead us to. Elections come and go, rulers too keep changing as per the wishes of the electorate, but never before had I witnessed a situation where the police department had practically come to a standstill. The biggest surprise was yet to come – and that was the slipping away of state's senior-most administrative officers, including the Chief Secretary, the Director General of Police along with another Secretary and an IGP, which was extensively covered by the media. Barely had I digested the news when I learnt that our SP too had gone underground. I cursed my fate as I inferred that the script of my solo performance had just gotten a little longer.

In the meanwhile, two sensational murders rocked Lumding. Finding an opportunity, the highway robbers became hyperactive. The workers of the Railway Transhipment Yard went on strike and many untoward incidents with a political undertone took place. As I applied myself to battling these raging bushfires, I never realised when my body fell prey to disease.

One day, I headed to the Railway Hospital to have a loose tooth extracted, while still in uniform. Asked about pre-existing illnesses, I confidently told the doctor that I had no issues and had previously undergone tooth extraction. The good doctor, relying on my words, pushed a few injections and asked me to wait for a few minutes. A few moments later, I felt severe pressure on my chest and breathing difficulty. I was immediately examined, placed on a stretcher and taken to another part of the hospital for further treatment. A short while later, I felt better. The doctor chided me, "Sir, you would have put me in grave trouble. Do you realise that your BP is 120/250? You may suffer a stroke at any time." I had little time to fret over the health issue at that moment as neither the OC nor the Second Officer of Lumding were available.

A few weeks later, a new SP arrived to take charge of the district. I was then fighting multiple battles at the same time and wanted to have a discussion with the SP about some of these matters. I called him up, extended a courteous welcome and sought time to see him. He replied, "Mr Chakraborty, you need not call on me, rather I will call on you." Obviously, he did not want me to leave the Lumding-Hojai area for even a few hours. I am sure that you now realise why I felt like a marooned soldier. After about a month-and-a-half of David *sahib's* departure, the new SP was the first senior officer to visit the affected area. The officer was well regarded in police circles for having discharged his duties successfully and honourably. After a discussion about the prevalent situation in the sub-division and its adjoining areas, the SP mentioned in a worried tone that the situation in other parts of the district was not happy either. Uncertainty loomed large over the state of affairs and there was an air of despair and despondency. He confided that he was trying his best to address the situation, even though he was unsure of the outcome. A few days later, he was handed over his transfer orders.

The nefarious police-politician nexus, frequent transfers of senior police officers and the outrageous disappearance of the top-most administrative officers of the state were among the hottest topics of public discussion in those days. Curiously however, the common people castigated the police more than the politicians. I would often think about the reasons for the difference in public perception. It is easier for a politician to recover from a fall in the public eye than for a police officer. A stain on the uniform is difficult to remove and can bring the hard-earned position and reputation of an officer to naught in an instant. The fact that senior officers are often scapegoats and that they have to undergo much trials and tribulations, is conveniently overlooked by the unforgiving public.

After the transfer of four SPs in five months, Shri Pallab Bhattacharyya took charge as SP Nagaon district. The officer's intense efforts soon bore fruit and the district police slowly returned on its track. During the few months of working with Shri Bhattacharyya, I noticed with admiration that he went beyond the call of duty as the District SP to address some of the fundamental issues that could potentially blow up into security threats in the future. I also concluded that upright officers who really intend to work, do so quietly, without blowing their trumpets or manufacturing newspaper headlines.

After camping continuously at Lumding for about four months, I returned to Hojai once the situation normalised. I carried with me memories of a few unsavoury incidents that took place during those four months at Lumding and had shaken me from within.

One such incident was the unfortunate killing of two brothers. The two siblings were political goons affiliated with two different political parties. The elder brother was associated with the party that had recently won the elections while the younger one was aligned with the previous ruling dispensation and had gone underground, fearing a reprisal. In such a situation, the elder brother had somehow convinced the younger one to join his party and took him for a meeting with other members of his party at a certain location. The elder brother was hopeful that if he was physically present, his brother would be forgiven and accepted into the fold. Unfortunately, his calculations went wrong and his party members attacked the younger brother, wounding him mortally. When the elder brother tried to intervene, he too was beaten to death. Political rivalry related murders have become an indispensable feature in most parts of our country nowadays. But this double murder, wherein member of a political organisation went to the extent of killing one of their own, underscored the extent of bitterness that was rife in Lumding at that point in time.

During the investigation of another murder case, I found from the case diary that the victim's mother, who was an eye witness to the murder, had refused to give a police statement or file any official complaint. One rarely comes across such an instance of hard-heartedness, so to probe a little deeper, I took the investigating officer along and visited the woman in the slum area where she lived. I tried to convince her to give a statement, which was necessary to bring the perpetrators of the heinous crime to book. The woman, however, remained firm in her decision. After much cajoling, the woman said, "Babu, I have already lost one son. I do not want to lose another one by opening my mouth." Apparently, the killers had warned her that they would kill everyone in her family if she dared to go to the police. She was fearful as she had witnessed that the killers roamed scot-free after committing heinous crimes, on multiple occasions and they had no fear of law. She therefore had little regard for the judiciary or police.

Admittedly, many people probably held the same view about the police as this mother. There was no dearth of those who held the other extreme view as well. These people believe that the police have the power to do anything if they want to – uncalled for and illegal violence included. I had the opportunity to meet a gentleman who belonged to this camp, at Lumding. The gentleman was a very senior Railways officer and was then putting up at the Lumding Railway Officers' Guest House along with his family. With no other accommodation available, I used to spend my nights at the same guest house. I had met the gentleman on a few occasions and exchange a few words. During one such meetings, the gentleman eagerly wanted to know what action was being taken against the anti-social elements that were responsible for ruining the Railway city. On another occasion, he raised the issue out of the blue again and furnished a list of the illegal activities of the anti-socials, who had by then gone underground. He added that one could do nothing against the will of these anti-socials and clearly he was traumatised with his experience with these people. Suddenly, he posed a question, "Can't the police stage an encounter?" Before I could respond, the visibly agitated gentleman shot, *"Khatam kar dijiye...haan...khatam kar dijiye.* (finish them off!)" I was aghast at the words and thought process of such a senior officer but inferred that he was probably nursing a wound. I fathomed that agitated officer might even offer a reward for the 'job.' Before the matter heated up any further, I politely excused myself on the pretext of some urgent work.

My transfer materialised

A few months later, another gentleman suddenly approached me with the offer of a percentage. He was known to be close to a senior party functionary of the incumbent government. He assured me, "You have done a great job of seizing a sizable quantity of illegal timber. We have decided to reward you with one-and-half percent of the proceeds of the auction." I remembered the case wherein 103 trucks loaded with illegally felled timber were confiscated from the Lumding forests. The timber had been handed over to the Forest Department and I had almost forgotten the episode. "So, there are still people around who value good work," I thought at the gentleman's assurances. But before I could find out the real reasons for the one-and-half percent reward, I was transferred.

In January 1997, the SP told me that he had learnt about my transfer through reliable sources though he had not received a copy of the notification. A few days later, I came to know that even the DGP did not know about my transfer. I wasn't surprised at the transfer at all as I was well aware that a political leader, nicknamed 'Veerappan of Assam,' who had acquired sudden wealth by looting the forest resources, had been pestering a very powerful secretary for my transfer for the past few months.

Predictably, the Hojai police underwent a major overhaul after the formation of the new government.

Except for an officer in-charge and the circle inspector of Doboka, all the other officers were replaced. The SDPO, too, was transferred. The criminals, especially the highway robbers, took advantage of the situation due to the inexperience of the new officers. I was not unduly disturbed with the rising crime graph as I was confident that everything would be brought under control with the cooperation of the entire team. I was wrong, as the Tughlak-like firmans of the aforementioned political leader and the nefarious activities of his cohorts put a spanner in our works.

Evidently, the cunning politician had realised that his electorate comprised largely of peasants and poverty-stricken people. For these people, 'government' meant the easily identifiable uniformed police personnel on the ground. Hence, he found an easy way out to make his electorate and supporters happy, by crucifying the policemen. Like a Nawab of the yore, he ordered the police officers in-charge of the Police Stations within his constituency to pay haziri (attendance) at his durbar (residence). Obviously, this politician was two steps ahead of his predecessors in making unauthorised interference with police work.

Things came to a head when it was clear that this politician's henchmen were creating many problems. With the blessings of the leader and with blatant disregard to the law, his supporters parked themselves in a few Police Stations and engaged in unlawful activities. On receiving complaints, the erring Police Station officers were issued warnings but those were conveniently disregarded, as they had received their postings due to the recommendation of the political leader whom they did not dare to antagonise. However, I visited a Police Station one night and realised that the water was flowing above the head. I had to take action and issued a stern warning to the leader of the group. As a result, all hell broke loose and large groups of members and supporters of the neta petitioned to him, demanding my transfer. But the political leader's boss was in agreement with my actions, and hence his effort went in vain. Vanquished and humiliated, the 'neta' thought it fit to tread the middle path in order to save his and his party men's honour. Finding himself pinned to the wall, he made a brief offer, "Give me a moment to have a cup of tea with my boys." Dear Ma, I could not have allowed the tea party. Call it a fault of my nature, but I did not oblige the politician. Since then, he nursed a grievous wound against me. The friction reached a point of inflammation when I became an obstacle in the hushing up of a case of brutal dowry death.

A month later, I visited Doboka Police Station where a new officer in-charge, who had the neta's blessings, had taken charge. After an introductory session, I sat in the OC's office to discuss a few matters. I noticed a middle-aged person peeping into the cabin but not finding the courage to enter. His long bearded face and sunken eyes clearly indicated that he was distraught. I had him summoned and asked him why he was in the police station. The man identified himself as Utpal Sarkar, a resident of Karbi Anglong district. Sharing his story, he said that about a week ago, he learnt from someone that his daughter, who was living in this town after her wedding, had died mysteriously. The death rites had also been conducted by the in-laws without informing him. Shattered, he visited his daughter's in-laws to know the exact cause of death. The in-laws told him that his daughter had died due to severe burns a few days earlier after an accidental stove burst in the kitchen. Asked why they did not inform him about his daughter's death, the in-laws refused to speak any further. Sarkar alleged that his daughter was being harassed for more dowry ever since her wedding a few years ago. Fed up with the atrocities, the couple had moved out of the house. They returned home only after being assured that Utpal's daughter would not be harassed any more. However, the in-laws did not keep their word and continued to assault her. Sarkar said that though he was aware of his daughter's continued harassment, he could neither fulfil the demands nor take any other step. Since his daughter was being harassed for dowry for a long time, he suspected that his daughter did not die due to an accident but was probably murdered. He had lodged an FIR at the Police Station and had come to enquire about the progress of the investigation.

From Sarkar's description, it was obvious that something was amiss in this case. Questioned about the progress in the case, the OC proffered that since the in-laws had reported the case as an accident, a case of U/D (unnatural death) had been registered. Perusing through the case documents, I noticed that though the case had been registered, no inquest *(surat-e-haal)* was done by the police. The OC had no answer as to why the procedure had not been followed. He was also unable to explain why a spot enquiry had not been conducted even after a case was registered or how the body could be cremated without police permission. The number of lapses in a single case was bewildering, deepening the suspicion. Was the ploy to inform the police about the stove burst an after-thought, aimed at concealing truth and escaping the law?

OC J. Ahmed had till that point not made any effort to further the investigation in the case; nor did he bother to visit the spot where the reported accident took place. Already much time had been lost, so I asked the officer to add legal provisions related to murder and other charges and proceeded towards the spot.

The deceased's father-in-law had a huge iron store in the middle of the town and lived in a large mansion next to it. By the time the police team reached, both the store and the house had large padlocks hanging on the gates. Obviously, they had been tipped off, enabling them to escape in good time. The police team returned empty handed that night. As the accused were educated people, their escape raised the suspicion further. I instructed the OC to arrest and interrogate the suspects, if required. I also asked him to keep a strict vigil over the in-laws' house, so that the remaining evidence is not tampered with.

Even after three-four days, the officer in-charge did not report anything conclusively or give any satisfactory explanation for the various lapses in the case. Perhaps, finding no other way out, he suddenly did the vanishing act. In the two-and-a-half years I had spent in the region, I found many cases of lapses and dereliction of duty. But the laxity in investigating a suspected dowry death case was perhaps the most diabolical of all.

I do not remember correctly now, but we were able to gain entry into the accused in-laws' house about a week later. Officially, the suspects were still untraceable. Since the investigating officer had absconded, another officer was entrusted with the investigation of the case and the police team entered the premises in the presence of credible witnesses. There was no evidence of fire in the kitchen. However, it was amply clear that a large fire had been lit in the bathroom. Inexperienced hands had also made efforts to remove the soot and stains by whitewashing the walls and cleaning the ceiling, sufficient tell-tale remains were available. Clearly, the bathroom's floor and the doors had been scrubbed clean. It was also evident that the bathroom's inner and outer door bolts had been tampered with. Many other damaging evidences were found at the spot and all of these tell-tale visuals were captured in a camera in my presence.

The spot inspection had cleared the air about a few things. The claim that the woman had died due to a stove burst in the kitchen was false. The fire had happened in the bathroom. Now, if that was the case, how did the fire take place? If, for the sake of argument, we assume that the deceased had set herself on fire, question arises as to why no one saved her? The event had occurred in the afternoon when there were enough people in the household. Besides, there were people in the adjoining iron shop and the neighbourhood. All of these are pointers to the fact that this was possibly not an accidental death. Then what was the truth? Only an interrogation of the accused could have revealed the real facts. Unfortunately, I was transferred at this crucial juncture of the investigation. It is pertinent to mention that some more evidence was gathered later, which went against the accused.

I am unaware of what the fate of this case was. I am still inquisitive to know if any crime was proven or if the perpetrators were punished for their misdeeds. Or, if they eluded their fate by making good use of the loopholes in our legal system and if the groom married again. As the supervisory officer, this case remained an unfulfilled task for me and I regret it to this day.

I can feel my belly churn whenever I reminisce about my more than three-year tenure at Hojai. The rot in the system was very apparent. Taking advantage of this rickety system, some lowly politicians get their will imposed by instilling fear of transfer in the minds of the inconvenient government officers. Unfortunately, this is blatant subversion of democracy, wherein the greater good is suppressed by a handful of selfish people who have access to vast money or muscle power or both. The most affected by this travesty are the poor and downtrodden. I know not whether this sickening situation will ever be fixed.

CHAPTER

17 Nothing Happens without Strong Political Will

After my transfer from Hojai, I took charge as the Additional SP (Border) of the North Lakhimpur District Police. The chief purpose of forming a Border Police unit was to identify the illegal migrants infiltrating from adjoining Bangladesh and take appropriate legal actions for their deportation. The biggest obstacle in this process, unfortunately, was the loopholes in the law under which such identification and deportation was to be effected. The influx of Illegal migrants from Bangladesh (erstwhile East Pakistan) has been a festering problem for Assam for decades and the cause of much political turmoil. During the '70s, the state witnessed the historic and prolonged Assam Agitation, spearheaded by All Assam Students Union (AASU), demanding action against illegal migrants. Bowing to the legitimate demands of the protestors, the then Congress government at the Centre enacted such a law in 1983, which eventually proved to be a protective shield for the illegal migrants. This controversial law was the 'Illegal Migrants (Determination by Tribunal) Act' or the IM(D)T Act.

Though foreigners elsewhere in the country are dealt with under the provisions of the Foreigner's Act 1946, the IM(D)T Act was enacted solely for Assam. A general dictum of law is that the burden of proof lies with the accused. However, the IM(D)T Act shifted the onus on the accuser. This resulted in a piquant situation. An accused person could easily claim in court that he was not an illegal migrant and walk away without furnishing any proof to support his claim. As a result, taking legal action against illegal migrants became difficult. Over time, this resulted in a decline in the annual detection rate, to the point of becoming negligible. According to a study, the number of deportations of illegal migrants between 1962 and 1984 was over 1 lakh. But after the enactment of the IM(D)T, only 1501 illegal migrants had been deported over a period of 12 years. Remarkably, 22 years after its promulgation, the Supreme Court of India struck down the IM(D)T Act, while hearing a petition filed by Shri Sarbananda Sonowal, who later became the Chief Minister of Assam (2016 – 2021), noting that, "The Illegal Migrants Act 1983 and Rule has created the biggest hurdle and is the main impediment or barrier in the identification and deportation of the migrants." But by then the damage had already been done. The massive influx of illegal migrants resulted in sea change in the state's demographic pattern. Anyway, that is entirely a different story.

As mentioned before, by the time I had taken charge of the North Lakhimpur Border Branch in 1997, the conviction rate was almost negligible. Making efforts to trace the migrants and filing cases against them was a futile exercise. Moreover, most of the IM(D)T Courts in Lakhimpur and other parts of the state had become defunct. The morale of the Border staff was extremely low and everyone was merely whiling away their time. Even after working through the few files that were dropped on my table, I had ample free time at hand. To pass time, I began pore over copies of the IM(D)T Court judgements. Browsing through a few papers, I noticed that in several cases, the accused persons had earned acquittals on the basis of government-endorsed documents. This struck me as odd. How did the accused manage to get hold of these documents? Were these forged and false? My interest was aroused and I began pursuing the idea with vigour, which, in turn, invigorated the other staff members as well. Preliminary investigations brought to light a few significant and surprising facts. To investigate the leads further, there was the need for some efficient subordinate officers who could act as decoys and easily mingle with the suspected migrants to get to the bottom of the murky affair. With some luck, a few such men were identified who could be entrusted with the task. One of them, Havildar Jalaluddin Ahmed, caught my attention. His courage, proficiency and above all, his devotion to duty, were exemplary. He was an asset for the Border Branch, which had acquired a bad name for being the dumping ground of the inefficient.

A team was constituted under Jalal's supervision, to keep an eye on the activities of some of the accused persons who had secured release from the court by producing government documents. The undercover team maintained complete secrecy and toiled hard for over six months. They were finally successful in identifying two gangs that were engaged in producing fake Indian citizenship documents for the illegal migrants. Apart from a few suspicious characters, these gangs also had the support of members of political parties, government officials and middle-men.

To take action, we now needed some solid evidence. Thanks to the determined efforts of the decoy team, one of the middle-men fell for the trap. Soon, we had in hand a fake document purportedly issued by the local Deputy Commissioner, which would allow the decoy 'illegal migrant' to claim Indian citizenship. A back-channel communication with the DC's office revealed that the seals were exact but the signature was completely forged in the document. A similar operation with the other group yielded a cache of documents purportedly issued by the Election offices in various parts of the State, all of which were fake.

The market seemed flooded with these fake Citizenship documents. But who paid for these documents? A search was mounted to identify the buyers. After painstaking efforts over several months, over a hundred suspects from across the district were identified. Meanwhile, a fake document maker fell for the lure of money and landed into the decoy team's trap. When we were absolutely sure of being able to catch him red-handed, I decided that it was time to swoop in. But, for a successful operation, we had to conduct simultaneous raids at the various hideouts, which required a good number of people. I had a detailed discussion with the District SP, Shri S. Hazarika, who knew about the undercover operation and was equally enthusiastic about the planned police action. Since secrecy and speed were of utmost importance, it was decided that we would not wait for reinforcements to arrive from outside the district. Rather, we would mobilise all available strength and swoop in as the miscreant would flee at the slightest hint of danger, bringing to naught the hard work of over a year.

On the first day of the raids, two gang members involved in preparing and delivering false documents were apprehended red-handed with the help of the decoys. During a search at their den, many forged documents and a large cache of fake seals of the DC and other senior government functionaries were recovered. The raids continued for the next few days across multiple locations in the district. Many fake documents pertaining citizenship were recovered and over two dozen criminals were arrested on charges of possession of false documents. Notably, the citizenship of the first two persons to be arrested was questionable. One of them has now become a Mandal Panchayat Pradhan, an elected representative belonging to a political party. The other one is a munshi at a Court and the Election Office. The citizenship of the others arrested during the raids was also questionable. Of these, three-four had been earlier deported. But they managed to re-enter Assam illegally. Cases also had been filed against them under the IM(D)T Act but they had managed to evade conviction in the court with the help of forged citizenship documents, and by exploiting the loopholes in the law.

Apart from these two, the others who had been arrested in the case, had become eligible voters by enlisting themselves in the voters list. The arrested persons confessed that that they had prepared over 20,000 false citizenship related documents. Readers can easily imagine how many lakhs of illegal migrants may have got themselves citizenship rights across the State with the help of such unscrupulous elements as many other gangs across the State may have been involved in the preparation of such forged documents. Notably, the first false citizenship documents case had surfaced in the Barpeta and Nagaon districts. Later, the tentacles spread across the entire State. Some of the documents recovered at North Lakhimpur had been prepared in Nagaon and a few other districts. It also became clear during investigations that in a few cases, the same document had been used by multiple persons.

About two weeks later, two more fake document gangs were busted and a large number of forged documents as well as fake official seals were recovered from them. These seals were of officers from the neighbouring Arunachal Pradesh and were used to prepare fake inner line permits and other documents required for entering the border state.

Though some readers may dismiss the arrest of a few fake document producers as a minor affair, it was actually extremely significant, considering the fact that illegal migrants have been a contentious issue in Assam for several decades. Had these initial detections been pursued to their logical conclusion with determined follow-up action, the results may have been spectacular. That the matter was taken seriously by some officials can be gauged from the flowing extract of a letter written by the Assam CID to the district Police Chiefs of Assam:

"The Border Branch of Lakhimpur district has detected an organised racket involved in preparation and distribution of false citizenship related documents and supplied the same to illegal migrants / foreigners. The involved person in the racket entered into a criminal conspiracy and has been preparing and supplying certified copies of N.R. C., P.R.C. and Voter's List to the suspected foreigners to assist them to support their claim to Indian Nationality for the last 10/12 years. It is reasonably suspected that foreign nationals accused in the IM(D)T Act and FT cases all over the state have been using such voters list, N.R.C.s in concerned courts and have succeed in securing judgement in their favour which has further encouraged influx of illegal migrants from Bangladesh...The North Lakhimpur Border Police has done a yeoman's service in this respect and that task must be carried ahead by us all."

In spite of the eagerness of the police brass to tackle the menace of illegal migrants claiming citizenship and making it to the voters list on the basis of fabricated documents, the political leadership of the day surprisingly gave the grave issue a cold shoulder. Perhaps, taking some strong actions at that point would have prevented the hue and cry over NRC clean-up that the State is currently facing.

Enlightened citizens would be aware that without strong political will and support, no significant work that may have some long-term ramifications or public reaction can be executed unilaterally by any government department or individual. Ironically, the political masters of the day were the ones who had used the illegal migrants issue as a ladder to climb to the seat of power. Their prolonged agitation had also led to considerable bloodshed. The government's indifferent posture, however, invited sharp criticism from various quarters, including the media. One regional newspaper made the following scathing remark (paraphrased):

"The Lakhimpur Police has proved yet again that the greed for illegal gratification of the Assamese kerani (government official), the seditious silence of the Assamese political leadership and sheer stupidity and nonchalance of the people of Assam are responsible for giving over 30 lakh illegal Bangladeshi migrants an opportunity to live freely in Assam."

It further wrote, "It is therefore pertinent to leave a note for the posterity and let the future generations know that they have to pay for the sins of today's characterless politicians, corrupt government officials and the silent and half-dead public. It is because of these entities that the Bangladeshis are trampling over Assam's soil, unchallenged."

You may now appreciate the fact that no one can help if those in power do not take timely and appropriate decisions for the welfare of the State and its people. The Lakhimpur Border Police had made a significant breakthrough that could have taken a festering problem to its logical conclusion. Unfortunately, the entire initiative came to naught due to the lack of political will power.

It is also unfortunate that the police had to ultimately pay the price for detecting four major gangs involved in making fake citizenship papers. The team's sweat, courage and painstaking efforts of over a year went down the drain. Havildar Jalal became a target of his own community and had to face two life-threatening attacks within three years of the incident. As I look back, I now realise that entire exercise was, after all, a futile one.

CHAPTER

18 Crisis in Bijni

In early 1993, I was posted as the Sub Divisional Police Officer (SDPO) of Bijni, then a sub-division under Bongaigaon district. Bodos were the majority community in the sub-division. It was a period of strife as the Bodo agitation for a separate homeland (Divide Assam 50:50) was at its peak, with Bongaigaon, Kokrajhar and Udalguri sub-divisions of Darrang district as its epicentre. Extremist elements had unleashed a reign of terror on the pretext of the political agitation, and chaos and blood shedding had become the order of the day. Police officers, especially the lower ranks and up to the rank of SP had to discharge their duties in spite of the myriad obstacles and perils posed by the tense and explosive environment. The extraordinary courage and dedication to duty displayed by the police personnel cannot be fully appreciated without an understanding the complex situation that fuelled the widespread acts of extremism and separatism across Assam at that point in time.

Assam had witnessed an intense period of decade-long unrest and agitation against illegal migrants led by students during the '70s. The agitation resulted in the formation of United Liberation Front of Assam (ULFA) in the late 1970s. The secessionist organisation's objective was to wage an armed struggle to liberate Assam and carve out a separate sovereign state. During the initial days, the cadres undertook some socially useful activities and earned tremendous public support. The organisation rapidly grew in stature and within a decade, ULFA had forged an alliance with two other notorious extremist organisations then active in the north-east – the Nationalist Socialist Council of Nagaland (NSCN) and the Kachin Independence Army (KIA). With support from these two terror outfits, ULFA amassed significant financial assets by looting banks, committing extortions and other such activities. Soon, it became an influential extremist organisation in South-east Asia and began using Bhutan, Bangladesh and Myanmar as bases for its operations.

Whilst Assam Police was still struggling to contain ULFA, another extremist movement cropped up. The Bodo Security Force (BSF), which was later renamed National Democratic Force of Bodoland (NDFB) and Bodo Liberation Tiger Force (BLTF), became active in the Bodo-dominated areas of Assam. The objectives of the two militant organisations were vastly different, adding to the complexity. While the predominantly Christian NDFB wanted to carve out to a sovereign Bodo homeland, non-Christian dominated BLTF was fighting to create a separate Bodo state within the Indian Union. Thus, the religious underpinnings of the militants created a bizarre situation with the two groups often being at loggerheads with each other.

Political aspirations of the ethnic groups and an alleged sense of political neglect were the primary reasons for the genesis of the Bodo agitation, which was initially spearheaded by the All Bodo Students Union (ABSU). The speed and nature of the agitation was so aggressive that the government rapidly lost ground control and there was no trace of the administration in about 80 per cent of the Bodo inhabited areas. Most of the government office building had either been razed to the ground or had been abandoned by the administration, fearing an attack. Roads and the transportation system were systematically destroyed to impede the movement of police or security forces. It was impossible to drive motor vehicles at most places. According to an estimate, about 429 big and small bridges across rivers or culverts were destroyed in the Bijni sub-division alone.

I was well aware of the situation in Bijni and therefore joined duty with a prepared mindset. But within a week of joining and interacting with the officers at the various Police Stations, I realised that there was practically no problem in the sub division. Crime and militancy in the area were completely under control. I perused through the records and found that the crime rate had also declined. "Is crime being supressed?" a suspicion arose in my mind. Circle Inspector Jawahar Paneri clarified, "No, nothing like that," and then went on to share the real reason for the decline in the crime graph. "More than 60 per cent of the population does not report any crime to the police any more due to the ongoing non-cooperation movement." I reflected on this conversation and thought if the impression of the severe conditions one gets from the outside were false. Everything seems hunky dory after all! Little did I realise that this was the proverbial lull before the storm. After years of severe unrest, the entities were lying low and waiting for opportune conditions for a revival. Within a few months, a few sporadic incidents occurred, making me sit up and suspect that something was brewing. I, however, expected only some showers but I was mistaken. It was a huge storm, the expansiveness, ferociousness and unexpectedness of which took everyone – including me – by complete surprise.

The incident I am referring to was the first of the six ethnic clashes that shook the Bodo region. The theatre of the high voltage drama was Aamteka, which fell under Bijni Sub Division, and the adjoining forest area that was part of the Kokrajhar district. As destiny would have it, I bore witness to the savage killings, fire incidents, other forms of violence and unending madness. For an agonising 17 days, I stayed put at the forests in the Bhutan foothills, trying to douse the fire – sometimes without food and sometimes without sleep.

Before I narrate the details of those 17 days, let me digress and share the context that led to the ethnic clash. Bijni area had two forests in its jurisdiction – Kuklong and a part of Manas. The prolonged agitation and the subsequent phase of militancy had resulted in the complete cessation of the activities of the Forest Department in that area. As a result, the militants had a free hand in the Manas forests. The Kuklong forest was practically destroyed due to unrestricted exploitation of the forest resources. Taking advantage of the situation, the Bodo and Muslim communities illegally occupied large tracts of forest land and villages sprang up overnight. The Bodo and Muslim villages were adjacent to each other and for some time, they coexisted peacefully. Over a period, however, differences and enmity between the two communities cropped up, which sowed the seed of discord, eventually culminating in the ethnic clashes of 1993.

As most of the government offices and even the police posts in the Bijni area were non-existent, communication lines had been completely disrupted. It was difficult to say with any certainty what was going on barely 15-20 kms away, let alone the far-flung interiors. The police officers were completely clueless and even reluctant to find out anything.

Another reason for the apathy was, perhaps, the lack of any incentive or motivation for putting in extra efforts. The political leaders too were reluctant to take any bold step to tackle the situation. They perhaps thought "Let them do whatever they are doing in the interiors." This utter state of neglect was exploited to the hilt and large tracts of forest land were illegally occupied, mostly by people of doubtful citizenship.

The clash-affected area was some 80-85 kms away from the Bijni town. Between Bijni and the clash site stood a lone police outpost at Aamguri, some 50 kms from Bijni, manned by one Sub Inspector and two constables.

Aamguri was, during happier times, a much bigger and more important trading centre than Bijni. Traders from neighbouring Bhutan would visit the market to purchase large quantities of foodstuff, clothes and other material. But Aamguri's fortunes plummeted with the rise of militancy. A number of large but dilapidated wooden double-storied structures bore testimony to the glorious past of the now almost deserted town. An armed picket had been set up for the security of the market. The picket had a wireless set, which was the only source of communication with the outside world. It was because of this wireless set that we had received information about the outbreak of violence within a few hours of its commencement, thus preventing much collateral damage.

In those days, the way to Aamguri from Bijni was through the Kuklong forest. After traversing for about 15-20 kms through the forest, one came across a rivulet, which had to be crossed on foot to reach the market, and then, the outpost. Crossing the river during the monsoons was a challenge. On the first day of my visit to Aamguri, I found that the run-down local Panchayat Office had been converted into an outpost. The room, made of cheap wood, was termite-infested. Sawdust dropped continuously from the roof. At one corner lay a cot used by the In-charge, Putul Ali. I felt sorry for Putul, who had been living in this condition for the past three years. Putul informed that the outpost could be shifted to any of the large empty mansions but he preferred to stay at the current location because of security reasons as it was close to the armed picket. Though the jurisdiction of the Aamguri outpost was quite large, hardly anyone approached the police due to the non-cooperation movement. The outpost stood desolately. Earlier, Aamteka, located at a distance of 15-16 kms, too had a police picket, but that was withdrawn in the wake of the agitation. The police had no presence there anymore.

I was surprised when the armed picket in-charge informed that no gazetted officer had visited the area in the last two years. Before returning to Bijni, I wished them well and instructed them to stay safe and alert.

A few days later, a piece of news made me fret over the security of the armed picket at Aamguri. A group of militants that had looted 150 Self-loading Rifles (SLRs) and five Light Machine Guns (LMGs) from the armoury of a Police Battalion at Charaikhola, Kokrajhar, a few months ago, was stated to be camping in the foothills near Bhutan, close to Aamteka. They could attack the armed picket at any moment to seize the weapons. I decided to visit Aamguri frequently. But visiting Aamguri was a pain as we had instructions to take an LMG along whenever passing through Kuklong forest. This meant an additional vehicle was required, which was often unavailable. Moreover, withdrawing the lone LMG at Bijni Police Station compromised its security. So I was in a fix. I consulted my Personal Security Officer (PSO) Havildar Umakant Singh. "Tell me a way to reach Aamguri on my Jeep. *Upay batlao.*"

Umakant had been in Bijni for many years. His knowledge about the roads and the prevalent situation was immaculate and trustworthy. Umakant was lucky to escape an Improvised Explosive Device (IED) blast while passing through the Kuklong forest, a couple of years ago. Mercifully, the vehicle he was travelling in had sandbags stacked on the floor as a safety measure, which reduced the impact of the explosion, saving his life. Umakant was fearless even after the attack. He had, however, become more cautious and alert.

At first, Uma tried to dissuade me. But finding me insistent, he thought hard. "There is a dirt track to Aamguri that bypasses the dense Kuklong forest," he said, adding that "the path was fraught with problems." A two-mile stretch in a completely desolate area is full of mud. If the vehicle gets stuck there, no one would be around to push it, he said. Then, there is a half-destroyed bridge over the river, crossing which is quite dangerous. I decided to try it out nonetheless. I took Uma and driver Roy in my bullet proof Jeep and set forth for Aamguri one day. You might be wondering from where did I get a bulletproof Jeep? Well, I had inherited the vehicle from my predecessor. I had learnt from the staff that SDPO Shri Sarat Phukan, who was posted during the height of militancy, had got 4-inch thick wooden planks placed securely on the sides of the vehicle as a safety measure. I used to mentally thank Shri Phukan for his foresight and the life-saver, which offered at least some protection.

After driving for about an hour, we were able to cross the muddy patch with much effort. Another short drive later, we arrived at the broken bridge over the rivulet. I realised the strategic importance of the bridge and the reason for the militants' attempt to destroy it. On crossing the bridge, one could access the gravel road to Aamguri. Fortunately, the militants were unable to destroy the two parallel iron bars over the bridge that were about a foot wide each. While the iron beams were wide enough for the vehicle to cross, it required an expert hand to drive the vehicle as a false move could be disastrous. The rivulet below had strong current. Driver Roy was reluctant to cross the bridge. He implored Uma, "Huzoor, madat karo." It was then that I came to know that Umakant was actually recruited as a Driver Constable. After much confabulation, Uma and Roy managed to take the vehicle over the bridge to the other side. We felt quite victorious at our success that day. Since then, the Kuklong path to Aamguri was forgotten for ever. Later, during the riots, I reckoned that had it not been for this path, we would have to endure much suffering.

During my next visit to Aamguri, I also visited Koila Moila and Aamteka towns. A river snakes around the Aamteka marketplace. On the other bank of the river is a vast forest. It was not apparent then that many villages had come up inside the forest. The market area comprised of a few tea stalls, shanties, a couple of provision stores, a few residences and little else. Earlier, the place had several government offices and a police picket. SI Putul Ali showed me the place where his earlier office used to stand. Now, even the foundation of that building was not visible. I visited the place Aamguri and Aamteka a few other times, cultivating an acquaintance with a few locals. I could also extract some information from these people and learnt that the Bodo student leaders were now the all-powerful. Their word was law. But another group, which used to rule the roost before, nursed a grudge against the student leaders. I had not anticipated then that the grudge would find a violent expression soon.

One day, I came to know that the situation in the Koila Moila-Aamguri area was quite tense. A group that was annoyed with the activities of the student leaders and had taken to the streets to lodge their protest. The news was disturbing. I had two recent experiences that made me realise how ruthless and inhuman punishments in these regions can be.

In one instance, a youth suspected of adultery was abducted from his residence and taken to a desolate place. The youth was tortured in an inhuman manner. Before being killed, his teeth were pulled out with pliers and innumerable wounds were inflicted on his body. He was then blindfolded and a burning tyre was placed on his body. The youth had died of the burns, in great pain.

The other incident also related to an abduction. I learnt that one of the militant groups had abducted a prominent member of another group. To ascertain the truth, I visited the youth's village only to learn that his family members had conducted the last rites of the youth. On enquiring where the body was found, the family members said that they had not found the body yet but had conducted the last rites nonetheless as no one who is abducted in this region ever returns.

So, on receiving the news of the probable attack on the student leaders, I rushed to Aamguri along with SI Neog of Bijni Police Station, a few constables and six armed battalion jawans. On reaching Aamguri, I learnt that the miscreants had thrashed student leader Ashok and his friend to death at Koila Moila and were now advancing toward the ABSU President's village. On reaching the village I found hundreds of irate villagers advancing towards the President's house. Their aim was to burn down the house. We positioned ourselves around the house. Then a warning was issued to the advancing miscreants not to come any closer. At this some of the miscreants stopped in their tracks. But soon, someone at the rear yelled, "*Bhoy nokoribi-re, eito*

Asom Police, guli nuphute-de" (Do not fear, these are Assam Police personnel and their guns don't fire.) The miscreants obviously had experience of fighting with the Army and other security forces, and did not think of Assam Police as a challenge. I concluded that if we didn't take action immediately, we would be charred along with the President's house, and ordered the team to open fire. The action put the attackers on the defensive and they began dispersing. Finally, we could heave a sigh of relief.

Dangers never come alone

Sometimes, life brings an avalanche of unsurmountable problems all together. October 1993 was a similar time for me. Sporadic information about the movement of 25-30 member strong groups of militants armed with sophisticated heavy weapons, including LMGs and mortars had been trickling in. Earlier, the militants moved around in much smaller groups and hence the veracity of the information about large groups was suspicious to me. But one day, the Additional SP Karim sahib, had a providential escape after accosting a similar large group of militants. Clearly, the militants had become emboldened and had adopted a new strategy. To flush these groups out of the forests, a raid was conducted on October 1 and 2. The campaign was tiring but I had no time to rest. On October 4, an armed group of about 40 militants stormed the Bijni weekly market and looted it. This was the first incidence wherein an entire market had been looted. My next 48 hours went into investigating this incident.

And then came the dreadful day of October 7. As soon as I woke up that morning, I came to know that the extremists and their supporters had been torching Muslim villages in Aamteka and the adjoining forests, and were continuing to move deeper into the jungles. There were many causalities. If immediate steps were not taken, even Aamguri would be affected. The ethnic clash between the Bodo militants and Muslims was a bolt from the blue because let alone the precedent of a violent clash, there was no prior information about any friction between the two communities. I informed the SP about the reported violence and immediately mobilised a team including the Circle Inspector, the Officer In-charge Atul Konwar and the available force, and rushed towards the spot. At that moment we had no idea about the extent of damage, its expanse or the possibility of facing a retaliation and everyone had left unprepared for a fortnight-long battle.

When we were about 5-7 miles from Aamguri, I noticed that a large number women of the Bodo community walking in the opposite direction along with whatever luggage they could carry. They were not using the road but were walking briskly through the adjoining woods and fields some distance away. I thought they are possibly fearful because of the violence and are vacating their villages. But then,

I noticed that the group comprised of women and children only. Where were the menfolk? And why should the Bodos be fearful, when the Muslims are reportedly the victims of the clash? There was no point in talking to the women as they would only create a ruckus or flee. Suddenly someone in the team said grimly, “Looks like an ancient war ritual.” Apparently, during the hoary past, the people of the region would send the women, children the elderly to a safe zone before the menfolk went to battle. This disturbed me further.

By the time we reached, Aamguri was already tense and edgy. The people expected a violent attack soon. The news of torching hundreds of dwellings inside the Aamteka forest had been received early in the morning. But thereafter, there was no news of what was happening for the last three-four hours as the movement of people had come to a complete standstill. No one knew what was happening in the interiors. Based on whatever sketchy information we could gather at Aamguri, I began mulling over what our next step should be, but could not come to a firm conclusion. At that point, I received a message from the SP, Shri Owatisimba Aao, to stay put at Aamguri till he arrived.

But what was the cause for the sudden eruption of this large-scale violence? Where did it all start? These were the questions that haunted me while we waited for the SP’s arrival. None of the locals could shed any light. In-charge Putul Ali too feigned ignorance. Finding answers to these questions was crucial for chalking out our future course of action. Besides, the major incident would have to be reported to the government, for which a credible and believable root cause was necessary. As I was lost in these vexing thoughts, my troubles were mitigated in a strange manner, as if through divine intervention. A newbie political leader from a particular community, with whom I had recently been acquainted, approached me quietly and said that he knew someone who could help me understand the genesis of the situation. I agreed to a confidential meeting with the person. However, I was quite disappointed on meeting the 'person' as I had expected to see someone senior with deep insights. Instead, before me stood a young lad, who hardly appeared to have any knowledge of the complex situation. I was mistaken. After hearing him out, I surmised that no one else could have perhaps shared such authentic details. Surprised, I asked the politician how the youngster knew so much? The politician revealed that the fair complexioned non-Bodo boy was an orphan who grew up in a Bodo village. He did menial jobs to earn a meagre living. Because he had lived in the village since his childhood, the locals considered him as one of their own. Like the others, he too would attend the public and secret meetings in the villages, and that is where he got a whiff of things.

According to the youth's statement, about a week ago, members of an extremist outfit conducted multiple public meetings to garner public support against the Muslim settlers in the forests. They alleged that initially, the Muslims abided by the dictats of the Bodo militants. But recently, they had not only stopped following any instructions, but also began openly opposing and defying them, and stopped paying any taxes to the militants. Two days earlier, on October 5, the extremists had called a large meeting wherein they provoked people by alleging that the illegal migrant Muslims had become a menace for the local Bodos. They further fanned the flames by alleging that the Muslims had crossed all limits by killing five members of the militant outfit in a planned, pre-determined attack. This was unpardonable, said the militant leaders, and urged the people to unitedly drive out the Muslim settlers. Soon thereafter, hundreds of people gathered, with beaten rice, jaggery and other requisites for the long haul, and set off for the jungles. The lad did not join the people but managed to quietly stay back, and later took refuge at the politician's house. "His presence has been under the wraps and it is unlikely that he will ever return to the village," the politician said. I requested the politician to take good care of the youngster and returned to the outpost.

A little later, the SP arrived with a platoon of battalion jawans, apart from his security staff and two SIs. Our combined strength was now about 50. Without wasting any time, we moved towards the affected area. From Aamguri, we reached Koila

Moila, only to be greeted by a deserted settlement that had 20-25 huts that had been burnt to cinders. The residents of this new Muslim settlement had obviously fled. SP Aao sahib may have thought that this was the main trouble spot and from his expression, it appeared that he was relieved to see that only a few huts had been torched and it was not as large a calamity as he had expected. However, on seeing the scenes that awaited us after traversing another 7-8 miles, all that could escape from his lips was, "Oh my God!"

What I witnessed after arriving at Aamteka will remain etched in my memory for ever. As far as one's eyes could see, one saw only fire and smoke. It appeared that the entire world was on fire. As we haplessly watched the all-consuming fire raging all around, I wondered whether the scene at Ravana's Lanka was larger than this when Lord Hanuman set it on fire.

By then, about 300 Muslims, who had fled their villages in the wake of the attack, arrived at the Aamteka market to take refuge. On seeing the police, they began relating their tales of horror. They described how their village as well as some of the neighbouring villages had been set on fire. Others came forward to complain about missing family members – children, husband, brothers or parents. Still others reported that hundreds of people have been killed. People fled wherever they could and some had fled towards the hills of Bhutan and some towards Dhali Gaon. But most of the homeless were stranded in the jungles.

These victims further revealed that the attacks had begun after dusk on the night before and large mobs had attacked multiple villages simultaneously, torching the huts. The pogrom continued through the entire night. Some of the villagers said that they were warned to leave the villages before being attacked, which suggested that the objective was to evict the settlers and free the lands rather than kill the people. It was also evident that a large number of people were still hiding in the jungles, fearing for their lives. Our first and primary task therefore was to rescue these trapped people and ensure their safety. A group of the victims agreed to lead us through the jungles. Without wasting any time, two teams were formed and we headed for the jungles. SP sahib stayed back at Aamteka market to collect more information and ensure the safety of the refugees.

On our way to the forests, we first encountered the river. The water was knee deep and I thought we could cross it in a few minutes. Setting foot in the river, I immediately realised that I was probably wrong. The water was very cold and the stones below were extremely slippery. After some struggle, we reached the other bank. I hoped that we would not have to face another water body ahead. I was wrong again as the area was full of mountain rivers and rivulets and we had to cross one every mile or mile-and-a-half.

It was clear to us that no living person could be found in any of the deserted villages, hence we did not go towards the villages. Instead, we focused on reaching the places where there was a high probability of the people hiding in the jungles. On seeing the police, many people came out of their own. They were asked to reach Aamteka market and take refuge there. Some of these people were so traumatised that they were fearful of going to Aamteka without police protection. They had to be convinced that the attackers were no longer around and no harm would come their way. Some of the homeless people were on bullock carts. They had sensed the danger after seeing huge flames in adjoining villages and had fled with whatever household articles they could gather. On the first day itself, we were able to rescue about 3,000 people. We came to know that many others were trapped in other parts of the forest. We returned to Aamteka market at about 11 p.m. that night. Thanks to the local traders, we did not have to go hungry. They had prepared *khichdi* for the team. After a laborious day, our eyes became droopy as soon as we had our meal. As there was no place to lie down, I spent the night in the Jeep. SP *sahib* too did the same.

The next day, we started for the jungles before dawn while the SP decided to visit a couple of villages in the vicinity, where many dead bodies were reportedly lying. Our destination was the Bhutan border area. After advancing several miles, we came across two adjacent villages that had been attacked. About 200 huts and shanties had been completely burnt. The large wooden structures and tin hutments, however, were left untouched, ostensibly for the use of the attackers later. Tell-tale signs of a military style attack were evident. In both the villages, two neat rows of ashes, possibly remnants of large torches (mashal), were visible. Evidently, after executing the arson the attackers had conducted a roll call parade to ensure that all member of their team were safe and accounted for. The attackers had destroyed all fruit orchards and private farms around the settlements, and poisoned the water sources to make sure that these places were inhabitable for the victims, even if they came back. We found around a dozen dead bodies in these villages on that day.

Millet fields stretched for miles around the two villages. Apparently, there was a huge demand for millets in Bhutan and the Bhutanese traders paid the villagers handsomely for their produce. Perhaps that was why people preferred to live in those villages despite the adverse living conditions. I wondered that had the Forest Department had taken control of these fertile lands and had done some cultivation, instead of allowing the encroachers to take over, the government coffers would have grown substantially. I later learnt that about five years ago, District Forest Officer C. L. Chakraborty had made a strong effort to evict the encroachers and free up the forest land. But the encroachers fought back and repulsed the government efforts to evict them. The situation had become so tense that eviction was impossible without loss of lives. In view of the grim situation, the magistrate had stayed the eviction proceedings. No effort was ever made by the government to evict the encroachers thereafter.

Aamguri Outpost In-charge Putul Ali also accompanied us that day. He said that the Muslims of these villages were actually prone to committing crime and were notorious. The writ of some 10-12 leaders, who were addressed as 'Sardar,' ran in this area. Recounting a horrific personal experience three years ago, Putul said that he had to visit a village to investigate a theft case. "Sir, the moment we set foot in the village, over a hundred people encircled us and angrily questioned us as to who had authorised us to enter their village. We were held captive for about an hour by the irate villagers, who raised slogans, 'Chor party zindabad, Police party murdabad.' After much heckling, the Sardars ordered our release, saying that, "We are letting you off because your name is Ali. But if we ever catch you again…". Putul's story was corroborated merely two days later. I will relate that story later.

That day, we visited a few Bodo villages apart from the Muslim villages. No houses had been torched there. None of the menfolk were visible in the villages. A few young girls and women occupied quite a few hutments. Evidently, they were not local people. On questioning, all of them replied that they had come for Church work from Udalguri and other parts. So, were these women here merely to evangelise in such a tense and sensitive situation? Something was fishy. But I had no time at my disposal to dig any further. We continued advancing.

That day, too, we were able to rescue some 3,000 people trapped in the forest. Aamteka now had over 5000-6000 refugees. There was space constraint and no roof over the heads of most people. Still, everyone feasted on meat that night. The farmers, who had livestock with them, had no means to keep them alive.

That evening, SP *sahib* shared that he had overseen the recovery of several dead bodies from a few villages. Since there was no means of sending the bodies for post mortem, the DM had been requested to send a medical team. That night, too, was spent in the vehicle.

Notably, we had not run into the militants during our jungle soirees on the past two days. Where were they? Had all of them fled to the Bhutan border? Experience said that except the hardcore militants, the rest may have quietly left for their own homes or were trying to do so. With that in mind, we decided to enter the forest at the rear on the south bank, which lay between Aamteka and Koila Moila, on the third day. Young and enthusiastic DySP Ejaz Hazarika was also with us. After advancing for a while, we heard the successive explosion of a few mid-sized bombs. On close scrutiny, we noticed that a group of militants were holed up about 300 yards away from a ravine. They were trying to dissuade us and the explosions were meant to warn us. When they deduced that we continued to move forward, two large bombs were set off in quick succession. From their devastating sounds, I could make out that these were not ordinary country-made stuff. We kept marching forward, as we had noticed that the militants were only exploding bombs at a distance and not firing at us. They would perhaps not dare to cross the deep ravine and come close enough for a combat or to cause any damage. But why were they trying to stop us, especially when we were passing through an unaffected area?

I got an answer to this question in about two hours when about two dozen suspected arsonists were arrested. The militants were trying to provide a safe passage to these people. The arrested persons were from far-off villages and interestingly, they had bottles of kerosene slung over their shoulders even at the time of arrest.

Instead of taking the same route while returning, we took a longer U-turn and trekked back to Aamteka through a different path. We found several senior political leaders of the main opposition party at the camp, who had reached the spot in spite of much discomfort. They were accommodated at the only empty space in the make-shift camp – the middle of the road. The arrested persons, bottles of kerosene still slinging on their shoulders, were paraded in front of the politicians. They also saw that over 5000-6000 victims had been rescued. As a result, they had to return without any ammunition to attack the ruling government alleging inaction.

That day, SP *sahib* had visited an affected village along with a medical team to conduct post mortems. After returning in the evening, he shared that the government had ordered the shifting of the homeless victims to the relatively safer Aamguri. The transit had to be effected the very next day.

Security of the refugees was a major concern for us, especially at night, as the Aamteka market was a vulnerable place from the security point of view. The non-availability of sufficient manpower to guard the camp site was another concern. The decision to shift the victims to Aamguri, therefore, was a welcome one. But executing the order was not a cakewalk. They would have to undertake a 16-17 kms trek through a hostile territory as Bodo villages lined both sides of the road. Trouble and danger were both evident. Unfortunately, there was no other way out, hence an announcement was made, asking the refugees to prepare for the transit, which would commence at dawn. They too welcomed the decision as the present camp site neither had enough shelters nor enough drinking water.

Almighty, the saviour of the new born

Preparations for the transit began at 3 a.m. the next morning. A three-mile long convoy stood all set for the arduous journey, which was all set to begin in about an hour. At that moment, the SP said, "You take charge of the convoy's security. I will stay back for some more time, just in case any more refugees arrive." Without uttering a word, I thought not a single refugee had arrived in the last 24 hours and the possibility of anyone else coming was remote. So there was no point in showing a reason – I would have unhesitatingly taken charge had I been told to do so. However, since I was under the impression that the SP would lead us, I had not bothered much to look into the security arrangements minutely. At the SP's orders, I hurriedly reviewed the security plan. I had a total of 35 officers and men, including 17 battalion armed jawans. Undertaking the precarious journey with so few resources was definitely a challenge. Paucity of forces has been a perennial problem but complaints had always gone unheard. I was therefore forced to improvise, much like today's T-20 cricketers. I instructed the constables and jawans to stay some distance away from the convoy and make frequent to-and-fro movements so that it gives the impression that we have a large presence.

OC Bijni Police Station was to lead the convoy whilst CI Paneri would manage the middle portion of the convoy. I would stay at the rear, we decided. Soon, the convoy was ready to move. The SP then suggested that it would be a good idea to take a round of the camp. The camp was entirely empty and all the refugees had lined up for the journey. I was tense with the convoy security and therefore did not respond as I felt the SP's suggestion was unnecessary.

At that moment, the Kokrajhar Additional SP, Shri Shubhrajit Hazarika arrived with a large armed contingent. He was on his way to set up a new armed police camp. The SP requested him to take a round of the camp site.

While taking the round, Shri Hazarika found a new born baby lying unattended. Dogs were eating up the umbilical cord and other tissue. I ran to see the child. Apparently, the new-born had been abandoned by its parents, who were more concerned about saving their own lives rather than their offspring's. It would be a difficult task now to find the parents. Of course, there was no question of leaving the new-born behind.

As I mulled over the problem, I suddenly remembered that an old woman had been pestering me to accommodate her in my Jeep. I sought her out and told her that I would let her travel in the vehicle on the condition that she would carry the infant. The woman readily agreed. She took out a cloth from her bag and wiped the new-born clean. I mentally thanked the invisible power, whose extreme compassion was evident in this incident. Was it the same power that had drawn Shri Hazarika to the Aamteka camp site? Was it instrumental in gently taking him to the place where the neonate lay haplessly? Moreover, the sudden arrival of a Nepali milk vendor, who had ventured out to sell milk that morning amid such a grim situation, was surely not a coincidence.

CHAPTER

19 The Convoy

The convoy moved. Everyone was on tenterhooks as over 6,000 humans lives were at stake. Among the refugees were elderly men and women, physically challenged people and expectant mothers with a flock of children. Even four-year-olds had to walk as their parents held their toddler brothers and sisters in their arms. Many of these vulnerable lives were on the verge of giving up mid-way. I could not proceed any further till they had moved on. We had to place some of these people in the few bullock carts that were part of the convoy. But that was not an easy task. The 'vehicle' owners were not too happy to accommodate the others. So, we had to use various tactics – from pleading to pressuring – to ensure that everyone reached the destination. Even though many people were unhappy or inconvenienced, I had no other choice. As we moved on, I noticed that the villages on either side of the road were deserted. Later, I learnt that the Bodo villagers had mistaken the long column of refugees walking towards them as a counter-attack and had fled. After about five hours, the convoy finally arrived safely at the destination. I informed the SP who was stationed at Aamteka. He was elated and replied, "You have done a miracle!" I too felt relived. Tired to the bones, I looked forward to some rest, unaware that trouble was brewing up ahead.

The Aamguri outpost was still about a kilometre away. The refugees ahead of me were advancing very slowly, impeding my movement. I mentally calculated how these 6,000 refugees would be accommodated and came to the conclusion that there was enough empty space around the Aamguri market, which could be utilised for the purpose. I was at that point oblivious of the fact that about 10,000 to 11,000 refugees from other adjoining areas had already occupied most of the vacant spaces. After moving at the proverbial snail's pace for about an hour, I managed to reach the Aamguri Police Station, only to find two groups of refugees engaged in a violent clash with each other.

"What is this violence all about?" I enquired.

"Sharing the spoils," came the response.

"What spoils?" I asked in bewilderment.

"The refugees had looted livestock – cattle and goats – anything that came their way during the transit from Aamteka to Aamguri. Now these warring groups are fighting amongst each other, staking claim on the spoils of the loot. What began as an altercation has now turned into a bloody fisticuff," said an onlooker.

I was aghast. Mercifully, the Bodo villagers on the way were in no position to protest, or else we would have witnessed another skirmish. I ordered the immediate use of force to disperse the squabbling refugees.

While resting briefly at the outpost, my thoughts suddenly turned to the new born baby. Where was it and where was the old woman who was taking care of it? SI Putul said, "Sir, while you were busy with the violence among the refugees, the infant's mother came to collect the child. We have made a General Diary entry in this regard." I was relieved and yet again thanked the Almighty for His compassion.

At about 11 a.m., a group of residents from the adjoining affluent village, Joynagar, arrived to inform that hundreds of miscreants were ready to attack their village and the situation was very tense. Though the village fell under Kokrajhar district, the District Police would take about 4-5 hours to reach the spot because there was no direct road access. Worried, they thought it prudent to seek help from Bijni Police. Joynagar was about 5-6 kms from Aamguri. On the way were two small rivulets. Since the situation was sensitive and time was of essence, I decided to take the plunge without bothering about jurisdictional issues. Today, after over two decades of the incident, I feel extremely proud of the courage, commitment and camaraderie displayed by my officers and men in the face of adversity. Everyone had been on their feet for the last 15 hours or more. In spite of being physically worn out, not one person shirked the call to duty. Platoon Commander Majumdar (his full name was perhaps Hemanta Majumdar) displayed tremendous leadership as led his jawans from the front.

We crossed the rivulets and reached Joynagar only to find a tense situation. The miscreants had attacked the Muslim village's market and torch a few shops. The residents had banded together to fight back and repulsed the attack. Though the miscreants had retreated briefly, they had regrouped again and had encircled the village from three sides. Another attack was imminent. Even after noticing the police deployment and the hearing the warnings, the miscreants stayed put. After about an hour, we resorted to intermittent blank firing to scare the miscreants. The ploy worked.

On returning to Aamguri in the evening, I learnt that two houses in the village had been torched. A group of refugees had broken into the private farm of two local Nepali speaking persons, destroying their fruit and vegetable orchards, and stealing firewood. When the owners resisted, the refugees responded by torching their houses. The two houses had suffered heavy damages. Mercifully, the houses in the village were constructed at a considerable distance from each other, and hence the fire did not spread.

Aamguri now was home to about 17,000-18,000 refugees, many of whom were hardened criminals. We had recently witnessed their indecorous activities and therefore, our new worry was how to protect the local residents from these undesirable elements. We continued to sporadically receive complaints against the refugees and had to plead with the locals to have some patience as it was impossible to initiate any legal action against the erring refugees in the extant situation.

The SP arrived from Aamteka late in the evening. Meanwhile, many inquires began pouring in from all quarters. I sat with the Wireless Transmission Set operator and instructed him what response to share for which query. This continued till 1:30 a.m. in the night.

Putul Ali had arranged for a rice and lentils dinner for us. After our meals, the SP and I shared Putul's cot for a brief rest. Even though I was very tired, sleep was sporadic. At early dawn, the SP gently nudged me and said, "Hi, I am going." He was returning to Bongaigaon. I tried to sit up but couldn't. Somehow, I managed to respond, "OK." I met the SP again after 12 days. But I will come back to that later.

Next morning – the fifth day – I visited the Bodo refugee camps. About 10 such camps had come up within a radius of 4-5 miles of Aamguri, all of which were in school buildings. The residents were mostly women and children. A few Bodo social service organisations were managing the camps and hence the living conditions were relatively better. People had taken refuge in these camps fearing retaliatory attacks. On returning to Aamguri, I learnt that Shri Sarat Chandra Sinha, former Chief Minister of Assam, who was then a leader of an opposition party, had arrived with his retinue to inspect the refugee camp. As I greeted him and introduced myself, he noticed my dishevelled state – I had grown a stubble, my uniform was crumpled and shoes were dirty – and said, *"Aapunak dekhi-ei gom paaisu Police-e kaam koriasey."* (After seeing you I am convinced that the Police is doing its job.) It is rare for opposition leaders to praise any activity of the government or its various organs. From the opposition's view point, everything is always inappropriate. Shri Sarat Sinha was among the few politicians who commanded respect for their honesty. He was also a good human being, and therefore spontaneously spoke his mind, disregarding political conventions. I have seen him – a respected former chief minister – travel in an ordinary city bus. He neither owned a personal vehicle nor a house. His final years were spent pathetically in penury and pain. It is ironical that those who dedicate their lives to the service of the people and lead an honest public life, often end up in such tragic situations in our country.

Uncalled for orders

A message was received indicating that the Chief Minister would be visiting the camp the next day. There was neither a senior police officer nor a senior administrative officer at Aamguri at that time. And neither did we have sufficient force. The DC had visited for an hour or two and the Sub Divisional Officer, the administrative head of the affected sub-division, had never visited the camp till then. On the other hand, an inspector of a paramilitary force met me to inform that a unit led by a Commandant that had flown in from Delhi was stationed at a distance of 20 kms. The officer requested for vehicles to ferry the troops to Aamguri. I explained to the officer that I did not have vehicles at my disposal and nor was it possible for me to arrange these at this juncture. The troops would have to bear some inconvenience and trek to Aamguri. The officer was offended and complained, "You (State Police) always try to dominate us." The officer was obviously oblivious of the ground conditions of the place where they were being deployed. I tried my best to explain that Aamguri is a remote, riot-affected place and not my headquarters. Since vehicles could not be arranged, the force did not come to Aamguri that day. I concluded that I would have to manage the impending VIP visit with whatever manpower I had.

On the sixth day after the riots, the Chief Minister arrived at about 11 a.m., with a large posse of ministers, party political leaders and two Secretaries. The DGP Assam, DC and SDO Bijni also accompanied him. The Chief Minister assured the refugees of all possible help and announced an ex gratia of Rs 1 lakh to the kin of those who had lost their lives and Rs 10,000 to those who had been rendered homeless. The announcement was received with a thunderous applause. All ended well and now it was time for the Chief Minister's departure. At that moment, a local trader walked up to the Home Secretary accompanying the CM, mistaking him to be a leader of the ruling political party, and demanded that the refugees be shifted away from Aamguri as they were creating a nuisance, affecting the day-to-day lives of the local people. The suggestion was not received well and the senior officer gave it a cold shoulder. The trader felt offended at this and it led to an altercation. The displeased Secretary asked me to arrest the person immediately and confirm the arrest in writing. I was in a fix as the order of the Secretary, who was well regarded as an honest and respectable officer, could not be neglected. On the other hand, the poor trader's intention was not bad; he was only trying to highlight the hardship of the local people. Arresting him would have sent out a wrong message and alienated the local people. I was still trying to grapple with the emergent situation when another issue cropped up.

I noticed the Police Chief gesturing me to come over. On doing so, he instructed me to provide six men for the SDO's security. I then realised why the SDO was hovering around the DC and the Secretary all the while. We were struggling with the lack of manpower, and the Police Chief was asking me to spare not one or two but half a dozen men. With all humility, I told the DGP that at that moment, it would not be possible to spare so many persons for security duty. The DGP shot back in Assamese, *"Dibo lagibo noholey moribi dei."* (You'll have to do it or you'll be dead). I could not trust my ears as I heard those words. I wondered how the senior-most Police Officer of the State could make such a negative comment with utter disregard to the ground situation. I later surmised that the DGP, who was from South India, had probably learnt a smattering of Assamese and had picked up the phrase from somewhere, and had used it unintentionally. Be that as it may, I was still perturbed. It pained me to no end to think that none of the senior officers even thought of how we were managing the situation. And if the Police Chief himself is not prepared to acknowledge, then it is imperative to raise the alarm and let everyone know about the ground realities.

As soon as the Chief Minster left, therefore, I wasted no time in in sending a message addressed to the DGP, regarding the security situation at Aamguri. I remember that I had mentioned "Force position in Aamguri, with eighteen thousand refugees is PATHETIC(.)" in the message. A copy of the message was forwarded to the Chief Minister and all administrative and police heads, right up to the SP. This worked. Within half an hour, IGP (Operations) himself called up to assure the availability of reinforcements at the earliest. I also learnt that he was camping at Bijni for the last two days. Mentally, I thanked him for not coming to Aamguri, since I would then have had to relinquish Putul's famous cot!

You might be wondering what had happened to the instruction to arrest the trader. The issue was finally resolved in the anecdotal "*Ashwathama hatha iti gajah*" (Ashwathama [the elephant] is dead) manner. A message was sent to the Secretary stating that the trader had been arrested. On the other hand, the trader was immediately given bail on personal surety, since the Secretary had only ordered his arrest and had said nothing about not releasing him on bail. The trading community reciprocated the good gesture that very night. As the paramilitary troops from Delhi arrived at about 8 p.m. after a 20 kms trek, the traders took it upon themselves to make proper arrangements for the large force's accommodation, taking a huge load off my chest.

Soon after the Chief Minister's ex gratia announcement, we started receiving fresh complaints of houses (all thatched huts) being torched. This was perplexing as the situation was fairly normal and the possibility of the miscreants launching any fresh attacks was remote. While investigating some of these claims we noticed that the huts were all illegally made on government or forest land and no furniture or other household items were burnt – only the hut had been charred. Obviously, the claims were bogus and aimed at unfairly usurping the ex gratia amount. The probe further revealed the handiwork of a gang that was instigating the people and ensnaring them with greed. The complaints whittled as soon as strong action was taken against the group.

One night, at about 9 p.m., we were preparing a meagre meal of rice and boiled potatoes when we noticed several large flares at a distance. How could any dwelling be torched in spite of so much security presence was our only thought as we left everything and dashed towards the fire. The young and dynamic DySP, Debraj Upadhyay, was also with us on that day. On reaching the spot, we realised that a few urchins had played a prank on us by lighting up pyres of firewood, trash and straw. We returned to have our half-cooked meals and catch a quick wink.

Relief operations had commenced after the Chief Minister's visit. Relief materials were air dropped from helicopters as the roads were non-existent. The two helicopters had to make several sorties every day to drop enough relief material including foodstuff, such as rice and lentils, for the 18,000 refugees. One day, I noticed that the helicopters were dropping very large packages that appeared like super-inflated footballs. However, the labourers on the ground were carrying those without much effort. Intrigued, I went up to take a closer look, only to find empty sack covers packed in those large packages. When I noticed the officials entrusted with the relief activities counting and stacking the empty sacks neatly, I fathomed what was going on. Apparently, empty sacks have a high statistical value during relief operations. If two hundred empty sacks can be planted along with two hundred sack of actual relief material, one could show that 400 sacks worth of relief material have been distributed. That the allegations of organised corruption during relief operations are not entirely unfounded was clear from what I witnessed.

Meanwhile, another nefarious game had started. Fresh claims of bodies, body parts or even skeletons being found from certain affected villages, which had already been thoroughly searched by us, started pouring. The claimants were mostly the refugees living in relief camps at Aamguri and the deceased were claimed to be a kin. The claims, however, were directed at a minister who was camping at Aamguri to oversee the relief operations. I am not aware of how the claims were disposed of.

The games people were playing on the backdrop of a massive humanitarian tragedy irked me to no end and pushed me to a state of despair and despondency. Soon, the government ordered the transfer of the refugee camps from Aamguri to Aamteka and I was entrusted with the security of the new camp. On October 18 or 19, I returned to Aamteka again. An Additional SP rank officer was entrusted with the security of Aamguri.

Divinely ordained relief at last

A day after I had arrived at Aamteka, my PSO, Havildar Uma Singh fell ill with malaria. He was transferred to a hospital at Bongaigaon, 125 kms away. I, too, was suffering from digestive issues due to the month-long disturbance. Moreover, there was no scope for receiving any medical aid. Eventually, even plain water seemed disagreeable to me. The situation was such that one could not even ask for leave. And even if I did so, there was no surety that leave would be granted. The days seemed to roll on without any respite.

I eventually received relief – in a rather dramatic fashion. On the early morning of October 23, the Inspector in charge of the Bongaigaon Police Station informed that Uma Singh's condition was precarious and he was restless to meet me. I was overwhelmed at receiving this information and decided to meet Uma at the hospital. I entrusted the other officers with the security of the Aamteka camp for a day and rushed to Bongaigaon, assuring them that I would return before dusk.

The road to Bongaigaon passed past the PWD Dak Bungalow at Bijni, which was then my Office-cum-Residence. Since I had been away for such a long time, I thought of dropping in to check if all was well. Entering the bungalow, I found that it was completely deserted. Not a soul, from the Home Guards to the office staff and even the cook, was around. As the saying goes, when the cat is away, the mice will play. I entered the bungalow and found everything was in order. The office files were neatly stacked. On the table was a small note under a paperweight. It was a telephone number. "Someone must have left it for me to call back," I thought as I immediately dialled the number. The person at the other end identified himself and said that he was speaking from the Guwahati City DySP's office. I asked if the DySP was in office, only to learn that he had been promoted the day before and had left to take charge of his new post. I told the officer that if your DySP has been promoted, then I too must have received marching orders. I requested him to look up the notification and tell me where I had been posted. He informed me that I had been posted as the 2nd in Command of the 2nd Assam Police Task Force Battalion at Lumding. "The DySP had probably called me to inform me about the promotion," I thought.

I then proceeded to Bongaigaon and met Uma. I also met his doctors and requested them to take good care of him. Thereafter, I met the SP and told him about my transfer, requesting him for an immediate release so that I could leave the very next day. The SP, in turn, requested me to stay back for a week at Aamteka. I could not refuse him and agreed to stay on till the month end. The SP was pleased at this and said, "You have toiled hard all these days. Spend the night at Bijni. I am arranging for another officer to oversee Aamteka for the night."

The final dilemma

While returning from Bongaigaon, I visited the Bijni and Manikpur Police Stations. At around 10 p.m., I reached the Dak Bungalow at Bijni. Rahman was waiting for me at the bungalow gate. Rahman was a petty shopkeeper and owned a small shanty next to the bungalow. I did not know him personally but he was a familiar face as he would wish me whenever we met. He was very happy and said, "Sir, you (people) have made me a (rich) man and I shall always be grateful to you." On enquiring what had happened, he said that he had undertaken an emergency contract to build roads in the riot affected areas after the reputed contractors of the area had refused the work due to the riots. At the SDO's insistence, he had agreed to execute the contract and had engaged 10-15 labourers who had completed the work in 2-3 days. He had received a large payment of several lakhs of rupees for the work that very morning. He further added that he could complete the work safely because of the constant police patrolling. He also shared how he could complete the task so quickly.

On hearing the details, I thought that Rahman and many others like him would be celebrating today, thanks to the help they received from nature and our system. You might be wondering what nature and our system did to enrich people like Rahman. Well, the dirt road made of river sand and gravel was already existing. All that the labourers did was create a demarcation on either side, in accordance with the width specifications laid down in the contract. The contractor neither had to use any material nor deploy any machine. Our system easily recognises such dirt tracks as roads and since this was an emergency work, the payment was released quickly too.

After freshening up, I had just laid down to rest when Additional SP Karim rang me. He wanted to know where I was. "Preparing to go to bed," I replied. "What? All those who have been promoted along with you have either taken charge or are on their way to do so. A few senior officers who have not received promotion have appealed to the High Court. If you do not join before the court assembles tomorrow and if an injunction is passed, you will be in trouble." Karim sahib's words put me in a fix. I rang up the SP and informed him of the situation. "Leave early tomorrow morning," he said granting permission. "We will discuss the outstanding matters later."

I had no sleep that night as I gathered whatever I could and packed my luggage in preparation for a 400 km dash to Lumding. At about 2 a.m., my cook handed me a cup of tea. Sipping the brew, my eyes fell on the paperweight under which was the note with the Guwahati City DySP's phone number. I asked the cook who had called up the day before. "No one," he said casually. "Then where did this note with the phone number come from?" I asked in surprise. The youngster said, "Oh that! While leaving the office room yesterday, I found it fluttering around on the table. I thought it could be something important and so I placed a paperweight on it." At that very moment, I recollected that a few days back, a colleague had given me that note with the City DySP's number for some reason. I had casually put it away along with the other papers in a tray, from where it must have blown on to the table.

Early next morning, as I said goodbye to Bijni while passing through the deserted streets, I could not help thinking about the marvellous drama that had just unfolded. If that telephone number had not caught my attention, no one knows how many days later I would have got the information about my promotion and transfer. As the Bengali devotional song goes, *"Shokol-i tomar eechha, eechha moyi Tara tumi..."* everything is truly Your Will.

CHAPTER

20 Some Unknown and Explosive Facts About the '62 Chinese Aggression

On occasions, extraordinary and praiseworthy work done by police officers often go unrewarded and unappreciated, especially if the officer belongs to a low rank. I believe this is due to an unholy combination of power-centre based politics, casual approach of senior officers and the media's penchant to flash the spotlight on those holding high positions rather than those who are actually worthy of receiving the credit. Let me share a striking example.

On November 19, 1962, in the wake of the Chinese aggression against India, a hand-written note scribbled by ASI Moloy Kanti Nandi, In-charge of the distant Missamari Outpost in Darrang district of Assam, was delivered by hand to the Tezpur City SP, Shri Nishi Nath Changkakoti. Overwhelmed on reading the note, the SP immediately promoted Constable Upen Bora, who had delivered the message. Bora was taken aback at his sudden and unexpected elevation. He could not fathom what the contents of the note could have been, which pleased the SP so much. He thought about this all the way back to Missamari. On reaching the outpost, he fell at ASI Moloy's feet and asked, *"O saar, chithikhonot baaru key nu aasiley je sahabe dekun mookey promotion di diley* (Sir, what did you write in the letter that pleased the SP so much that he gave me a promotion?)" Upen had no clue that the note had recorded a fact that had a bearing on the national security, which no other organisation had brought to light till then. ASI Moloy Nandy's hurriedly scribbled note that contained the highly sensitive information read:

SP,

I respectfully beg to state that Chinese Army has launched a two pronged attack on 4th Div. Army H.Q. in Missamari and 4 Core H.Q. at Tezpur from Thang La via Charduar. Enemy is expected at Missamari Border (Foot Hills) in the morning. Kindly send sufficient arms and ammunition so that we can utilise our lives profitably.

Jai Hind.
M. K. Nandi
I/C, Missamari

The SP, Shri Changkakoti (who went on to become the Director General of Assam Police later) felt reassured that his suspicion about the advancement of Chinese troops was correct, after receiving Moloy Nandi's note. The Army and the media had been painting a different picture all the while by claiming that all was well at the borders. Changkakoti was unable to convince the government about his assessment for want of credible information. Moloy Nandi's note was a vindication of his stance. Apart from a confirmation of the Chinese incursion, the note had brought to light another surprising fact: The Chinese troops were about to launch a two-pronged attack by advancing from Khang La to Missamari via Charduar and then go to Tezpur whilst bypassing the well-fortified Sela Pass.

The rest of the story is well known. On the basis of the ASI's note, the District Police Superintendent was the first to inform the government about the Chinese incursion. The government, anticipating an attack, ordered the evacuation of Tezpur city. Though the government tried its best to ensure a safe evacuation, the citizens of Tezpur had to suffer heavily as the arrangements were unplanned and insufficient.

On November 20, China declared a unilateral cease-fire. The reasons for China's sudden declaration of cease-fire continues to be debated. Unfortunately, the Chinese decision was used as pretext by many Congress leaders to criticise the Chief Minister's decision to order the evacuation of Tezpur, on the basis of an 'ordinary' ASI's note. Shri Moloy Nandi wrote the following in a letter:

"After declaration of unilateral cease-fire by the Chinese, I came under severe criticism by the powerful vested interests of the state for my said report. Thus, my activism outside my routine police duties, even on the matter of national importance, had invited trouble for me."

In 1959, His Holiness the 14th Dalai Lama, the Tibetan Buddhist religious leader, had taken shelter at Missamari after escaping from Tibet, along with thousands of Khampa warriors. During that historic event, ASI Moloy Kanti Nandi, then a 24-year-old officer, was posted as In-charge at Missamari to oversee the law and order situation. He discharged his duties honourably and with great efficiency in that position for about five years. His smart appearance, officer-like qualities, amiable demeanour, sharp wit and a friendly attitude enabled him to get acquainted with many young Army commissioned officers. These relationships helped him collect vital national security related information with ease.

In September 1962, the Chinese troops had already captured the Thang La Army post, located about 200 miles from Missamari. The post was located at what was then known as North East Frontier Agency or NEFA (presently Arunachal Pradesh). Ever since he received this information, ASI Moloy Nandi kept a sharp eye on the day-to-day developments and made strenuous efforts to collect as much information as he possibly could.

About 48 years ago, I was filled with excitement as Nandi related his experience at Missamari. I had requested him to recount those historic incidents and share them in writing with me. Nandi, who retired as DySP (CBI), kept my request and in spite of health issues, he wrote to me on January 10, 2015. Reproduced hereunder are excerpts of his letter:

"...For the proper appreciation of my story of the Chinese aggression, 1962, it is perhaps essential to give you an idea about the place, Missamari. It was a sleepy village with an abandoned air strip of World War II. The area of the Police Post was about 300 sq miles, stretching up to the border of Arunachal Pradesh (NEFA).

Immediately, after the fleeing of the Dalai Lama from Tibet followed by the hotting up of the border with Tibet, the Headquarters of the 4th Infantry Division of Indian Army was hurriedly raised at Missamari.

Besides, Missamari was also the headquarters of Border Roads Tusk Force, known as Tuskers, which was responsible for building strategic road networks connecting Misarmari with Tawang and other forward posts of the Indian Army. At that time, only a narrow road capable of allowing only one-ton Nissan Trucks (Japanese make) and Jeeps to ply existed. The road and these vehicles were the only means of carrying men and materials to the forward areas besides the Army's age old Animal Transport Unit of mules.

My office and quarter was located in close proximity to the Army's ASC Officer's Mess and was surrounded by different units of the Army. I was then in my early twenties. In the course of time, I became very close to the officers of my age group, mostly of Captain rank.

Following the Thang La incident, forward posts at Buma La, Dhu La and Khinzemane were run over by the Chinese troops in quick succession. I used to get information of day-to-day developments on the border through my above sources. The developments on the border resulted in a sudden spurt in the activities of both Army and the Tuskers by way of movement of men and materials from Missamari towards NEFA. After a lapse of some time, Tawang also fell to the enemy. Increased reinforcement including Tanks were seen being rushed to the border areas. I was told by my source that an impregnable defence had been built up at Sela Pass in between Bomdila and Tawang to thwart any Chinese move.

Endless fleets of brand new Japanese one tonner Nissan trucks were found reaching Missamari and there were endless of sorties of Fairchild transport planes. Maximum sorties started landing from second week of November '62 carrying troops from faraway places like Bangalore etc. The situation was visibly tense. Every night troops were found passing along the road in front of my quarter for forward posts with loud war cry of 'Jai Bajrang Bali Ki!'

On the night of 18-11-62, at mid-night, I woke up on hearing the kicking sound of boots on my door. On opening the door, I was astonished to see my friends, Captains Nirmal, Pritam, Bhatnagar and others in full uniform. They were in a hurry and started dumping their personal belongings including camera and tape recorders on the floor of my house. They told me that they would collect the same back if they return alive, otherwise they asked me to give the camera, tape recorder as a gift to "my would-be wife." They then informed that they would dig in that night itself to meet the enemy. I was also informed that one of our friend, Captain Sharma's convoy had been ambushed at a place called Khelong in NEFA, which was about 11 kms from Assam border (as a crow fly). Hearing all these I was fully convinced that the situation was really grim.

On that night, I could not sleep and wrote a report addressed to SP Shri N. N. Changkakoti, IPS and sent it immediately through Shri Upen Bora (LC). My said letter was written in my own hand and ended with 'Jai Hind' and inter alia with a request to provide us with sufficient arms and ammunition so that we could profitably use our lives.

As against the ground realities, the Liaison Officer of the 4 Corp. (Brigadier) was not sharing any information about the Chinese advancements with the civilian local authorities. It was subsequently learnt that on 19-11-62 (the day I reported about the two pronged attack by the Chinese Army) the GOC of 4th Infantry Division sought permission to withdraw (from Missamari) from the 4 Corp Commander Lt Gen B. M. Kaul. But Lt Gen Kaul could not be reached to act on the said request from the GOC. It was gossiped that on that very day, Lt Gen Kaul was away from 4 Corps HQs for angling in a tea estate club (near Tezpur).

However, in the light of my report, New Delhi was informed about the latest Chinese advancement. The local Army authorities, after enough loss of time, had informed the civil authorities of Tezpur that the Army had lost its power to resist the Chinese advancement. The Civil Administration then swung into action and order evacuation and burning of currency notes (of Tezpur treasury and Bank). All these rapid developments resulted in confusion and mass exodus of people in a most disorderly manner, causing miseries. This fuelled a political blame game within the ruling Congress party. In this connection, Minister Biswadev (MLA from Rangapara) brought out a pamphlet in Assamese captioned *'Mukhya Mantri-loi Mukali Chithi* (Open letter to the Chief Minister), blaming the Chief Minister for his unwise decision of ordering the evacuation of Tezpur merely on the basis of (a report) of an ASI.

At this time of national humiliation, it came to my notice that some unpatriotic elements attached to Border Roads Tusk Force (Tusker), taking advantage of the situation, conspired with the carrying contractors, to cheat the government and in furtherance of the said conspiracy had falsely shown dispatch of huge quantity of defence stores toward Bomdila, before its fall, and diverted the same to various places in Darrang and North Lakhimpur districts. They showed the materials as fallen into the hands of the enemy. My source, who was a driver himself, together with his other colleague, had carried those materials to various destinations spreading over an area of 150 miles. None of those stacking places were within my jurisdiction (Missamari OP). However, I made necessary recce and found cement, rods, motor tyres, barbed wire, foodstuff, diesel drums, etc. at various places and reported the matter to SP, Shri D. K. Kakati. The SP was pleased to order search and seizure of the defence stores. As a result, huge quantity of defence stores was recovered. I along with Circle Inspector Jadav Das had to spend a whole day only at one place, namely Benjuli Tea Estate in making search and seizure. Thereafter, many more seizures were made by various police stations.

But after some days, when I noticed that the case was not progressing well, I again approached the SP and brought to his notice the whole development. The SP was pleased to forward the case to CBI, Shillong Branch, headed by Shri Sontosh Kumar Chakraborty, IPS, for investigation. The CBI took up the case and registered case no. RCI/63-SHG. I extended all help and cooperation to the CBI team till the case was returned in charge sheet against Col Thambia, contractor S. S. Agarwalla and others. The case came up for discussion in the National Parliament also."

A retrospective analysis of ASI Moloy Nandi's work during the Chinese aggression in '62 reveals his extraordinary commitment and dedication with a matter having a direct bearing on the national security. Unfortunately however, instead of receiving rewards and recognition for his extraordinary work, all he got was undue and unfair criticism. In spite of such adversity, ASI Moloy Nandi did not buckle down, get demoralised or hide himself in a shell. Instead, he worked diligently with double the energy. His untiring efforts and detailed reports were instrumental in the recovery of diverted Army supplies, worth crores of rupees, from various parts of Assam. This proves that those who want to work for public good, do so under all circumstances. They are the pride of the Police Department and the civil society. Unfortunately, it is a matter of shame that such efficient and accomplished officers are not given the right opportunity or the right and timely recognition. In spite of standing first among 600 candidates in the SI promotion examination, Moloy Nandi had to wait for three long years before he got his due. Moloy Nandi's delayed promotion is an apt example of how officers at the lower levels of the hierarchy have to suffer due to red tapism.

CHAPTER

21 Respect and Recognition is Independent of Uniform

Dear Ma, as the day turns into dusk without one realising it, I too have already written a fairly long letter without realising. I prostrate at your holy feet and would like to conclude with a few more words.

Ma, people do not realise that police work cannot be confined within any boundary, unlike the activities of many other government departments. The expanse of this profession is vast and the responsibilities are boundless. To deal with the myriad challenges, many police personnel work in plain clothes for specialised units such as Special Branch, CID (Crime Branch), Vigilance, etc. During my career, I have spent more years in plain clothes (including over 10 years with Sikkim Police Special Branch) than in uniform.

So far, the experiences I have related to you pertain to my career in uniform, or more plainly, Police Station postings. The main reason for this is that the general public associates 'police' with the uniformed personnel only. The public perception about police – for good or for bad – is shaped largely by the actions or otherwise of the uniformed police. That is why I have tried to highlight some of the peculiar problems, issues, complexities and inevitable conflicts faced by the uniformed police personnel, whilst trying my best to remain within limits.

Undoubtedly however, believing that the activities of uniformed police is all that there is to policing would be similar to the case of the blindfolded man and the elephant. I believe that from an internal security perspective, the contribution of the plainclothesmen, who are part of various specialised units such as the Special Branch, is as significant as the work done by the uniformed men, if not more vital and challenging at times. The satisfaction one derives from the success in such operations is much greater than those obtained by solving cases of murders and dacoities. Since plain clothes activities are done under cover and are bound by secrecy, the general public remains unaware. To be successful in CID or Special Branch, one needs extreme patience, commitment and skills acquired after painstaking and prolonged effort, besides exceptional acumen. Many people believe that plainclothes work is neither glamorous nor does one get the deserved respect. This cannot be farther from the truth. Let me share two examples.

I have previously mentioned that in 1968, a massive student agitation had been held to protest against the division of Assam and the carving out of a new state, Meghalaya. In its aftermath, an Enquiry Commission had been set up to investigate the alleged lapses on the part of the administration, which led to huge losses being incurred by the business community and damages to the Borjhar Airport near Guwahati. The Commission began its hearing and on the dock were the Police Chief, the DC Guwahati, SP and DIG. The anxiousness among these senior officers at the prospect of facing the Enquiry Commission was evident. I noticed that all the senior officers were seeking out DySP Phoni Roy and receiving his counsel before replying to the Commission's queries. I did not know much about Phoni Roy then and was therefore intrigued by the respectful behaviour of these senior officers towards a relatively junior DySP. More surprise awaited me during the lunch break that day when I noticed that the Police Chief was vying with the other senior officers for DySP Roy's exclusive time. All of them wanted DySP Roy to board their car and the reason was obviously to discuss the next steps and gather as many points as possible in their defence, within the short period of the lunch break. Predictably, it was the Police Chief, who won the tussle as DySP Roy boarded his car with a smile on his face. I was quite impressed with the goings on and the 'demand' for DySP Roy. I later learnt that DySP Roy had joined as an ASI. An exceptional talent, he had cleared the Law examinations and was posted as DySP with the CID's Legal Cell.

After about four-five years, I had another opportunity to see Phoni Roy in action. The sensational Sudadiya murder case was then being heard at the Shillong Sessions Court. The accused, that is, the victim's younger brother, had engaged a reputed Barrister from outside the region to defend him. But the legal representative for the State was not a professional lawyer; it was the SP – CID, Shri Phoni Roy.

The case, as mentioned before, was sensational. The Sudadia brothers were extremely rich tea estate owners. Differences arose between them due to property matters and they had filed cases against each other. On the fateful day, after a hearing of one such case at the Nagaon Court, the elder brother was returning to his residence at his tea estate in his car, along with two others. The tea estate was located near the Burapahar range, close to Kaziranga. Unfortunately, the elder Sudadia had not anticipated that his own younger sibling had meticulously planned his murder. As soon as the car reached a culvert on a desolate stretch at the foothills of Burapahar, the younger brother accosted his brother and obstructed the car's further movement. He thereafter rained bullets on the unsuspecting elder brother and the other two co-passengers, in a bid to ensure that there was no eyewitness. Once he was sure that his victims were dead, he transferred their lifeless bodies to the car's boot. He then turned the car around and speeded back towards Nagaon, travelling west. Thereafter, he crossed Nagaon,

Raha, Jagi Road, Khetri, Sonapur Town and Jorabat, entered Meghalaya and headed towards the State's capital, Shillong. Driving through the hilly tract snaking up, the assailant hatched a plan to dispose of the bodies. Finding a dark, deserted stretch near Barapani in the dead of the night, he pushed the car down a precipice, convinced that his woes would end once the vehicle fell 5,000 feet below and either caught fire or got mangled beyond recognition. He then nonchalantly returned home, 200 miles away, feigning innocence. However, the truth in the saying 'truth is stranger than fiction' was proven yet again as the next act of the drama unfolded.

The next day, a few Khasi village women, who lived in a settlement at the foothills, walked up to the jungle area to pick firewood and other forest produce. The group suddenly noticed a vehicle hanging among the trunks of a few pine trees, about 200 feet above the trail they were walking on. As accidents on the hilly roads were common, the women dismissed this as another case of road accident. A few curious women, however, climbed up to the vehicle to inspect it. They were surprised to hear moans and a muffled voice, crying for help. The women immediately informed the menfolk in the village and the police. With everyone's help, the vehicle was retrieved and one person was recovered alive, along with the two dead bodies, from the car's boot. On the basis of the survivor's statement, a case of murder was registered against the younger brother at the Barapani police station.

The tale of the man who had a providential escape (let's call him Amar) was an incredible story of human survival, stranger than fiction. The younger Sudadia had first fired a few shots his elder brother, killing him on the spot. Then, he had shot the other person who was accompanying them. Amar anticipated that it was his turn next. The moment he received a hit, he lay still as if he were dead. The assailant shot him again, but Amar remained unmoved in spite of the unbearable pain. Fortunately, neither bullet had hit any vital organ or blood vessel, because of which he survived, even though he was grievously wounded. The younger brother had then carried him first and threw him in the car's boot. The other two bodies were then piled on him one by one. In spite of severe blood loss and excruciating pain, Amar lay still and endured the arduous journey in the car's boot with two dead men for company, for several hours. According to Amar's statement, he was unconscious when the car was pushed down the cliff and had regained consciousness only early in the morning, when the car was precariously perched among the pine trees. He had somehow found his voice and summoned all his strength to cry for help.

Let me now return to Phoni Roy's story. It was the first day of this sensational murder case's hearing. The time was exactly 10 a.m. The small frame of Shri Phoni Roy strode into the court room, smartly dressed in a pair of trousers, a crisp shirt, tie and a blue blazer. A team of constables led by a Sub Inspector followed him, carrying two massive steel trunks. I first thought that the trunks probably carried exhibits related to the case. I was later surprised to find that trunks were filled with law books and copies of AIR. These were neatly flagged. Obviously, the flags marked important rulings that would have a bearing on the case.

No sooner had the judge taken his seat, about 8-10 senior advocates of the Shillong Court walked into the courtroom. I initially thought they were either the defence or prosecution lawyers, but was surprised to see them make their way to the gallery and take their seats among the audience. Some senior lecturers of Shillong Law College too arrived in the courtroom. I then thought they might have come to watch the presentation of the well-known barrister defending the accused. The hearing commenced. That day, only Shri Roy had the opportunity to present his case. The legal luminaries sat through the entire presentation, observing the proceedings from the gallery without batting an eyelid. I then realised that they had actually come to witness Shri Roy's presentation. I was really overwhelmed to note that these senior advocates had taken time out of their busy schedule to listen to Shri Roy - a police officer. This was perhaps an incredible acknowledgement of a police officer's legal acumen.

About 20 years later, I had the opportunity to meet Shri Roy again. He had by then retired a long time ago. I was tasked to meet him and take his opinion on a particularly sensitive and complex legal matter. On learning the issue for which Shri Roy's counsel was being sought, I thought, "There are many competent people who could have given an opinion on the matter. Why is a retired man being disturbed unnecessarily?" I reluctantly met Shri Roy, who was not keeping well, and explained the purpose of my visit. In spite of his illness, he agreed to undertake the assignment on learning who had asked me to meet him. He then made me run around and provide him with various inputs and legal books. I toiled for two days to fulfil all his demands and provided him with all that he required. Since it was difficult for him to sit up and write, I intermittently acted as his stenographer. On the third day, he handed me a three-page note containing his opinion. I said, "Sir, you have worked so hard for the past two days only to produce a three-page note?" Roy sahib laughed and said, "After all, this is Phoni Roy's opinion." I did not question him again as I concluded that such confidence was perhaps the reason behind his being so successful and sought after, in spite of being in a so-called unglamorous post.

Shri Roy's incisive legal wisdom and tactful presentation had eventually resulted in the conviction of the younger Sudadia in the murder case, who was handed a life term. I believe that if only all our Public Prosecutors study the case diary diligently and put in even half the effort exerted by Shri Roy and the Court Inspectors of the past, the conviction rate in police cases could improve drastically. My opinion has its roots in my personal experience, wherein I have had the misfortune of noticing that the public prosecutor was unaware of the case details – at times those related to heinous crimes including murders, investigated by me – even on the day of the final hearing. Instead of being counselled, I was nonchalantly asked, "Umm…so what was your case all about?"

In the early 1990s, a significant and high-level conference of the senior police and military intelligence officers active in the entire North East was held. The conference was attended by the police and intelligence chiefs of many north-eastern states apart from high ranking military officers, such as Lt Generals, Major Generals and a few Brigadiers. No police officer below the rank of DIG has been invited to the event. I had been posted there as part of the Special Branch Security Cell. All the senior police and military officers had taken their designated seats. I noticed that a certain officer was conspicuous by his absence. A discussion on matters related militancy and internal security without his presence struck me as odd. "What could be the matter? Was he being neglected? If so, this meeting is doomed to fail," I thought. Meanwhile, all the delegates had taken their seats a few minutes ago but the meeting did not commence. Everyone was quiet. "Are they waiting for someone?" the thought crossed my mind. Suddenly, I noticed the officer whom I had been expecting, walk in from a hidden door at the rear. This officer was none other than the Assam Police Special Branch DIG, Shri Bipul Kalita. Immediately, another thought flashed through my mind, "In spite of always being so punctual, the DIG has handed over a battering stick to the military brass present here by being late." The very next moment, I witnessed something incredible. The rank-conscious senior military officers were warmly greeting a relatively junior ranked police officer, which, I believe, is a rare occurrence in our country.

As soon as Shri Kalita walked up the dais, the senior Army officers and Police Chiefs of different States rose to shake hands with him and exchange greetings. The warmth and camaraderie on display unmistakably cleared the mist around who the show stealer was that day. I did not have an opportunity to hear the officer speak as it was a closed-door meeting and I had to leave the hall. But the point remains that Shri Kalita had earned the incredible affection and respect of his peers and seniors by the dint of hard work and extreme penance.

Shri Bipul Kalita had joined Assam Police as a DySP and had retired as an Inspector General. As far as I know, he had served as a District SP only for short period and was part of the Special Branch almost throughout his illustrious career. Having worked with him for many years, I fathomed that he not only loved his work, but also thoroughly enjoyed it. And because he enjoyed his work, he was never upset even if a mountain of work was piled on him. He never stopped working even if he was unwell or bed-ridden. That was so because his sources would share many crucial and secret details even when he was indisposed. I also learnt the secrets of how he built his sources and observed from close quarters the extraordinary manner in which he managed them. His sources came from all walks of life – from students, teachers, leaders, actors, ordinary farmers or traders to extraordinary people. He had once told me that he believed in the adage 'catch them young' when it came to creating sources. He would then nurture these sources painstakingly for 10-12 years.

The unblemished reputation enjoyed by Shri Kalita was a result of his infinite patience and incredible hard work. I had many opportunities to visit the offices of central Intelligence agencies in Delhi for official purposes. On all of these occasions, my identity as an officer from the Assam Police Special Branch enabled me to accomplish my work with relative ease. On uncountable occasions, senior officers in Delhi asked me with a tinge of admiration in their voice, "Oh, so are you from Kailta sahib's office?" Clearly, Assam Police Special Branch had become synonymous with Shri Kalita, even though he was not the head of the department. Credibility, respect and glory therefore, does not depend on one's uniform only.

Ma, I conclude with a caution to the fault finders with the following words of the Deathless Yogi, Sri Sri Mahavatar Babaji (whom you fondly address as 'KESAR MURARI,'): "Judge not all for the faults of many."